LAW IN CRISIS

THE CULTURAL LIVES OF LAW

Edited by Austin Sarat

RUTH A. MILLER

Law in Crisis

The Ecstatic Subject of Natural Disaster

STANFORD LAW BOOKS

An Imprint of Stanford University Press
Stanford, California

Stanford University Press
Stanford, California

Printed in the United States of America on acid-free, archival-quality paper

Library of Congress Cataloging-in-Publication Data

Miller, Ruth Austin
Law in crisis : the ecstatic subject of natural disaster / Ruth A. Miller.
p. cm.—(The cultural lives of law)
Includes bibliographical references and index.
ISBN 978-0-8047-6256-4 (cloth : alk. paper)
1. Law—Philosophy. 2. Subjectivity. 3. Natural disasters—Law and legislation. 4. Law—Political aspects. I. Title. II. Series: Cultural lives of law.
K240.M55 2009
340.1—dc22

2008055820

Typeset by Thompson Type in 10/14.5 Minion

Contents

LAW IN CRISIS

CHAPTER ONE

Introduction

Introduction

This book is in part a plea to revive ecstasy as a point of departure in the study of law.[1] Ecstatic subjects—shattered, dispossessed, displaced, and beside themselves—have never disappeared completely from legal or political analysis.[2] Since the 1970s and 1980s, the subject in ecstasy has been invoked in a number of books and articles, especially in the fields of religion, metaphysics, and literature.[3] The idea, however, that ecstasy is, or should be, central to legal structures or legal study is one that has not found proponents for a number of centuries.[4] I make the case in this book that legal ecstasy is still very much with us, that it remains an effective framework for politics, and that ecstatic subjects—or their off-center, eccentric counterparts—have been key players in the articulation of modern and contemporary political norms. I do so by focusing on what has increasingly been called "disaster law"[5]—defined broadly here as the legal and political structures that appear in the aftermath of crises such as earthquakes, floods, or fires. What I suggest throughout this book is that the dual purposes of disaster law are, first, to make the disaster intelligible by, second, assigning a politically normative function to the subject in ecstasy.

I admit that the subject in ecstasy is a strange place to start a book that is not being written thirty years ago, when discussions of subjectivity were more widespread.[6] What I propose over the following chapters, however, is that at that moment thirty years ago, there was a potential connection, a possible linkage, among ecstasy, eccentricity, and the law that could have been made but that was not—an association that was momentarily formulated, but that then unraveled. My starting point in this book, therefore, is that this brief, potential, or possible linkage needs to be rearticulated—especially now that crisis and disaster have become common tropes in contemporary political and legal rhetoric. Over the following pages, I argue that during a disaster or crisis, the law assumes not bounded, distinct, definable subjects, but rather eccentric subjects or subjects beside themselves—subjects in ecstasy. Furthermore, this assumption of legal ecstasy or eccentricity produces not just bodies beside themselves, but also displaced spaces and shattered narratives—the reality associated with what can be represented giving way to a reality associated with what cannot.

That law might deal in ecstatic rather than in bounded subjects—in what cannot be represented rather than in what can—may at first appear paradoxical. One of the most common assumptions in legal studies today is that legal systems, regardless of their ideological bases, both demand and define discrete, unitary, and above all bounded subjects. The rights-bearing individual, for example, is assumed to enter the liberal social contract only after taking on the rational, unitary subjectivity that is citizenship. The state becomes sovereign and thus a state—capable of engaging in international law systems—only when it is recognized to possess distinct boundaries enclosing a definable space.[7] Even the racialized body that is regulated by shifting, decree-driven totalitarian law is a body capable of being represented and made (sometimes hyperbolically) distinct.[8] Although a number of scholars have criticized this emphasis on the bounded subject—trying, for example, to preserve the notion of rights while doing away with the categorization and dependency demanded by the social contract,[9] or highlighting the racism that underlies the valorization of the inviolate national boundary[10]—few have questioned the more fundamental assumption that law demands a unitary subject.[11] I focus on the law of disaster in this book in order to challenge this assumption.

At the same time, I emphasize that my focus on disaster has less to do with its aberrant nature and more to do with its normative, routine functions. I argue, in other words, that the law of disaster is not in fact different from the law that operates in the apparent absence of disaster—that the subjects of what is termed the jurisprudence of the "day-to-day"[12] are as much subjects in ecstasy as their counterparts in the midst of an earthquake or flood. As so many scholars have noted in other contexts, that is, I argue in this book that the crisis has become the norm.[13] My final point, therefore, is perhaps a counterintuitive one, especially in a book purporting to address disaster law: rather than aiming at some (legal) resolution to crisis or disaster situations, rather than attempting to solve the problem that is the crisis or disaster, I suggest that we should instead develop a legal vocabulary that recognizes disaster as the endpoint of law.

The rest of this introductory chapter is devoted to building a framework for addressing these points. First, I outline the major themes that appear throughout the book, and second, I introduce some of the theoretical work with which I engage. In the three sections that follow, for example, I address a number of broad trends in the literature on ecstasy, subjectivity, and truth. I describe ecstatic subjects of law as they appear in late twentieth-century work, and explain how my own interpretation of ecstatic subjectivity both draws on these descriptions and departs from them.

The sections "Ecstasy," "Ecstasy and Subjectivity," and "Ecstasy, Subjectivity, and Truth" explore the law of disaster—addressing recent theories of political exceptionalism, comparing these theories to emergency measures taken during crisis situations, and describing the ways in which these disasters and crises are made meaningful. My purpose in these sections is to situate my analysis of the crisis or the disaster—and more specifically the *subject* of the crisis or the disaster—within these broader theories of the state of exception. Again, in the section "States of Exception," I suggest that although the subjects of disaster law are very much related to the subjects of the political exception, they are also distinct in significant ways.

The sections "Natural Disasters and Metaphysical Disasters" and "Disaster Law and Feminist Theory" set the groundwork for the chapters that follow by bringing together my working definitions of the subject in ecstasy and my working definitions of the subject of disaster law. The literature on subjectivity and the literature on disaster have both relied heavily on a rhetoric of crisis. In the first of these sections, I suggest that these natural disasters and metaphysical disasters are in many ways the same thing. Then in the second section, I define "disaster law" for the purposes of my argument, I describe how its constituent parts interact to produce the ecstatic subject, and I discuss broadly the importance of feminist theory to these relationships.

Ecstasy

It is difficult to dissociate ecstasy from subjectivity. As the next section shows, each has been repeatedly defined in relation to the other, and each lends itself easily to a relational definition. Before I get to this relational definition, however, I want to sketch a few characteristics of the former detached from, divorced from, or even prior to the latter.[14] Literally, therefore, *ecstasy—ek-stasis*—means a "being put out of place" or a "standing outside of." It is a term that describes a process—and a process alone. Who or what the subject or object of this process might be—what is put out of place, or what stands outside of what—is a question that is for the most part left unanswered. It is in fact only in the secondary definition of the term in Greek, a "being disoriented," that the existence of a subject is implied at all.

Despite this relatively open literal definition of "ecstasy," the usual definition that we see in contemporary political philosophy—a "being beside oneself" or a "being outside of oneself"[15]—seems to rest on the notion that the self or the subject[16] *should* be a part of the conversation. The state of ecstasy in its initial articulation, that is, does not require a self. Contemporary discussions of the state of ecstasy do. What I would like to do in this section and the next, therefore, is begin with this initial articulation of ecstasy as a process, and then move on to ecstasy as an aspect of subjectivity—to the quite reasonable tendency to understand ecstasy primarily, or even only, in relation to the self.

What, then, does it mean to "be put out of place" or to "stand outside of?" First of all, each implies a process of decontextualization. Being put out of place means being deprived of a context, of reference points, of a meaningful framework. Being put out of place means being offstage; it means, more broadly, being incapable of representation. Being put out of place—like being eccentric (off center)—is thus to be constantly shifting, disintegrating, and reintegrating elsewhere. This is not a state of transcendence, not a process of othering or being othered.[17] There is no movement from one defined or finite state to another. Rather, this is a state of constant and simultaneous isolation, disintegration, and reintegration.

What I suggest in this book is that the law of disaster seeks to produce precisely this state of ecstasy. Instead of understanding law—or law's violence—as something that defines, represents, rationalizes, and forces into a meaningful frame, that is, I understand law as something that insists upon a process of decontextualization, a gradual move toward the indefinite. If there is a coercive character to disaster law, therefore, I suggest that it manifests itself by shifting what can be represented into the realm of what cannot—not by forcing complex subjects to conform to simple, rational, or recognizable legal and political norms.

This does not mean, however, that subjects and subjectivity are irrelevant to legal ecstasy. "Being put out of place" and "standing outside of" each imply, at least, some object, subject, space, or narrative that is undergoing this process of decontextualization—each almost demands a thing that might be fractured, shattered, or placed beside itself. And to the extent that this thing is the body or mind, the subject does gradually begin to enter the picture. If ecstasy means standing outside of the body, standing outside of the mind, or standing outside of the self, in other words, it is in many ways an aspect of subjectivity.

Although I take as my starting point ecstasy as a process, my fundamental working definition of the term is "a decontextualizing," or "a rendering incapable of representation." In many instances, it is the subject who becomes decontextualized or unrepresentable. In some instances, however, it is not. Nonetheless, what I want to do now is turn to the work that *has* addressed ecstasy primarily in relation to subjectivity—to the work that has described the various ways in which ecstasy has indeed become a means of describing or even defining the subject.

Ecstasy and Subjectivity

Much of the late twentieth-century work on subjectivity took as its starting point the so-called Cartesian subject—seeking variously to challenge, critique, defend, or re-create the bounded, rational self that was invented, it was contended, by René Descartes.[18] As Matthew L. Jones has argued, the story of Descartes' invention of the modern subject became "a comforting fable" in many scholarly fields—a narrative in which "knowledge and truth" were assumed to "rest upon the individual subject and that subject's knowledge of his or her own capacities."[19] Jones's purpose in this analysis of Descartes is to emphasize the complexity of what has often been described as almost a caricature of the rational, modern, self—to rescue Descartes, at least in part, from the critiques of modernity in which he has been entangled.[20] By focusing on the mathematical exercises that "Descartes highlighted as propaedeutic to a better life and better knowledge,"[21] for example, Jones states that Descartes' philosophy valorized "the will to recognize and to accept freely the insights of reason . . . not just following the passions or memorized patterns of actions. It meant essentially recognizing the *limits* of reason and willing *not* to make judgments about things beyond reason's scope."[22]

My purpose in this section is not to argue in favor of, or against, the complexity of Cartesian subjectivity, or the validity of holding up the "Cartesian subject" as an actual product of Descartes' philosophy and mathematics. Nor do I attempt in this section an extensive review of the late twentieth-century literature that addresses subjectivity in general. Given the hundreds of books and articles on the modern subject, its crisis, its death, and its revival that were published throughout the 1970s, 1980s, and 1990s—and that continue to appear, although with less frequency, today—such a comprehensive review would in any case be excessive. Rather, what I try to do in this section is paint in broad strokes some of the major themes that helped to shape this intellectual moment—and explain why I am seeking to return to it now. In particular, I emphasize the persistence of what has been called Cartesian reason, related or not to the philosophy of Descartes, as a trope in discussions of subjectivity—even, or especially, in those discussions that announce the death or crisis of the rational subject. I address, that is, the enduring assumption that truth and knowledge must be situated in bounded, self-conscious, rationality—even when this rationality is critiqued, challenged, or set aside.

At the same time, I should note that my point in this section is not that the critical writing on subjectivity is inconsistent or contradictory in its simultaneous dismissal of, and insistence on, Descartes' rationality. It is true that even while grappling with the Cartesian subject, even while announcing the death, disintegration, irrelevance, or revival of this subject, much of the work on subjectivity seems to have treated this apparently dead, dispersed, or irrelevant subject as the norm. It is likewise true that although the modern, rational subject has been described as a subject in crisis for many decades or even centuries, it remains an often overwhelming presence in academic work today. I think that this is so, however, less because of the often paradoxical nature of scholarly writing, and more because there has been a misreading of the nature and development of modern law and politics. As I argue in the following chapters, the key figures in the development of political and legal structures over the past three centuries have not been the bounded, rational, self-conscious subjects of precrisis Cartesian rationality, but rather precisely the postcrisis subjects—the subjects in ecstasy, beside themselves, unrepresentable, and at the margins—described by these critical works.

With that in mind, I am not going to start this discussion of ecstasy and subjectivity in the 1980s, but rather in the first couple of centuries CE, with the treatise of the literary critic, Longinus, *On the Sublime*. Longinus's purpose in this treatise is to analyze different types of rhetoric and to evaluate their efficacy in moving a public audience. Indeed, although he addresses a variety of styles of speech—poetic as well as political—he makes a point of asking early on (and repeatedly afterward) "whether we shall have theorized on something useful for men in political life."[23] Throughout the text, Longinus remains interested above all in politically useful speech—and in the type of speech that forms a politically useful subject. Moreover, according to Longinus, at the heart of this question of political speech rests the relationship between the rational subject who can be persuaded by logical discussion and the subject in ecstasy who is irrelevant to such discussion. "What is beyond nature," Longinus argues,

> drives the audience not to persuasion, but to ecstasy. What is wonderful, with its stirring power, prevails everywhere over that which aims merely at persuasion and at gracefulness. The ability to be persuaded lies in us, but what is wonderful has a capability and force which, unable to be fought, takes a position high over every member of the audience.[24]

A number of pages later, he continues that the "final end of poetry is the astounding of those who hear it," and that both political speech and poetical speech "are seeking the sublime and the state of sympathetic excitement." Finally, in a concluding section, he repeats, "you see—as I never stop saying—the works and emotions which come near to ecstasy are a release and a cure-all for every audaciousness in spoken and written style."[25]

According to Longinus, in other words, there is a clear and distinct division between unitary, rational subjects—subjects capable of being persuaded—and ecstatic subjects beside themselves, astounded, and in an altered state. As the editors of the text argue in their notes, the difference between being persuaded and being moved to ecstasy is that ecstasy is a "hypernatural" state that is "almost mystically beyond *logos*," whereas being persuaded "indicates voluntary acquiescence as a result of *logos*."[26] Being astounded—"a synonym of 'ecstasy'"—"knocks you out" and results from a "direct sensation" or "images of such sensations," and "is one of the principle jobs of the public speaker."[27] I want to emphasize this point: in Longinus's universe, there is the same dichotomy between the unitary subject and the ecstatic subject that we see in current work on subjectivity. Unlike the literary critics writing in the 1980s, however, Longinus assumes almost automatically that the *normative* subject—the subject produced by both political discourse and political structures—is the latter of these, the subject in ecstasy. Truth, power, politics, and life are a function of being beside oneself.[28]

Two thousand years later, Michel Foucault addressed similar aspects of this trend in the work of classical ethicists and philosophers. In a series of lectures given in 1981 and 1982 on *The Hermeneutics of the Subject* and in 1983 on *Fearless Speech*, he goes into detail about the relationship among classical Greek and Roman subjectivity, existing outside of oneself or in an altered state, and having access to the truth.[29] Starting with the Socratic admonition to "know oneself" and "care for oneself," Foucault makes the case that spirituality (as distinct from theology),[30] subjectivity, and truth were interconnected issues in the world of antiquity. Spirituality, he argues, "postulates that for the subject to have right of access to the truth he must be changed, transformed, shifted, and become . . . other than himself."[31] He continues that the insistence on "care of the self" in Socratic philosophy "designates precisely the set of conditions of spirituality, the set of transformations of the self, that are necessary conditions for having access to the truth."[32] As a result, he concludes, "the philosophical theme (how to have access to the truth?) and the question of spirituality (what transformations in the being of the subject are necessary for access to the truth?) were never separate."[33] Like Longinus, Foucault recognizes that persuasion through *logos* was neither invested with an obviously positive moral value nor particularly closely associated with truth or reality in the classical world. He argues that in Greek thought, for example, "you *metanoei* (you change opinion) when you have been persuaded by someone," and this process "always has a negative connotation, a negative value."[34]

Foucault continues by comparing this classical relationship among subjectivity, spiritual transformation, and truth to modern variations on the same theme. In the process, he develops two further points. First of all, he argues that the "Cartesian moment"—a term he uses as shorthand for a general modern shift toward unitary rationality in ethics and philosophy—marked the point at which "know yourself" was "requalified," and "care of the self" was "discredited."[35] Rather than linking truth to an altered or transformed state, Foucault suggests, modern philosophers instead insisted that "the condition for the subject's access to the truth [was] knowledge, and knowledge alone."[36] In *Fearless Speech*, he elaborates on this notion, stating that,

> before Descartes obtains indubitably clear and distinct evidence, he is not certain that what he believes is, in fact, true. In the Greek conception of *parrhesia* [speaking freely], however, there does not seem to be a problem about the acquisition of the truth since such truth-having is guaranteed by the possession of certain *moral* qualities: when someone has certain moral qualities, then that is the proof he has access to the truth—and vice versa.[37]

According to Foucault, in other words, there is a distinction between the modern assumption that truth exists outside of the subject—and thus requires a self-conscious, knowing subject capable of grasping it—and the classical assumption that truth and (altered) subjectivity are the same thing. In the classical period, he argues, something could be true only via recourse to the transformed, uniquely virtuous, or ecstatic subject. In the modern period, contrarily, something could be true only via recourse to knowing, rational, unitary subjects—subjects who were, by definition, *not* beside themselves.

The second and related point that Foucault draws from both his analysis of classical subjectivity and the distinction he posits between classical truth and modern truth is that the *ecstatic* subject of Greek and Roman texts had no relationship to law or politics. For example, *ascesis* (or *askesis*—exercise or the practice of caring for oneself) is not, for Foucault, "a way of subjecting the subject to the law; it is a way of binding him to the truth."[38] More emphatically, he argues that "in the culture of the self of Greek, Hellenistic, and Roman civilization, the problem of the subject in his relation to practice leads . . . to something quite different from the question of the law."[39] Indeed,

> however pressing the city-state may be, however important the idea of *nomos* may be, and however widespread religion may be in Greek thought, it is never the political structure, the form of law or religious imperatives that can say what a Greek or Roman . . . must do concretely throughout his life. In Greek classical culture, the . . . art of life is, I believe, inserted in the gaps left equally by the city-state, the law, and religion regarding this organization of life.[40]

In addition to positing the Cartesian moment as the end of the normative ecstatic subject, in other words, Foucault is likewise arguing that, even in antiquity, subjects beside themselves had little to do with law or politics. The care of the self, the truth that was accessed by the transformed subject, had nothing to do with the world of the city-state and the legal structures that defined it.

These two points—the shift marked by the Cartesian moment and the irrelevance of any but the Cartesian subject to law and politics—have been extraordinarily influential in writing on subjectivity. Judith Butler, for example, operates in an analytical framework in many ways similar to Foucault's and, like him, understands the ecstatic subject as a marginal figure in law and politics. It is true that rather than positing a chronological break—the Cartesian moment—as the thing that differentiates the ecstatic subject from the bounded subject, Butler instead posits a narrative or discursive break. But the dichotomy is nonetheless clear. On the one hand, for example, she argues that terms such as "*my* sexuality" or "*my* gender" indicate not so much possession but "*modes of being dispossessed*, ways of being for another or, indeed, by virtue of another."[41] On the other hand—and in opposition to this fractured subjectivity—she states that in the context of law, politics, and rights,

> we have to present ourselves as bounded beings, distinct, recognizable, delineated, subjects before the law, a community defined by sameness. Indeed, we had better be able to use that language to secure legal protections and entitlements. But perhaps we make a mistake if we take the definitions of who we are, legally, to be adequate descriptions of what we are about. Although this language might well establish our legitimacy within a legal framework ensconced in liberal versions of human ontology, it fails to do justice to passion and grief and rage, all of which tear us from ourselves, bind us to others, transport us, undo us, and implicate us in lives that are not our own, sometimes fatally, irreversibly.[42]

On the one hand, she continues, "to assert sexual rights" means "struggling *to be conceived as person* . . . [and] intervening into the social and political process by which the human is articulated."[43] On the other, failing to engage effectively with political, legal, and social structures renders certain people less than real—renders "their loves and losses less than 'true' loves and 'true' losses."[44]

Like Foucault, that is, Butler also draws a number of distinctions between the unitary, knowing subject and the dispossessed subject in ecstasy. First of all, it is the unitary subject who is the subject of legal and political structures. Ecstatic subjects—even if they are "what we are about"—remain irrelevant to the language of law and rights, reminiscent of Foucault's subjects of *askesis*. Second, something can become (politically or legally) true or real in this context only via recourse to the unitary subject. The subject in ecstasy—eccentric to these structures—can never produce effective (political or legal) truth.[45] In the work of Butler, it is precisely a "Cartesian" type of law or politics that renders the loves and losses of those beside themselves less real and less true than the loves and losses of those who are self-contained. Although she does spend time in her work trying to redefine rights and law such that they might be relevant to fractured subjects, therefore, I want to emphasize that Butler's starting point and assumptions are not far removed from Foucault's: law as it exists *now* assumes a bounded, unitary subject. Access to (recognized political) truth has nothing to do with the subject in ecstasy.

Rosi Braidotti, who has also written extensively on subjectivity, draws conclusions that are in many ways different from Butler's but, again, seem founded on the same assumptions about bounded and ecstatic subjects. In her *Nomadic Subjects*, for example, Braidotti asks "how can we *affirm* the positivity of female subjectivity at a time in history when our acquired perceptions of 'the subject' are being radically questioned?"[46] She asks furthermore whether it is possible "to avoid hegemonic recodification of the female subject . . . to keep an open-ended view of subjectivity, while asserting the political and theoretical presence of another view of subjectivity."[47]

Throughout much of her writing, Braidotti proposes a number of possible answers to these questions. Drawing on the work of Luce Irigaray, for example, she argues that the crisis of the Cartesian subject should be recognized as "only the death of the universal subject—the one that disguised its singularity behind the mask of logocentricsm."[48] Drawing on the work of Deleuze, she argues that the subject is a "process," and "can no longer be seen to coincide with his/her consciousness but must be thought of as a complex and multiple identity, as the site of a dynamic interaction of desire with the will."[49] According to Braidotti, in other words, the way out of the crisis of the Cartesian subject is to recognize that its defining (violent) characteristic was its "logocentric" claim to universality. Similarly, the particular danger that faced feminists and critical theorists—a danger against which Braidotti convincingly warns—was that their work would simply recodify this unitary, universal subject under different terms.

Where, though, does this place law? In a relatively familiar move at this point, Braidotti associates law—in some ways conflated with logocentrism in her work and in other ways not—with the dead Cartesian subject. Law becomes irrelevant, that is, when the unitary, rational subject has disappeared. Indeed, in her

1994 discussion of biopolitics as an (undesirable) manifestation of this postcrisis thinking, Braidotti argues that,

> the biopower world is marked not by the sovereignty of the law but by prohibitions, rules, and regulations that bypass, overflow, and disregard what used to be the law. The bodily matter is directly and immediately caught in a field of power effects and mechanisms for whom legislation, when not archaic, is simply redundant.[50]

A year later, Giorgio Agamben would make the case that sovereignty and biopolitics are much more closely—or at least ambiguously—related to one another than this.[51] Rather than going into more detail about his argument now, though, I simply want to highlight, again, the assumptions under which Braidotti appears to be operating. Unlike Butler, who remains convinced that—despite the metaphysical crisis—both the unitary subject and the language of law are ideas worth engaging, Braidotti argues that the crisis has effectively killed both. Butler advocates some sort of working relationship between the subject beside itself and the legal rhetoric that apparently ignores this subject. Braidotti—like Foucault in his analysis of classical theories of the self—disregards law and its unitary subject altogether. At the same time, however, all three nonetheless see the same, and I think familiar, relationship between law and subjectivity: law produces a bounded, rational subject; law thus has nothing to do with the ecstatic subject; law is therefore (a) irrelevant, or (b) in need of redefinition.

The ecstatic subject, in other words, died with Descartes, and the Cartesian subject died soon after, during the repeated critiques of modernity throughout the late nineteenth and twentieth centuries. And now we are left with—something else. What I want to argue in this book, however, is that this something else is none other than our original ecstatic subjects—and that it is these ecstatic subjects, far more than their ephemeral Cartesian counterparts, that have been the normative subjects of modern, if not necessarily classical, law and politics. In particular, it is the ecstatic subject who has been the focus of disaster law and politics. And, to the extent that disasters have in many ways become the day-to-day norm, the subjects that they have produced have likewise become far more—paradoxically—central than they might initially appear.

Again, my purpose in this section has not been to attempt a literature review—or even an extended definition—of "the subject" as a theme in philosophy and ethics. Rather, I have tried to pinpoint some common trends that appear and reappear in writing on subjectivity, ecstasy, and truth. In general, regardless of perspective or prescription, much of the work on these issues seems to be founded on the same assumptions. First of all, whether the break is chronological as it is in Foucault, or discursive as it is in Butler, there appears to be a distinct dichotomy set up between the unitary subject and the subject in ecstasy. Second, there is likewise an assumption that whereas in the premodern period ecstatic subjects could be the political norm—truth accessed and produced by subjects beside themselves—in the post-Cartesian world, unitary, rational subjects became the norm, and (political and legal) truth was derived from what could be verified rationally and externally. In general, that is, despite the fact that the Cartesian subject has died repeatedly over the past century and a half, it still appears in work on subjectivity with a perplexing frequency.

I argue that this is the case, however—that Descartes' subject will not die—not because of some intellectual paradox, not because of some lag between metaphysical crises and political ones, but rather because of a misreading of politics, law, and truth in the post-Cartesian world. It is not, I suggest, the unitary subject that has been the basis for political and legal structures over the past three centuries. Rather, the political and legal norm has been the subject in ecstasy—that subject theorized so many centuries ago by Longinus and his contemporaries, and that subject who has survived so many floods, fires, earthquakes, and disasters.

Ecstasy, Subjectivity, and Truth

Although I began to describe the relationship between ecstatic subjectivity and access to the truth in the previous section, I pause here to explain in more detail how this relationship will play out in this book. As Foucault, Butler, Braidotti, and others have argued, the truth accessed by ecstatic subjects and the truth or reality accessed by rational, bounded subjects seem completely distinct from one another. Ecstatic subjects alter themselves, internally or spiritually, as a means of apprehending truth in its totality. According to Foucault, for instance, "during the Hellenistic and Roman period there is the increasingly marked absorption of philosophy (as thought concerning truth) into spirituality (as the subject's own transformation of his mode of being). With this there is, of course, an expansion of the cathartic theme . . . [H]ow must I transform my own self so as to be able to have access to the truth?"[52] Spiritual, cathartic transformation, that is, predisposes subjects to engaging with truth.

Rational subjects, contrarily, alter the external world such that they can gradually gather knowledge, which will then, piecemeal, lead to a different sort of truth. This does not mean, however, that rational subjects are not concerned with their internal state. As Jones argues with respect to Descartes' work, for example, "Descartes' geometry was . . . a spiritual exercise [*askesis*], meant to counter instability, to produce and secure oneself despite outside confusion, through the production of real mathematics. Descartes' famous quest to find a superior philosophy took place within this therapeutic model."[53] The difference between these two approaches to truth and subjectivity, therefore, is less that one ignores the self whereas the other takes the self as a starting point. More, it is that in the latter, truth follows from anchoring the self, whereas in the former, truth follows from shifting or transforming the self. Whereas the ecstatic subject changes, or even loses, the self in order to internalize truth, suddenly, in its totality, the rational subject secures, or even asserts, the self in order to comprehend truth, progressively, through the gradual accumulation of evidence.

What I suggest in this book is that the law of disaster operates at the intersection of these two approaches to subjectivity. It does seek security of the sort demanded by Descartes, but what it secures is the subject in, and state of, ecstasy. It secures each of these in a *rational* way—defining, representing, and contextualizing them. But it defines them as indefinable, represents them as unrepresentable, and contextualizes them outside of context. As a result, the subjects of disaster law access a truth that is both total or immediate *and* dependent on gradual, rational alterations to the external world. The ecstatic subjects sought, described, and produced by disaster law, that is, have unique access to a truth that is simultaneously spiritual and rational. In turn, the legal narrative of disaster that these subjects produce is a narrative that is more than total—that describes not just public and private, but internal and external, spiritual and rational, ecstatic and bounded.

When I say that the state of ecstasy—or more narrowly, the subject in ecstasy—endows the disaster with meaning, therefore, I am making a very distinct and narrow claim. I am arguing that as the law of disaster is elaborated, what may or may not have happened in the disaster area is less meaningful than the shattered, decontextualized condition of the subjects of disaster law. What broke, what died, what burned down, what was destroyed becomes in some ways irrelevant as disaster law is articulated. Instead, what becomes key to determining the existence of the disaster is the state of the subject, the partner, the slightly less than real *other* actor, who may or may not have even existed when the disaster struck.[54] Moreover, it has been primarily via reference to these shattered subjects that legal narratives of disaster—and that the legal meanings of disaster—have been formulated, reformulated, and put into play.

States of Exception

I turn now to interactions between theories of subjectivity and theories of exceptionalism in writing on disaster. Many recent analyses of law and disaster have taken the state of exception as a starting point, drawing in particular on the work of Carl Schmitt and Giorgio Agamben. These discussions have addressed both the concrete relationship between natural disasters and states of exception—the extent to which catastrophes blur the line between law and politics and provoke emergency measures—as well as the more theoretical relationship between disaster as a concept and the political philosophy of the exception. What I do in this section, therefore, is talk briefly about Schmitt's and Agamben's theories of the exception and then explain in more detail how my subjects in ecstasy reflect Agamben's *homo sacer*, and also the ways in which they do not.

At the beginning of his *Political Theology*, Schmitt argues that a sovereign is "he who decides on the exception."[55] According to Schmitt, sovereign existence is in fact predicated on the state of exception—the relationship between sovereign power and the exception identical to the relationship between divine power and the miracle. "The exception in jurisprudence," he argues, "is analogous to the miracle in theology," and just as the divine suspension of the laws of nature proves the existence of God, so too the sovereign suspension of the sovereign's law proves the existence of the sovereign.[56] Each is situated in precisely the destruction of a system of objective legal norms.

In his critique of Schmitt's arguments, Agamben reevaluates this discussion of sovereign power and develops a useful and peculiarly *spatial* theory of the exception. The state of exception, he argues, "represents the inclusion and capture of a space that is neither outside nor inside" the juridical order that constitutes the norm.[57] The exception instead has a unique relationship with the norm, in which,

> in order to apply a norm it is ultimately necessary to suspend its application, to produce an exception. In every case, the state of exception marks a threshold at which

> logic and praxis blur with each other and a pure violence without *logos* claims to realize an enunciation without any real reference.[58]

A number of pages later, Agamben turns to a concrete example of this process—"periodic anomic feasts" such as the Roman Saturnalia[59]—which "dramatize this irreducible ambiguity of juridical systems" and "celebrate and parodically replicate the anomie through which the law applies itself to chaos and to life only on the condition of making itself, in the state of exception, life and living chaos."[60]

The state of exception is, in other words, a disaster. Moreover, as Ellen Kennedy has argued, this theoretical link between the political exception and the natural disaster became gradually more concrete over the nineteenth and twentieth centuries, as the "definition of political power became more closely associated with power in exceptional circumstances."[61] According to the 1807 U.S. "Insurrection Act," for example, the president can use military force to restore order in response to "a natural disaster, epidemic, or . . . terrorist attack," as well as an actual insurrection.[62] By the early twentieth century, the American Red Cross reports were conflating riots and rebellions with famines and floods.[63] In nations like Italy, the "law specifically recognized 'riots and plagues' as instances where governmental (political) power was required and imminently justified."[64] In both their theoretical and practical application, that is, the politics of disaster and the state of exception seem in many ways interchangeable.

More fundamental to my own argument, however, is the subject assumed by these theories of politics and disaster. Although neither my brief analysis of Schmitt nor my brief analysis of Agamben refers directly to the subject produced by the state of exception, a certain type of subjectivity is nonetheless implied in the work of both. In the work of Schmitt, for example, the subject is nonrational, nonverbal, nonobjective—at home in a universe of sudden miracles and (quite classical) alterations of state and self. According to Agamben, subjects of the exception are both outside and inside the sphere of politics, simultaneously temporary and permanent—they are subjects that manifest themselves most concretely when law, governing chaos, embodies chaos. Put another way, subjects of the state of exception appear at first very much to be subjects in ecstasy. They are eccentric subjects, offstage. They are explicitly indefinable, occupying a limit space, straddling multiple contradictory positions, and beside themselves. They are the seeming opposite of the bounded, definable, unitary subject of the Cartesian moment.

So the state of exception produces something that looks like subject in ecstasy—and it would seem, therefore, that we have an excellent frame of reference for thinking about the law and politics of disaster. I want to pause here, however, and make clear that, in my analysis, the law and politics of disaster are *not* in fact identical to the state of exception. Again, as I argue throughout this book, the subject in ecstasy, the subject of the disaster, has unique access to a particular kind of truth, is in a unique position to endow the disaster with meaning. The subject in ecstasy *defines* the disaster, provides a link between the world of disaster and the world of law. The relationship, therefore, between the subject and the disaster is, if anything, an *inverted* version of the relationship between the subject and the exception. Just now we saw that the state of exception demands what looks like a subject in ecstasy. Over the following pages, however, I argue that subjects in ecstasy are far more active than their exceptional counterparts—central to the production of legal and political truth.

As a result, although related to Agamben's *homo sacer*,[65] the ecstatic subject is in many ways quite different—being, if nothing else, a more optimistic figure. *Homo sacer*, for example, represents both the starting point and the end point of the inscription of bare, biological life into political structures.[66] *Homo sacer* is manifested concretely in the hyperbolically passive "neomort," refugee, or *Muselmann* of the Nazi death camp. The death of *homo sacer* is a nonevent, is irrelevant, because *homo sacer* is defined first by a politics in which all that matters is the regulation of bare life, and second by a bare life that has been stripped of political meaning. And so the life, also, of *homo sacer* is irrelevant, spiritually[67] meaningless, reduced to bare biological markers.

When I argue that ecstatic subjects endow the crisis or disaster with meaning, therefore, I am understanding these subjects to be something quite different from *homo sacer*. I thus approach Agamben's work in a manner similar to Braidotti, who criticizes

> the extent to which *zoe*[68] gets coded in negative terms, for instance in the post-Heideggerian work of Agamben, as a liminal state of extreme vulnerability of being human: a becoming-corpse . . . [T]he potency of *zoe* as the defining trait of the subject displaces the unitary vision of consciousness and the sovereignty of the "I". Both liberal individualism and classical humanism are accordingly disrupted at their very foundations. Far from being merely a "crisis" of values, I think this situation confronts us with a formidable set of new opportunities.[69]

I therefore argue that ecstatic subjects are hyperbolically active. Their death,[70] unlike the death of *homo sacer*, is in every way a catastrophe—of the utmost importance. Indeed, with the death of the ecstatic subject, all truth, all meaning, any link between law and disaster disappears. If ecstatic subjects *produce* politics, their nonexistence is unthinkable. Unlike the life of *homo sacer*, the life of the ecstatic subject is if anything *over*determined, spiritually critical, situated in, but also far beyond biology. It is a life that must have active, political, narrative meaning in order for political and legal structures to function. Although I address in this book the violence, racism, sexism, and straightforward butchery that dog both legal ecstasy and the politics of disaster, therefore—just as they dog the politics of the exception and "day-to-day" politics—I also insist that there are less ominous qualities that can and do attach themselves to eccentric subjects in ecstasy.

Natural Disasters and Metaphysical Disasters

It will have become clear by now that although the focus of this book, narrowly defined, is natural disasters or crises—fires, floods, earthquakes, and the like—I am also defining both "disaster" and "crisis" as broadly as I can. I am doing so primarily because when we move away from the bounded subject of day-to-day law and start to address the ecstatic subject of the law of disaster, we are faced with the problematic, fractured, and indefinable character of disaster itself. The day-to-day has recently been resituated as a site and state of constant violence (if also occasional transcendence), incapable in many ways of representation.[71] In the process, however, the disaster or the crisis—what the day-to-day has now become—has to some extent been emptied of even its earlier idiosyncratic meaning. What I do now, therefore, is look briefly at what has historically been defined as a disaster or crisis, and what, historically, has not. In doing so, I start with the nineteenth- and twentieth-century rhetoric of the natural disaster, and then move on to what has been called more generally the metaphysical crisis of the rational subject. I suggest in the following section that the relationship between the natural disaster and the metaphysical disaster is much closer than it might at first appear—that both produce systems of law and politics arrayed around decentered, eccentric subjects, subjects in ecstasy and beside themselves.

With that in mind, I begin by addressing two early twentieth-century texts that unambiguously seek to define "disaster." The first is a 1909 article written for the American Geographical Society discussing an earthquake in Messina, Italy. It begins:

> On May 3rd 1887, an earthquake might have been felt in many places scattered throughout about one-half Old Mexico as well as over two-thirds of Arizona and New Mexico. This shock was not chronicled in the world's centers of culture, and even up to the present it has been vouchsafed but little attention; yet it was undoubtedly a far heavier shock than that which has just stirred the emotions and aroused the sympathies of the entire civilized world. The area of the destructive shocks of the earlier disturbance exhibits an alternation of mountain and arid plain, much of it inhabited only by Indian tribes with a few scattered ranches and mining camps. Had it been much more thickly settled than it was, it is probable that the loss would have been small. If an army in tents had encamped upon the site of Messina on the morning of the 28th of December last, the loss of life and property would have been insignificant.[72]

The second text is from an American Red Cross report summarizing Red Cross activities between June 1917 and June 1918. In this report, "military relief" is carefully differentiated from "civilian relief," with "great disasters" or "calamities" appearing as subsections of the latter. Among the acts of military violence relieved in 1917 and 1918 were battles and famines in France, Romania, Russia, Serbia, Belgium, Italy, Syria, and Palestine. Among the calamities and disasters relieved over the same period were "six large fires, four floods, four tornadoes, two earthquakes, one shipwreck, one storm, one race riot, one explosion in a munitions plant, one ship sunk by submarine, and one explosion of a munitions ship in harbor."[73]

Each of these passages contains a straightforward definition of disaster, calamity, or crisis—followed immediately, however, by what is arguably an undermining or shattering of this definition. Each assumes that the line between disaster and not-disaster is clearly distinguishable, but each in turn seems to blur this line into effective nonexistence. In the first passage, the disaster is apparently differentiated from the not-disaster by the existence of a settled population in the disaster area. What seems to be important in understanding disaster, in other words, is not only that a shock occurred, but that there were recognizable people around to feel it.[74] The passage brings the disaster's destruction to life not only via reference to what happened, but also—and perhaps more so—via reference to what this destruction, what this disaster, what this crisis, was *not*. According to the article, the Messina earthquake did not occur in the implicitly empty space of the American Southwest, it did not occur beneath a tent city, and it was not at the margins of the civilized world. Again, I want to make this reference point clear: what makes the Messina earthquake understandable is not just that it occurred at a center of civilization—where people could feel it—and that it therefore produced *x*, *y*, or *z* meaning; more so, what makes it understandable is that there may or may not have been *another* earthquake that occurred *beyond* the bounds of civilization, where no one would have noticed the shocks.

This may seem like an insignificant shift in perspective, but I suggest that it is fundamental to both the law of disaster and to its ecstatic subject. First of all, realizing that what makes a crisis real is not its proximity to centers of civilization, but rather an alternative, marginal, *other* disaster's *lack* of proximity to centers of civilization moves us beyond the usual discussions of national or imperial subject formation that appear in so many analyses of both political and natural violence.[75] The point here is less that certain spaces or bodies occupy certain rungs on racist or colonial civilizational hierarchies, and that, depending on this placement, the suffering or violence that occurs in these spaces or to these bodies becomes more or less real or meaningful.[76] The point is less that crises that occur at what has been defined as the center of civilization demand more attention, produce more emotional arousal, and attract more sympathy among the comfortable, secure, imperial subjects who develop these hierarchies in the first place. Rather, like premodern dream manuals, these narratives link the reality of a disaster to the eccentric subject offstage or to the ecstatic subject in flux.

What is important in deciding on the reality of a disaster or crisis, in other words, is not just that it happened—empirically—or that it caused destruction—measurably—at some imperial or neoimperial center. What is important is that another crisis may have been glimpsed briefly, out of focus, outside the frame, at the same time. The 1887 earthquake *might have* been felt by *hypothetical* Indians, ranchers, and miners. The unknowable space of the American wilderness, or the ephemeral and never built tent city, could *possibly* have been wracked by disaster. And *therefore* the Messina earthquake occurred. The crisis here is above all a crisis of what cannot and could not be represented, defined, or understood.

If we turn to the conclusions reached by the American Red Cross, they seem if anything more clearly addressed to the political subject in ecstasy. Once again, among the implicitly apolitical calamities and disasters relieved by the organization were not just fires, floods, tornadoes, earthquakes, storms, shipwrecks, and explosions, but also "race riots" in the American Midwest and submarine attacks in the Atlantic Ocean. To reiterate: according to the American Red Cross, a race riot or a submarine attack resembles a flood or a tornado more than it does a battle or a revolution. Why should this be? One simple explanation is that the organization is sending a message about what can and cannot be endowed with political meaning. Unlike the meaningful, if unfortunate, devastation caused by a battle or a revolution, the violence associated with the race riot or submarine attack is without meaning. Like an earthquake or a storm, a race riot or a submarine attack is chaotic, uncontrolled, and without purpose. There is no cause or effect, no rationality or reason, associated with these disasters. They are nothing more than pointless, formless destruction—asking for political whys and wherefores is as absurd as asking why, politically, a flood affects one city but not another.

Although this interpretation of the American Red Cross reports is in many ways a convincing one, I think there is also more going on in the organization's counterintuitive process of categorization. If we think about what sort of subjects are involved in both the race riot and the submarine attack, we can see that the report is conforming quite clearly to the paradigm established by the American Geographical Society. By the end of the First World War, the submarine attack had become associated almost exclusively with what was termed "illegal" German military activity—so much so that many analysts were designating submarines as pirate ships and hence the "enemies of all mankind."[77] Detached from any sort of definable political identity, placed on the boundless open seas, incapable of representation, the submarine-as-pirate had, by 1917, *already* become a fractured subject. On the one hand, it was part of the rapidly disintegrating sovereign state that was Germany. On the other, it was outside any sovereign system—isolated and in flux.

The American "race riot" was even more closely associated with the not-quite-sovereign eccentric or ecstatic subject. Incorporated into political systems in much the same way that pirates were, the dissatisfied "race" was simultaneously outside and inside, shattered, multiple by definition. Although the American Red Cross's process of categorization is without question a means of delegitimizing what in other circumstances would look like quite legitimate political violence, therefore, it is also more than that. In the very process of emptying the race riot and submarine attack of political meaning, the report is revealing the ecstatic state of the subjects associated with them. More important, the report is then invoking these shattered subjects as a means of determining what *is* a "disaster" and what *is* a "calamity." In the same way that the Messina earthquake became real at the same time as—and *because*—imagined Indians became real, the floods, tornadoes, and earthquakes relieved by the American Red Cross became real only alongside the pirate submarine in its disastrous destruction, and the race riot in its calamitous fury. These disasters could *only* occur once the ecstatic subject had been situated as the norm.

These two passages are anecdotal ones, indicative of broader trends in the politics of disaster or crisis that I discuss later on. For now, I just want to emphasize, again, that the process of defining a certain event as a disaster, a calamity, or a crisis is more complicated than it might at first appear. Most fundamentally, an earthquake, flood, fire—or for that matter submarine attack—becomes a disaster not only, as has been theorized before, because certain spaces, bodies, or narratives occupy certain places on an imperial civilizational continuum, and are thus endowed with greater or lesser value or meaning. Rather, an earthquake becomes a disaster precisely because shattered subjects beside themselves are briefly more real, more valued, more meaningful than their bounded, rational counterparts. The rhetoric of disaster is aimed at the ecstatic, eccentric subject, not at the unitary, self-conscious one. Indeed, the crisis so relentlessly decenters these rational, bounded subjects, that in many ways they disappear altogether. One talks about the Messina earthquake by invoking hypothetical Indians, miners, and ranchers. One relieves a flood by turning to submarine/pirates and racial storms. The disaster becomes a disaster only in the presence of the subject incapable of representation.

If we turn from the natural crisis or disaster to the metaphysical crisis or disaster, we can see almost identical themes playing out. Indeed, the crisis of the rational subject has been one of the fundamental points of reference in the past two hundred years of political philosophy—often used to signify a reinterpretation of truth or reality. In order to address this crisis, I highlight one analysis of it—Braidotti's—and then re-situate my study of natural disaster within it. In her 1991 book, *Patterns of Dissonance*, Braidotti seeks, first, to address what she calls modernity's metaphysical crisis—the "crisis of the rational subject"—second, to analyze the rhetoric of the "feminine" in the political philosophy that has responded to this crisis, and finally, to ask why it is that despite this emphasis on the feminine, feminist theory and discussions of actual women have remained so marginal in the work of contemporary philosophers.

In addressing these issues, Braidotti invokes the work of a number of political theorists, but her starting point is, again, Descartes, and particularly the Cartesian interpretation of (and attack on) the body. According to Descartes, Braidotti argues, the body conforms "to a very precise geometry: it has a volume that occupies a certain amount of space so as to exclude from it all other bodies."[78] This body, the site of "pre-rational susceptibility" and "multiple other perturbations," is held up in opposition to "thought," which is "defined as the principal of intellection" and "is the driving force of the will thanks to which man can dominate the powerful sensory perceptions which invade him."[79] As a result, the body becomes "the favorite target of Cartesian method, and thus forms the battleground for the combat between reason and its other."[80]

From this point, Braidotti traces the various ways in which modern political philosophy has critiqued, undermined, or simply moved away from Descartes' rational subject, with its antagonistic intellect/body paradigm, and toward a reevaluation of subjectivity. According to her analysis of Foucault, for example, the subject is "eccentric in relation to him/herself . . . situated in the void opened up by the discourse on him/her," and "in this space, which nudges nihilism whilst at the same time resisting it . . . it becomes possible to think anew about the modern subject."[81] Addressing Deleuze, who plays a significant role in her analysis, Braidotti likewise discusses the transition from "thinking" in "Western metaphysics," which "always means thinking about something" to "the new intransitive status [of thinking] reached by contemporary theories of subjectivity."[82] The fundamental strain that runs through all of her argument, however, is again that first, these new theories of subjectivity represent a crisis and, second, that this crisis is inextricably linked to gender studies[83] and feminist theory.[84] As a result, she emphasizes, alongside "the rejection of the alleged universality of the knowing subject, and the critique of the complicity of masculinity and rationality," there must be "a renewal of intent in the sex-specific nature of the subject," that begins "with the idea of embodiment."[85]

What, though, does this metaphysical crisis have to do with earthquakes that afflict hypothetical Indians in the imagined American Southwest, or with submarines and race riots that code as fires and floods? Most obviously, both the crisis that is the natural disaster and the crisis of the rational subject are concerned with addressing the meaning of destruction—and in particular the relationship among destruction, reality, and subject formation. The American Geographical Society wants to describe and define the Messina earthquake and wants to know what Messina and its inhabitants are, now that they have been destroyed. The American Red Cross wants to do the same with its myriad floods, fires, tornadoes, and explosions. Similarly, Foucault and Deleuze want to know what Descartes' rational subject is, now that it has been demolished. Braidotti wants to address the disintegration of his mind/body dualism.

More to the point, however, both the natural disaster and the metaphysical crisis produce identical responses—responses addressed first and foremost to what cannot be represented. Foucault's subjects are eccentric to themselves and situated in a discursive void. His subjects, in other words, are in many ways a collection of fantasy Indians, ranchers, and miners who exist offstage in the discursive emptiness that is the imagined American Southwest. Deleuze's thought is intransitive above all—there is no cause or effect, no rational progress narrative that imparts depth to his thinking subject. His thinking subject is thus likewise in many ways a submarine attack or a race riot—emptied of meaning, but representative of a new embodied subjectivity precisely in its shallowness.

Braidotti's discussion of the "feminine" as representative of the limitations, gaps, and deficiencies in an apparently precrisis rhetoric of the rational subject in this way becomes quite significant in my analysis of disaster. I do not think that these similarities in defining, discussing, and responding to the metaphysical disaster and defining, discussing, and responding to the natural disaster are arbitrary. Each type of crisis demands a new subject, and each type of crisis brings ecstasy within reach. Moreover, to the extent that the crisis of the rational subject has destabilized two centuries of juridical truth—even while most contemporary legal rhetoric remains resolutely blind to its destructive potential—the law of disaster must be operating on multiple levels. I therefore suggest in this book that metaphysical and natural disasters do not just explain one another, but that they produce one another—and that as much as legal responses to them cry out for a rational subject, it is the subject in ecstasy that is eventually revealed.

I conclude this section by saying that although I started with a plea to revive ecstasy as a category of legal and political analysis, in many ways I end with a plea to shift gender studies and feminist theory to the center of the study of law and politics. If ecstatic or eccentric subjects are as foundational as I suggest they are, then the methodologies developed by scholars of gender will be indispensable in addressing them.[86] Likewise, *if* there is a field in which the ecstatic or eccentric subject—the displaced, decentered, shattered, peripatetic object of law and politics—has been effectively theorized, that field is gender studies or feminist theory.[87] In the same way, therefore, that I am calling for a return to the emphasis on ecstasy that occurred in the 1970s and 1980s, I am likewise calling for a rereading of the theories of gendered subjectivity that appeared alongside it in the 1980s and early 1990s. Returning to these discussions will be essential to an effective reading of the politics of disaster and the types of subjects that these politics describe.

Disaster Law and Feminist Theory

I define "disaster law" broadly in this book. Although the cases, statutes, codes, and regulations that compose the legal doctrine of disaster play a significant part in my argument, I pay equal attention to the literary and cultural discourse of disaster law—and deliberately ignore the boundaries that are thought to exist between legal texts with legal meaning and cultural texts with cultural meaning. When I invoke disaster law, therefore, I invoke not only, for example, the trials of criminally negligent building contractors, but the popular response to these trials, and the political management of this popular response—without privileging any one set of texts over the others as more truly legal. I describe not just the regulations that have ordered postdisaster refugee camps, but also the spatial manifestations of these regulations, and the autobiography or poetry produced within these spaces. My contention is that it is precisely as these legal, cultural, political, and literary texts intersect that disaster law is elaborated. My working definition of disaster law is the simultaneously legal, cultural, political, and literary production of the subject in crisis.

At the same time, I am well aware that such a broad definition of disaster law runs the risk of becoming not only broad, but also diffuse. I therefore devote this section to explaining my understanding of disaster law in more detail, anchoring it within the discussions of ecstasy, truth, exceptionalism, and metaphysical crises that came before. More specifically, I answer two questions: first, how is it that a poem or a pamphlet *can* be as effectively legal—as much "law"—as a case or a statute, and second, how is it that the subject in ecstasy can operate within this broadly defined legal sphere? Underlying both questions is a more fundamental one that I also address in this section—namely, why gender studies or feminist theory methodologies are the most effective means of describing both disaster law and its political subjects.

The three major chapters of this book all follow a similar plan. In each, I begin with a specific case, code, or narrative that is not obviously relevant to the legal doctrine of disaster—a case, for instance, that is ordinarily studied for its bearing on medical ethics, a code that has meaning primarily as a foundation for interwar sovereignty, or a narrative that initially operated only in the universe of nineteenth-century imperial geography. Each of these examples serves as an introduction to a more targeted discussion of the law and legal discourse of a specific disaster. All three chapters then end with a return to the realm of what is ordinarily assumed to be normal or everyday law.

I have arranged the chapters of the book in this way in order to emphasize the continuity between everyday law and law in crisis—to demonstrate the extent to which one seems always to serve as the endpoint to the other. There is a second sort of continuity that this arrangement suggests, however—and that is the continuity among legal, cultural, political, and literary texts. As each of these texts gives way to the other, the boundaries among them become difficult to discern. Moreover, the reason for this imprecision, I argue, is that each serves the same fundamentally *legal* purpose. Whether we are talking about the liberal citizen-subject of social contract theory, or the subjected self of critical theory, a (and perhaps *the*) fundamental purpose of law is the production of a political being[88]—and it is toward the production of this political being that these texts all tend. When I say, therefore, that cultural or literary texts are as much a part of law as legal doctrine is, this is not just because law operates within a cultural context, or because something called "law" is "entwined" with something called "culture."[89] More so, it is that each—the poem, the pamphlet, the code, and the statute—does the same, and the same quite specific, work in determining political subjectivity.

To that extent, it is not only reasonable to suggest that "disaster law" consists of both legal doctrine and cultural or literary texts, but it is perhaps irresponsible *not* to do so. It is after all only by following the crisis from its appearance in the trials of contractors or looters, to its appearance in newspaper accounts of these trials, to its appearance in the shattered responses of the populations who follow these media accounts that the multiple meanings and effects of disaster law become clear. It is only by looking simultaneously at the military or camp regulations legislated in the aftermath of disaster, at the building and rebuilding plans that draw on these regulations, and at the demographic studies that populate and repopulate these plans, that the strange continuity of what is supposed to be a unique, ad hoc legal response to crisis begins to make sense. This, then, is why I understand the poem or the pamphlet to be as effectively legal as the case or the statute—because all of these texts are part of the same political process, equally fundamental to the production of the political subject.

The problem, however, is that this political process is by no means a straightforward one—especially when the subjects of disaster law are, as I suggest, ecstatic, shattered, and far removed from the bounded, autonomous citizens of liberal theory. Indeed, there is a circularity in the relationship between the subject in ecstasy and the elaboration of disaster law that will become increasingly apparent as my argument progresses. I do not try to dispel that circularity here or elsewhere in this book. I do, though, address it briefly and explain in more detail how it helps to formulate both ecstatic subjectivity and the politics of disaster.

My contention that the law of disaster both assumes and produces a subject in ecstasy is a problematic one. If law assumes a subject, then that subject must already exist; if law produces a subject, then that subject cannot have already existed. The contradiction is obvious and becomes only more so when we add that the ecstatic subject is likewise both defined by the disaster and makes the disaster politically intelligible. This circularity—or contradiction—however, is by no means unique to my own take on law and subjectivity. It is rather a question that has motivated a great deal of recent political theory and that has inspired a number of responses, especially since the 1980s.

Since my interest here is not to take on or to resolve this contradiction, but rather to explain how it affects my own argument, I address only one of these responses here. Regardless of their methodological approaches, many twentieth-century political philosophers started with the notion that neither the assumption nor the production of the political subject was a single, discrete act. Rather, they argued, the relationship between law and the political subject was an iterative one, each constantly producing and assuming the other. In liberal theory, this process was articulated via various theories of consent—the unique act of hypothetical consent to the social contract giving way by the end of the nineteenth century to the repeated, tacit acts of actual consent that represent daily life in a liberal state.[90] Psychoanalytical theorists—recognizing the violence implicit in this repetition—reformulated the relationship between law and subjectivity as a traumatic one, the political subject's compulsive dependence on law for symbolic existence described as hysterical and sometimes even pornographic.[91] Critical theorists developed increasingly sophisticated theories of interpellation, noting in particular the guilt that must underlie such repeated, consensual acts of subject formation.[92] In general, that is, the relationship between law and the political subject was necessarily circular, necessarily contradictory, and necessarily ongoing.

In this sense, therefore, the circularity involved in the production and assumption of the *ecstatic* subject of disaster law is by no means unique—and I situate my analysis of these processes within a well established, preexisting field of literature. At the same time, however, the fact that I focus in particular on disaster law and in particular on the ecstatic subject does raise some additional issues. First of all, disaster law is by definition something unique, discrete, and even accidental, whereas the law described by the theories above is supposed to be continuous, repetitive, and deliberate.[93] Second, according to my analysis, disaster law produces and assumes the subject in ecstasy precisely in order to make the disaster intelligible. This supplementary function of the political subject requires some explanation.

With that in mind, I return now to my point that gender studies or feminist theory methodologies are the most effective means of describing disaster law. The continuity between ordinary law and law in crisis is not new to feminist theory. As Braidotti argues, many critical theorists have sought in the supposed feminine their desire for a crisis of metaphysical, political, and legal structures.[94] As Carole Pateman argued some years earlier, many liberal theorists likewise *feared* in the supposed feminine the *threat* to metaphysical, political, and legal structures.[95] It can indeed be argued that as ordinary law has increasingly come to be viewed as law in crisis, women have in actuality become the neutral or normative figures of this metaphysical, political, and legal crisis.[96] It is this gradual materialization of what was once thought to be a metaphorical disaster, then, that gender studies methodologies can help to describe—this gradual movement from the ongoing subject formation of the everyday to the ongoing subject formation of the crisis. In the chapters that follow, it will become clear that far more often than not, the concrete realization of the subject in ecstasy—the actual citizen involved in the repetitive and circular process of ecstatic subject formation—is first and foremost a gendered subject.

That being the case, the interaction between ecstatic subjects and intelligible disasters is an interaction very much also embedded in feminist theory. Just as gender studies methodologies have been indispensable to describing the theoretical relationship between the field of the intelligible and the nonfield of the unintelligible,[97] they will be equally indispensable to describing the concrete relationship between the intelligible disaster and the unintelligible subject in ecstasy. When I say, therefore, that disaster law—defined, again, as simultaneously legal, cultural, political, and literary—assumes the subject in ecstasy in order to endow the disaster with meaning, I am making a distinct, specific claim, situated in feminist methodology. I am arguing that the disaster becomes a politically viable event at precisely the moment that *all* subjects become not just gendered, but *unthinkably* gendered. The assumption and production of the ecstatic subject of disaster law, that is, involves precisely the negation and the unraveling of this subject.

It is for this reason that I have brought together in this section three seemingly disconnected issues—my working definition of "disaster law," my brief analysis of subjection and subjectivation, and my claim that feminist theory methodologies are essential to any analysis of disaster law. Although not immediately relevant to one another, each gets at a key aspect of the assumption, production, negation, and unraveling of the ecstatic subject. By defining disaster law broadly, as the product not just of legal doctrine but of literary and cultural texts, I recognize that the political field of the intelligible can only be defined through the interaction of *multiple* discourses. By acknowledging the circularity of the legal and political relationship, I situate disaster law and its ecstatic subjects within a well established, existing literature. And finally, by describing the subject of disaster law as a subject specifically relevant to feminist theory, I shift my study into the methodological realm with arguably the most potential for radically rethinking these interactions and relationships.

Historical Context and Chapter Outlines

Throughout this introductory chapter I have drawn in an impressionistic way on descriptions of a number of different disasters. I have also cobbled together a variety of theoretical discussions of crises, exceptions, and subjects beside themselves. Over the remainder of the book, I ground these theoretical analyses within a more detailed history of four major case studies: the 1894 Istanbul earthquake, the 1906 San Francisco earthquake, the 1923 Tokyo-Yokohama earthquake, and the 1999 Istanbul/Marmara earthquake. Readers may be taken aback by the case studies I have chosen, and particularly by my privileging of the (repeated) destruction of Istanbul. Rather than writing a further section in which I explain or defend my choice of case studies, however, I instead relate a paragraph from a work that deals with similar political issues.

> I have not respected the academic division of labor between area studies and the disciplines. I offer no modest apologies for this. Europeanists universalize European

> milieus and experiences all the time. Instead of provincializing Europe, I have attempted a necessarily provisional universalizing of one corner of postcolonial Asia. Humanity (and theorizing about it) is, after all, an interminable work of collaboration and comparison.[98]

Needless to say, I write under the same assumptions.

At the same time, I note that these disasters and the narratives surrounding them are all unique and specific to their chronological and geographical contexts. They also, however, share key similarities, especially with regard to the legal and political responses that followed them and the legal and political subjects demanded by these responses. Each, I suggest, produced a political context in which the ecstatic or eccentric subject became the norm. And each invoked the subject in ecstasy as a means of endowing the disaster with meaning.

As for the usual facts and figures that accompany histories of destructive earthquakes, the first Istanbul quake occurred at 12:24 on Tuesday afternoon, July 10, 1894. It consisted of three major shocks, lasting thirteen seconds, and would have measured around 7 on the Richter scale. The epicenter was in the Sea of Marmara, eight kilometers from the shore of the European side of the city. According to official figures, 138 people were killed, but likely many more than that lost their lives, and hundreds of houses and public buildings were destroyed.[99] The San Francisco earthquake occurred at 5:12 on Wednesday morning, April 18, 1906. It consisted of a number of shocks lasting forty-five to sixty seconds, and would have measured between 7 and 8 on the Richter scale. The epicenter was about three kilometers offshore. According to official figures, 375 to 478 people were killed, but, again, the estimates as to the actual death toll are much higher. Tens of thousands of homes and public buildings were destroyed in the quake and in the fire that followed it.

The Tokyo-Yokohama earthquake occurred at noon on September 1, 1923. The shocks measured 8.3 on the Richter scale. The epicenter was in Sagami Bay, southwest of Tokyo Bay. At the time, an estimated 100,000 to 140,000 people were killed in the quake and in the fires that followed. The city of Yokohama was completely burned, and in all over a billion dollars worth of property was destroyed. Finally, the second Istanbul earthquake (the Marmara quake) occurred at 3:02 in the morning on August 17, 1999. The first two shocks lasted thirty-seven seconds, and the largest measured 7.4 on the Richter scale. The epicenter was seventy kilometers south of Istanbul in the gulf of İzmit. An estimated 15,000 people died, and 600,000 were left homeless in the months that followed.

I provide these figures less because they will be important to my later analysis than because this is the sort of information that is expected in discussions of disasters of this kind. Again, though, my particular interest in this book is not so much what happens during or after a disaster as what defines the disaster in first place—and what sort of subject is at the heart of this process of definition. As a result, the book is divided into four major chapters, each of which addresses one aspect of subject formation during moments of crisis. Chapter Two consists of a literature review of both historical and contemporary writing on disaster. In it, I address, first of all, the meaning of earthquake metaphors in political speech—what happens to the disaster, that is, when revolutions, rebellions, and economic crises are explained via recourse to the "convulsions of the earth." I then turn to historical discussions of actual earthquakes and how these have drawn on this political rhetoric. Finally, I discuss the concerns of contemporary scholars of catastrophe studies—and the various tropes and events that they invoke in order to make disasters understandable.

Chapters Three and Four engage with ecstatic life and ecstatic death as they have been defined by the law and politics of disaster. In Chapter Three, I complicate the story of postdisaster blood transfusions, organ transplants, and disease prevention measures by arguing that each is as much a means of articulating the subject in ecstasy as it is a means of providing sanitation and security to the self-conscious, bounded subject. Framed within an analysis of U.S. Judge Benjamin N. Cardozo's historic 1914 decision on the right to bodily integrity, this chapter suggests that these various "gifts of life" are methods of physically and bodily manifesting citizens in pieces—citizens quite physically beside themselves. Chapter Four concerns itself primarily with the repeated, if counterintuitive, granting of rights to dead bodies during moments of disaster—with the reiteration, for instance, of the right to property and the right to bodily integrity possessed by the respectable dead citizen, and the suspension of the right to life forfeited by the living looter or "ghoul." Addressing the postdisaster rhetoric of death tolls, democracy, and decomposition, this chapter describes one functional process by which the dead body—a disintegrating body almost proverbially in ecstasy—becomes the norm of disaster law.

Chapter Five turns to the spaces defined by the law and politics of disaster—and particularly the extent to which these spaces become ecstatic backdrops for the articulation of ecstatic subjects. Contextualized within a discussion, first, of Henri Lefebvre's critique of capitalist or fascist space, and second, of Achille

Mbembe's critique of postcolonial space, it addresses the ways in which unitary, sovereign spaces can become fractured, distorted, and thus definable by the law of disaster. Drawing on the tropes of the camp, the cemetery, and the demolished monument or public square that appear in postdisaster narratives, I suggest that each of these areas is a deliberate political construction, each is key to demonstrating the truth or reality of the disaster, and each is fundamental to the production of subjects beside themselves.

Finally, in Chapter Six, I return to the arguments that I outlined above. First, I elaborate on the notion that the disaster or crisis has in many ways become the legal and political norm. I then make the case that understanding disaster as the endpoint to law may be the most effective way to address the inconsistencies (and violence) associated with contemporary disaster response. In the end, I return to feminist theory as both a means of addressing and a means of redefining disaster law, subjects of disaster, and disaster response in the twentieth and twenty-first centuries.

Conclusion

Although I have not addressed it explicitly, this book is clearly indebted to the past decade of work on the everyday or day-to-day. As the line between the extraordinary and the day-to-day has been blurred, and as politics, violence, and subject formation have been gradually reframed within the overlapping spheres of the exceptional and the normal, disaster has become a prominent topic of debate and discussion. In so many ways singular, and yet in so many ways the norm, the disaster—and particularly the natural disaster—represents an intersection between the political violence of daily life and the political violence of the unexpected. My intention throughout this book is to keep both approaches to subject formation in mind. As a subject of disaster law, the ecstatic subject is simultaneously a product of the day-to-day and a product of the emergency. As the subject who endows the disaster with meaning, the ecstatic subject is likewise both the aberrant and the norm. At the same time, however, these dual roles are by no means paralyzing—representing as they do a possible way out of the confusion that is and has been a part and parcel of the law and politics of disaster.

Writing About Disaster

Metaphors in Crisis

Introduction

This short chapter contextualizes my study of the Istanbul, San Francisco, and Tokyo earthquakes within the extensive literature that already exists and addresses natural disaster. The scholarly field of catastrophe studies has grown over the past decade, generating a number of methodological conventions that I both adopt and challenge throughout this book. The second section of this chapter describes many of these conventions and the points at which my work intersects with and diverges from them. However, writing about disaster is certainly not unique to the beginning of the twenty-first century. Disasters—and the various ways in which they might be endowed with meaning—have generated political and literary interest for a long time. As one scholar has pointed out, many European historians describe the 1755 Lisbon earthquake "as a watershed event dividing the premodern from the modern age."[1]

I do not argue that any one disaster ought to serve as such a distinct historical signpost. I do, however, address much of the literature that does make these types of claims, and the first section of this chapter, "Historical Disaster Writing," is thus a broadly conceived review of three centuries of writing on disaster. In it, I analyze the ways in which, historically, various earthquakes have been endowed with meaning, and I make the case that a disaster's political meaning has been determined via the production and invocation of the subject in ecstasy. In the second section of the chapter, "Contemporary Disaster Writing," I argue that despite this historical trend, the contemporary historiography of disaster is in many ways split—divided into texts that insist upon a bounded subject and subtexts that insist upon a shattered one. I conclude by situating this study within both the modern history of disaster writing and the contemporary historiography that constitutes catastrophe studies. In the process, I set a foundation for the more detailed discussion of subjects beside themselves that appears in later chapters.

Historical Disaster Writing

My particular interest in this section is the metaphorical life of the natural disaster—and especially the earthquake—between the mid-eighteenth century and the mid-twentieth century. It was over these two hundred years that both modern disaster response and modern political relationships were developed, and so it makes sense that disaster metaphors should also have taken on a distinct political meaning over this same period. There are indeed a number of clear and common themes that seem to run through the modern rhetoric of disaster. In general, for example, these metaphors all invoke in different ways the disintegrating, eccentric, ecstatic subject—and in general they all seem to do so in order to turn the political or natural situation they are describing into something recognizable. At the same time, the modern earthquake metaphor is a shifting trope in which it is never entirely clear what precisely is signifying what. What I do over the course of this section, therefore, is address, first, a few examples of disasters as politics, second, a few more examples of politics as disaster, and then finally, a couple of examples where the referent is not obvious. My focus is the gradual process by which the politics of disaster became a politics of ecstasy—and by which the metaphor of the disaster gradually became a concrete reality.

Before I get to these eighteenth-, nineteenth-, and twentieth-century discussions of disasters, however, I turn to a mid-seventeenth-century earthquake that does not conform to my theories of subjectivity and disaster law. This is an early modern analysis of earthquakes that in a number of ways supports Foucault's point about the contradiction between the rationality of theology and the ecstatic potential of spirituality[2]—an analysis that distinctly invokes the unitary, bounded, self-conscious subject as a means of revealing the rational and verifiable *religious* truth of the disaster. It thus serves as an effective jumping-off point for the story I tell in the remainder of this section about the gradual articulation of a modern politics of disaster and of ecstasy.

In 1668, in response to an earthquake that struck primarily the European provinces of the Ottoman Empire, the Dutch writer, Leopold Wettersteint de Hodenstein, determined that the disaster promises (1) "good and prosperous success to Christians," (2) that "the infernal powers shall be converted and turn'd against one another," (3) that "the *miscreant Turks* by internecine wars and divisions shall tear the very heart of the *Ottoman Empire* asunder," and finally (4) that "he that has hitherto been invincible, and proudly insulted over Christian Kings and Princes, now the very earth (the lowest, basest, and vilest of all creatures) scorns to bear him and begins to shake him off."[3] This discussion is a relatively straightforward example of natural disaster understood as, first, a tool in religious prophecy and, second, a punishment from God for religious and political misbehavior.

At the same time, it can likewise be read as something of a variation on Cartesian rationalism and dualism, where the base earth/body responds to the will of the exalted government/mind. Natural disorder—described elsewhere in the text as the "commoting of the earth"—is analogous to political disorder—internecine wars—and each is subservient to religious truth. Nature or the body personified as Earth, "the creature," is obedient to rational Christian will and Christian need, attempting to shake off the Muslim Ottomans altogether. What I highlight in this passage, however, is less the relationship between political disorder and natural disorder in Wettersteint de Hodenstein's universe—a relationship that is relatively obvious—and more the way in which this disorder is made understandable.

First of all, there is a direct causal relationship between God's displeasure and the "commoting of the earth." This is a disaster, in other words, that is logical above all else—the meaning is there for anyone to see. More to the point, the political subjects involved this disaster are likewise the political subjects that take center stage in Wettersteint de Hodenstein's analysis of it. There are Christians and there are Turks. Each is directly affected by the earthquake. There are, contrarily, no offstage Indians or pirates to make this disaster meaningful. Indeed, given that the earth is seeking in the future to throw the Turks offstage, their central role in the present is quite clear. This is a rational, logical earthquake that is made intelligible—and the political meaning of which is made clear—via reference to central, unitary subjects.

Almost one hundred years later, the natural disaster remained for many writers a rational and logical event that assumed a similarly bounded, unitary subject. According to a 1750 article in the British *Gentleman's Magazine*, for example, earthquakes were "evidently placed among those methods by which God punishes a rebellious and wicked people . . . all [of] which makes it abundantly plain, that Earthquakes are under the divine management, and are made use of by God to fulfill his pleasure."[4] Nonetheless, disasters were also becoming more complicated throughout the eighteenth century and, as Maxine Van de Wetering argues in her study of earthquakes and Puritan sermonizing, the process of endowing them with meaning was becoming increasingly fraught.

One Puritan thinker, for instance, divided earthquakes into two categories—natural and supernatural—the former occurring "at the climax of an observed sequence of 'meteorological warnings,'" and the latter "delivered apparently without sequential physical warning."[5] The former, this writer suggests, was "lawful," whereas the latter was the consequence of "God's direct intervention into His own lawful mechanism."[6] Van de Wetering's analysis of this division is that "to action-driven Puritans, such an [irrational] God would have been morally immobilizing, and the obvious disjunction between the natural and the moral governments would be ethically crippling to the community."[7] As a result, "the Puritan God was forever being startled, so to speak, out of His normal habits of operation through natural law by some kind of human behavior."[8]

But there is an additional reading of this interpretation of natural and supernatural earthquakes. Again, the supernatural earthquake, unbounded by law and a function of, as the *Gentleman's Magazine* notes, God's pleasure, remained prophetic and punitive, functional in the realm inhabited by Leopold Wettersteint de Hodenstein. The natural earthquake was quite different, a product of law and legal structures, seemingly unrelated to God's desires. The supernatural earthquake proved the existence of God; the natural earthquake proved nothing more than the existence of law. Supernatural earthquakes occurred without any direct reference to law; natural earthquakes occurred without any direct reference to God. I suggest, however, that despite all of these differences, these two types of earthquakes were by no means disconnected from one another in the broader politics of eighteenth-century Puritanism.

Given that God made the laws that governed the natural earthquake, and that the supernatural earthquake proved the existence of God, neither the natural earthquake nor the legal system it followed could exist *without* the possibility of a supernatural earthquake. It was the supernatural earthquake, in other words that, in its very lawlessness, made law possible. This was an articulation of disaster and politics that in almost every way prefigured Carl Schmitt's analysis of the state of exception. For Schmitt, the exception proved the existence of the sovereign, and thus the existence of the day-to-day jurisprudence (even in its suspension) as it was overseen by the sovereign.[9] For the Puritans, the supernatural earthquake proved the existence of God and thus the existence of the natural law (even in its suspension) that was overseen by God.

Put another way, it was the very thing that was unknowable, that was by definition ecstatic—God in his decision to wreak divine destruction or the sovereign in his decision to suspend day-to-day jurisprudence—that endowed law with meaning. Even when God was, as it were, ruling by decree, however, it is important to keep in mind that these decisions made rational and logical sense: men were evil, God responded. The difference between Leopold Wettersteint de Hodenstein's analysis and this early eighteenth-century Puritan analysis, therefore, is not that one is rational, embedded in causal relationships, while the other is not. Rather, it is that one is *unitary* while the other is not. In the late seventeenth century, in the apparent era of Cartesian dualism, there was a one-to-one correspondence between religious will and natural disaster—between political disorder and natural disorder. There was none of this questioning of the relationship among law, politics, and divine decree, between legal subjects and their religious or political counterparts. The early eighteenth-century Puritans, however, in their very religious fervor, brought law, and thus legal subjects, into the picture. In the Puritan analysis, the Cartesian structure was shattered. And the result was a situation in which the rational, *lawful* mechanism and its rational, *lawful* subjects could be real, could be endowed with meaning only via reference to that hyperbolically ecstatic and offstage being—that being who is defined above all as He who is outside of the law—God. We have the beginning here, that is, of legal systems, of laws of disaster, that become real only via reference to the ecstatic subject.

My point in bringing up Puritan analyses of disaster is not to suggest that religious belief or the lack thereof is what is key to this transformation in seventeenth- and eighteenth-century earthquake metaphors. Rather, I argue that by the eighteenth century there was a gradual shift in focus away from the unitary subject and toward the ecstatic, eccentric one. Indeed, if we turn to one of the most famous eighteenth-century European discussions of natural disaster—Voltaire's poem on the 1755 Lisbon earthquake—we can see precisely this transformation in action. Voltaire's poem on "the axiom 'all is well'" plays with two themes. The first is that God's existence is becoming increasingly dubious in the face of the enormous human suffering that follows disasters such as the 1755 earthquake. The second is that it is more ethical to relate to human beings as discrete individuals than it is to relate to them as members of an undifferentiated religious or even national group. As such, the poem appears at first glance to be very much in opposition to the Puritans' religious sermons and very much in support of the unitary, bounded, rational subject. Although the poem can be placed superficially into these categories, however, in one important way—in its invocation of the ecstatic subject—it is identical to the Puritan writing.

As Rita Goldberg argues, for example, "what made Voltaire's evocation of suffering caused by the Lisbon earthquake unusual was that most eighteenth century writers remained more interested in the compassionate response of the observer than in suffering itself."[10] Voltaire, contrarily, "devotes himself entirely to the victims of the earthquake in his poem," and thus "the shattered domesticity of Lisbon offers a challenge to representation as well as belief."[11] Voltaire's "audience," she concludes "is not his subject."[12] His audience is not his subject. What does this mean? Most clearly, as Goldberg suggests, it means that the poem is not just a poem about religious belief; it is a poem about shifting modes of representation. Whereas other eighteenth-century writers collapsed subject and audience into one—attempting to produce sentimental political subjects by talking *to* and *about* sentimental political subjects—Voltaire's scene is fractured. He, too, is trying to create (political) subjects, but he is doing so by talking *to* citizens and philosophers *about* the suffering population of Lisbon.

Just as the Puritans' rational system of natural law could become meaningful only by invoking the eccentric, ecstatic subject that existed outside of it, so too Voltaire's rational, thinking individual could become meaningful only via recourse to a shattered Lisbon both at the center of, and at the margins of, the political scene. To repeat, rather than talking to the population of Lisbon about their suffering, rather than talking to citizens or philosophers about their sentimentality, Voltaire is instead talking to citizens or philosophers about the suffering population of Lisbon—in order to make a broader point about political and religious identity. Producing a split in the scene—a divide between audience and subject—Voltaire is arguably understanding ecstasy as the most effective starting point for a conversation about subjectivity.

Just as the 1668 earthquake was a political metaphor for Wettersteint de Hodenstein, that is, the 1755 earthquake was the same for Voltaire. Unlike Wettersteint de Hodenstein, however, Voltaire does not read the disaster as something relevant only—or even primarily—to the population in the disaster zone. What has occurred in Lisbon is explicitly *not* that the people misbehaved and that therefore they were punished. Rather, the 1755 earthquake is relevant to a population far removed from Lisbon—a population on the verge of becoming rational, progressive, and aware of its various rights—a population, however, whose liberal existence is predicated precisely upon reference to the ecstatic subjects of Lisbon.[13] Voltaire's poem is thus in many ways an example both of disaster as politics and politics as disaster. It operates, therefore, as an excellent jumping off point for my next collection of earthquake metaphors. What we will see in the following passages is a number of moments at which politics become disaster, rather than disaster politics. I emphasize again, however, that it is still Braidotti's metaphysical crisis that is at the heart of these metaphors—and it is still the subject in ecstasy that makes them intelligible.

The first of these metaphors was published in 1788, when *The Columbia Magazine* reprinted an essay by David Hume, "On Civil Liberty." In this essay, we learn that "private property seems to me almost as secure in a civilized EUROPEAN monarchy, as in a republic; nor is danger much apprehended in such a government, from the violence of the sovereign, more than we commonly dread harm from thunder or earthquakes."[14] Second, and at around the same time, Edmund Burke was gradually popularizing the rhetoric of disaster—his reference to the French Revolution, for instance, as "the greatest moral earthquake that ever convulsed and shattered this globe of ours," and his insistence that only "justice" could "defy" it, was reproduced repeatedly in early nineteenth-century British journals as a textbook example of flawless political eloquence.[15] By the 1850s, *Blackwood's Edinburgh Magazine* was arguing in reference to the 1848 revolutions, variously, that "Canada has lately shared largely in the moral earthquake which has so violently shaken all parts of the British Empire,"[16] and that, but for the Reform Act, "the British constitution would infallibly have been overturned during the moral earthquakes in Europe which followed the French Revolution of 1848."[17] Two years later, the editors noted in another essay on "earthquakes": "so violent were the shocks of the revolutionary earthquake in the Fatherland [i.e., pre-unification Germany], that the entire disruption of society and ruin of the national independence seemed to be threatened by its effects."[18] The *Saturday Evening Post* argued ten years later that "since the time when the throes of 'that world's earthquake, Waterloo' convulsed and changed the destinies of

Christendom, nothing has so powerfully excited the public mind as the present revolt in India."[19]

Switching focus to the United States, an anonymous writer of 1815 attacked inappropriate political violence in France and England by insisting that, "if the island of Great Britain and the whole territory of France, should now be sunk by an earthquake, the loss of lives would perhaps be less than what has been occasioned by the voluntary and anti-Christian wars of the two nations."[20] The author then concludes by asking whether "the people of the United States [should] continue to follow the bloody examples of these nations in *offering human sacrifices*? God Forbid!"[21] Finally, jumping ahead a number of decades, the Civil War in the United States, according to Sheila Hones, was "presented most often . . . in the image of a gulf, or chasm," produced by "the national 'earthquake,'" and creating "a metaphorical dislocation . . . both spatial and temporal at the same time."[22] She continues that the war "was remembered as 'unnatural,' first because of its association with the absence of intelligent, moral leadership [on the battlefield] and second because of its image as a war of massacred armies rather than thoughtful individuals."[23]

I could continue with these examples of politics as disaster ad infinitum, but since my primary interest in this book is disaster as politics, and since all of this serves principally as context, I will stop here. What I want to highlight, however, again, is the type of political subject that these inverted politics/earthquake analogies assume. What is it about these various political activities—the sovereign seizure of private property, various revolutions and anticolonial movements, inappropriate declarations of war—that turns them into *disasters*? And why is it that, to the extent that protective solutions are advanced, these have to do with variations on the rule of law? First of all, this decision to render various forms of political activity disastrous or calamitous is identical to the decision to differentiate between "military violence" and "great disasters" in the early twentieth-century American Red Cross reports. Doing so delegitimizes certain types of political activity, empties them of meaning, and dehumanizes their perpetrators. At the same time, however, just as in the Red Cross reports, there is also something more going on in these disaster metaphors than a simple process of delegitimization.

If we consider the last example, for instance, we can see that the Civil War in the United States is defined as an earthquake above all (if perhaps paradoxically) because it is "unnatural." It is, in turn, "unnatural" because there is an apparent absence of thoughtful, rational leadership on the battlefield, and a turn toward undifferentiated armies massacred without reason. What makes something an earthquake in this rhetorical space, therefore, is quite specifically the invocation of a mass of irrational, shattered, butchered bodies—bodies that, by definition, are beside themselves, dismembered, that can in no way become unitary subjects. Similarly, in the second to last example, what makes an earthquake different from warfare is that the latter is "voluntary" whereas the former implicitly is not. What makes an earthquake the *same* as warfare is that each is a form of "human sacrifice." Once more, therefore, the way in which warfare becomes an earthquake in this passage is via reference to irrational, butchered (in this case sacrificed) bodies—bodies that are, again, in no way part of the seemingly voluntary logic of nondisastrous political structures. To emphasize, the issue that is key to defining the meaning of the political violence here is less agency or activity—"voluntary" warfare, after all, is made rhetorically identical to involuntary disasters. Rather the issue that is key is the condition of the bodies—the shattered state of the physically ecstatic subjects of war/disaster.

The rhetoric that turns anticolonial and revolutionary violence into disaster is slightly different in that it takes spaces or states as its subject rather than bodies or citizens—but it nonetheless plays on almost identical themes. A revolution is an earthquake because it convulses land, changes the course of history, threatens independence, and disrupts society. A revolution is also an earthquake because of what can prevent it, namely constitutional law. The way in which an act of political violence becomes an earthquake, therefore, is via the invocation of a shattered, indefinable, spatially and temporally disrupted *land* that can never function, like a state, as a rational political subject. Contrarily, the way in which this political violence remains undisastrous is by invoking the rational, unitary subject that is apparently demanded by the rule of law—a point made clear in Hume's positing of respect for "civil liberties" as the thing that differentiates civilized sovereign activity from its disastrous counterpart.

Again, my interest in this book is less the way in which various political events have been defined as disasters, and more the ways in which disasters are turned into politics. My last set of examples of metaphors in crisis, however, also suggests that the line between these two rhetorical positions—the difference between referent and reality—is not as obvious as it might appear. Indeed, what follows now are a number of muddled metaphors—hypothetical disasters in the imagined future turned into present political realities, or hypothetical political violence in the imagined past turned into a future natural disaster. What I suggest in these last few paragraphs is thus, first, that politics and disaster are far too entangled to address separately, and second, that both disasters and the political structures that develop out of them become intelligible only via reference to the ecstatic, eccentric subject.

I begin, therefore, with a typical example of politics, in this case imperial politics, colliding with disaster rhetoric. In March 1894, *New Peterson Magazine* conducted an interview with the geologist and earthquake expert John Milne. Rather than inviting Milne to discuss the physical causes or effects of earthquakes, the interviewer asked him instead to satisfy his readers' curiosity about their "moral effects,"[24] and concluded the conversation as follows:

> in such places as Japan and Naples, we find light hearted carelessness and disregard for the morrow more prevalent than elsewhere, and in all earthquake countries, the arts conducive to pleasure are highly cultivated. If, says, Professor Milne, the seismic force of South America were turned loose in England or Germany, it would ultimately produce a people with no idea of permanency among whom everything spiritual would collapse and might result in sinking Germans and Englishmen to the lowest level in the ranks of civilization.[25]

This passage is a straightforward and unremarkable example of nineteenth-century racism and civilizational rhetoric.[26] The climate and geology of England and Germany have led to civilizational superiority; the climate and geology of Japan, Naples, and South America have led to civilizational inferiority. I bring it up, however, less to highlight the relationship between scientific rationalism and imperial violence that developed over the nineteenth and twentieth centuries, and more to stress the extent to which the eighteenth- and early nineteenth-century politics/disaster metaphors that I discussed above had become a concrete reality by the turn of the twentieth century.

If we compare this discussion of civilization and disaster to a second one published thirty years later, we can see that this transformation had by the 1920s become complete. By 1923, in fact, Germany had fallen into precisely the trap foretold in the above passage, and in an article entitled "Germany in Earthquake," we discover the following: "Germany is sick. And a bulletin on her condition is inevitable. The question is no longer whether she has suffered for her sins but whether, as Germany, she will survive."[27] In 1894, in other words, we were told that civilizations existing in earthquake zones are impermanent and civilizationally inferior. In 1923, German politics are in fact "in earthquake," and—as expected—Germany has become sick, backward, and impermanent.

Although related to the nineteenth-century discussion of the "revolutionary earthquake" that had disrupted society and threatened the "Fatherland's" independence, therefore, I want to emphasize that this analysis is also something of a departure. Before, politics and natural disaster were *analogous* to one another, each serving in different ways as a reference point for the other. Here, the analogy has disappeared. Politics per se—revolutions, elections, battles—do not show up at all in the text; they have been consumed entirely by the disaster. Germany is in earthquake. Period. And, biologically, it is sick. There is no longer any political reference point, there is only material, scientific discussions of *actual* natural disasters and *actual* biological illness. What had once been a literary device has become a reality. More to the point, however, this device has made the subject offstage, the subject in ecstasy even more insistent than before. The *only* way to understand Germany, to make Germany intelligible, to make Germany a political subject, and—most important—to comprehend Germany's disaster in this analytical universe[28] is to invoke the fantastic, pleasure-loving Japanese, Neapolitans, and South Americans. It is only by turning hypothetical subjects in ecstasy into a legal and political norm that Germany as a concept—and the German disaster in particular—makes any sense at all.

Throughout the late nineteenth and early twentieth centuries, in fact, we see repeated anecdotal examples of the new *reality* of the disaster/politics metaphor and the paradoxical centrality of the eccentric subject appearing in analyses of earthquakes. In the context of the U.S. empire, for instance, an American correspondent writing in 1902 on the occupation of the Philippines stated the following:

> A certain well-known Pacificator of Provinces confessed that, though not a cruel man, if a tidal wave had to follow upon the earthquake, he hoped it would sweep with overwhelming force over a certain district where, despite frequent announcements of peace, the rebellion rages. "We might drown them out, but this rubbing out process is proving too expensive."[29]

Switching scenes, Said Nursi, a late nineteenth-/early twentieth-century Ottoman and Turkish philosopher, engages in an analysis of God's use of earthquakes and other natural disasters to "wake up" the careless.[30] In a reversal of Leopold Wettersteint de Hodenstein's position, however, Nursi understands God to afflict believing populations with disasters in the here and now so that they will not have to suffer in the next world.[31] Moreover, Nursi speaks a careful language of law, religion, and civil officialdom quite divorced from Wettersteint de Hodenstein's, where functionaries who behave in a treacherous or illegal manner in the name of "law" are identical to earthquakes, droughts, illnesses, or storms.[32] Finally, altering the context one last time, the 1954 Japanese film *Godzilla* encapsulates the concrete reality of political violence as natural violence in what has now become an almost paradigmatic manner. The story of a monster that wakes up and destroys Tokyo following American nuclear testing, *Godzilla*, as Susan J. Napier argues, "demonizes American nuclear science in an obvious reference to the atomic tragedies of Hiroshima and Nagasaki."[33]

Although occupying vastly different cultural and aesthetic positions, each of these discussions is an example, first, of the now concrete nature of the disaster/politics metaphor and, second, the increasing centrality of the subject in ecstasy. In the American colonial context, the "pacification" of the Philippines and the "rubbing out" of rebellious soldiers will ideally conform to the overwhelming force of a tsunami. If it should operate in conformity with an actual tsunami, however, so much the better. In the Ottoman Empire and Turkey, the treachery of functionaries and their political misbehavior writ large occupy the same category as natural disasters. They are not *like* earthquakes or famines; they *are* earthquakes and famines—each undermines in exactly the same way the health and prosperity of the population. Finally, in *Godzilla*, this trend is brought to its logical conclusion. In the years following the Second World War, the bombings of Hiroshima and Nagasaki were increasingly depicted as natural disasters rather than as deliberate, politically motivated acts of violence. *Godzilla*, therefore—ironically or not—turns this rhetorical point into a concrete reality. Again, it is not that these bombings were *like* a natural disaster—they *were* a natural disaster. The connection is direct, and it is the monster, not the bomb, that ends up destroying the urban center.

Moreover, in each of these examples, as the disaster metaphor becomes increasingly concrete, it relies increasingly on the ecstatic subject to determine its political meaning. The discussion of the Philippines, for example, takes the assumptions underlying the American Red Cross reports one step further, and turns not just the rioting "rebels"—the equivalent of rioting "race"—into a force of nature, but also the U.S. military's response to them. The only way in which military violence can make sense in this context is in reference to indefinable subjects. Likewise, the rule of law in the Ottoman Empire can be defined only via recourse to the treacherous official as natural disaster. And finally, Godzilla is essentially playing the same role as the Puritan God was two hundred years before. He is irrational, destructive, and quite obviously outside the rule of law—but it is only by making him the subject of the legal and political narrative that the deliberate, politically motivated bombings of Hiroshima and Nagasaki can make any sense at all.

Once more, my purpose in bringing up these anecdotal examples of the disaster metaphor is to emphasize the extent to which Braidotti's crisis of the rational subject remains very much with us, and the extent to which the legal and political rhetoric of disaster assumes an ecstatic subject. I have provided a number of different variations on the metaphor—earthquake as politics, politics as earthquake, and earthquake/politics situations in which the referent is not clear. I repeat, however, that my interest in this book is predominantly the first of these associations. And I address the legal and political structures that develop when a disaster becomes the reference point for politics. At the same time, as I have suggested, the line between these two types of metaphor is not in any way an obvious one—and it is precisely this ambiguity that lends the subject in ecstasy its rhetorical power.

Contemporary Disaster Writing

Having touched on the historical literature that addresses disaster, I turn now to the more recent work that has appeared in the field of catastrophe studies. In particular, I am interested in the various ways that this scholarship has grappled with defining the disaster. Again, my own hypothesis is that a disaster comes into existence when the ecstatic subject becomes the normative figure of law and politics. Obviously, however, there are other ways of approaching this issue, and the purpose of this section is to address these alternative approaches, to examine some common themes that emerge in them, and to try to find points of overlap between these conclusions and my own. I address, especially, three broad arguments that appear in contemporary discussions of the disaster.

The first of these is the notion that disasters become disasters when they occur at some commonly accepted center. According to this argument, a disaster occurs when it has been effectively framed within a coherent cultural, civilizational, or geographical context. The second approach suggests that disasters become disasters only upon their articulation as well-worn narratives. Scholars who implicitly or explicitly support this position argue that disasters come into existence only when they are articulated via a coherent and rational story that is already comforting and familiar. And finally, the third position that I address concerns the everyday—it rests on the notion that a disaster becomes a disaster when the everyday or daily life becomes a template for politics.

I would like to begin with what is probably the most common thesis about the relationship between reality and disaster—namely, that a disaster happens when it destroys some "cultural center." As a 2006 law school textbook on Hurricane "Katrina and Beyond" puts it:

> the flooding destroyed New Orleans, the Nation's thirty-fifth largest city. Much as the fire that burned Chicago in 1871 and the earthquake and fire that leveled San Francisco in 1906 destroyed the economic and cultural centers of an entire region, so too did Hurricane Katrina destroy what many considered to be the heart of the Gulf Coast. The destruction also called to mind the Galveston Hurricane of 1900, which thoroughly devastated the town of Galveston, Texas. At the time, Galveston was an economic and cultural center of Texas and was the State's fourth largest city . . . [Y]et, Hurricane Katrina not only damaged far more property than any previous natural disaster, it was also the deadliest natural disaster in the United States since Hurricane San Felipe in 1928.[34]

It is, in other words—and repeatedly—the destruction of a *center*, a heart, that turns something into a disaster. New Orleans, Chicago, San Francisco, and Galveston are moved to the center of the cultural scene, and it is as a result of this centrality that their destruction is a disaster. Indeed, there is an implicit assumption in this writing that loss of life itself becomes disastrous only when it happens at the center. Violence thus codes as a crisis if and only if it is central—with all of the political consequences that this association implies.

This approach to disaster—along with critiques of it—has become common in recent years. At the same time, however, much of the recent writing that accepts the center of culture paradigm also attempts to subvert it in some way, or at least to shift its meaning. While accepting that a reference to the center defines a disaster, these discussions also seek to destabilize the notion of centrality itself and to reevaluate the political rhetoric that is produced via references to centers. In an analysis of the 1923 Tokyo-Yokohama earthquake, for instance, one writer states first that "on Saturday, 1 September 1923, a devastating earthquake hit the Tokyo-Yokohama area. The initial jolt lasted nearly fourteen seconds. Over 100,000 people were killed, many more were injured, and hundreds of thousands of homes were destroyed by the quake and the ensuing fires."[35] He then continues, "a lesser known disaster . . . followed fast on the heels of the 1923 earthquake. This was the massacre of hundreds of Koreans in Tokyo, Yokohama, and other places in the days immediately following 1 September."[36] In a very different context, a second writer argues in a discussion of "Peru's Five Hundred Year Earthquake" that "the society that confronted the major seismic event on the afternoon of May 31, 1970, was in many ways already a catastrophe."[37] The reason for this, according to the author, is that the economy was "characterized by acute boom-and-bust cycles and chronic mal-distribution," meaning that "Peru was and continues today to be in a vulnerable condition."[38]

Although operating in different frameworks, and seeking to prove different points, these two writers are nonetheless working with the same assumptions about what precisely makes a disaster meaningful. In the first passage, there is a reference initially to the destruction of a cultural center that killed *x* number of people. The point of invoking this destruction, however, is to recenter a "lesser known disaster," the massacre of the Koreans. By accepting the relationship among disaster, cultural centrality, and mass death, the writer is able to reframe what for him is the real catastrophe—the politically motivated persecution of Koreans in the disaster area. In the second passage, we can see a similar rhetorical process at work. There is first the disaster at the center—in this case the 1970 earthquake. By invoking this disaster, however, the writer is, again, able to reframe what he sees as the real calamity. What is important in this passage is not that an earthquake occurred, not that centers of culture were destroyed, not that many people died; rather what is important is that Peruvian society was "already a catastrophe"—that Peru's vulnerable economy was in crisis. Each of these writers is simultaneously reinforcing and reinventing the connections among centrality, death, and disaster.[39]

A second theme that appears in catastrophe studies is that unitary narratives are key to making disasters intelligible. The question that gets asked in this scholarship is less what makes a disaster meaningful than what the media does to make a disaster meaningful. The starting point of much writing on media and disaster is indeed that media representations of disaster insist (inappropriately) upon discrete, bounded, unitary narratives, even if these narratives are in turn linked to shattered, unthinkable bodies. As one analysis of "The Media Response to Oil Spills in Great Britain" argues, for instance,

> the disaster narrative frames employed by the media vary surprisingly little from one disaster to another, drawing upon existing broad underlying themes which serve as templates for cultural constructions of reality . . . [I]n so-called environmental disasters such as oil spills, the focus is generally on the effects of the ecology, and not on the effects on the human communities. This is an attempt to naturalize the disaster.[40]

A second discussion, which links media narratives of disaster to "body horror," rests on the idea that "the thrill of disaster reports does not derive from close up photography of corpses or body parts but from restrained imagery tied to stories of fatally bad luck . . . [I]n picturing disasters, bodies are generally absent or signified by spatters of blood."[41] In one final passage that describes, in this case, apocalyptic literature rather than news media representations of disaster, we learn that the "ultimate object" of apocalyptic literature is "an image of purity so absolute that it denies the organic messiness of life."[42] At the same time, however, "the end result of apocalyptic purification often seems of less importance than the narrative pleasure derived from the bizarre and opulent tribulations of the bodies"—bodies that are "perverse . . . unstable and mutating from maleness to femaleness and back again."[43]

In each of these discussions of disaster and the media, there is an emphasis on—or critique of—the discrete, unitary, ordered narrative that ignores or redefines the disordered, pained human or body. In each, indeed, the very incomprehensibility of the human or body is rendered comprehensible when it is, quite literally, incorporated back into the narrative. In the first, the human cost of oil spills—and the oil spill itself—are subsumed under a master narrative of "nature" and ecological catastrophe. In the second, the narrative is a story of fatally bad luck—a story that requires a restrained evocation of the destroyed body rather than a direct photograph of it. Finally, in the apocalyptic literature, although the "narrative pleasure" derived from experiencing bodies in ecstatic pain often overwhelms the apparent goal or purpose of the genre writ large, the "ultimate object" remains: hyperbolically disordered bodies are reordered in the name of a coherent, meaningful narrative of redemption.

The last recurring trope in catastrophe studies that I want to discuss here is the trope of the everyday. The notion that a disaster occurs when something called the "everyday" is either disrupted or revealed as the template for politics is certainly not a new one. What many of these more recent studies do, however, is question the very notion of the everyday. Like the analyses of the media narratives, these discussions frequently maintain a certain rhetorical distance from the disaster itself—asking not just what makes a disaster real, but what makes the things that it destroys and disrupts real. As one sociologist argues, for example, a compelling reason to study disasters is that "disasters provide opportunities to examine aspects of social structures and processes that are hidden in everyday affairs," and are "invaluable opportunities to study sense-making mechanisms, at both collective and individual levels, in their most visible forms."[44]

Other scholars have examined the mobilization of the everyday as a response to, or a model for, the politics of disaster—often coming to quite different conclusions about its desirability or efficacy. On the one hand, for instance, Veena Das has suggested that it is possible to make "a space of destruction our own not through an ascent into transcendence but through a descent into the every day."[45] On the other hand, some feminist scholars have argued that since "disaster management tends to be a male-dominated, top-down process" reinforcing "existing masculine-dominated gender relationships," the "return to 'normality' sought by emergency planners tends to be an oversimplified picture. The ordinary and the everyday need to be seen as difficult and requiring interpretation."[46] Obviously these interpretations of the everyday are quite different. The one attempts to obviate the occasionally hysterical "vulnerable spaces" rhetoric by invoking *personal* normality. The other attempts to rescue the everyday from a sexist "normality" that operates at the level of emergency planning and procedure.[47]

All three of these discussions, however, seem to be drawing on similar assumptions. According to each, a disaster is endowed with meaning upon the invocation of the everyday. Moreover, although this everyday is open to interpretation, it is always a clear, coherent, concept. It is knowable and decipherable. Above all, it orders. In the first passage, it in fact orders so effectively that it can "hide" key social structures and processes and obscure sense-making mechanisms. In the second, it orders (or reorders) lives wracked by destruction. It is the opposite of transcendence—the opposite of ecstasy with all of its eccentric messiness. Finally, in the third, it orders the normality sought by patriarchal emergency planners. It orders the male-dominated gender relations that appear in the days following the disaster. What makes the disaster intelligible, in other words, is the invocation of yet another unitary, bounded narrative—the narrative of the everyday.

Conclusion

My own approach to catastrophe studies engages all three of these trends in the existing literature, but it also diverges from them in significant ways. What I have shown over the past few pages is that the ecstatic, eccentric subject is by no means alien or unrelated to contemporary writing on disaster. When the "center of culture" trope, for example, is rhetorically subverted, we are seeing in one sense a new focus on the eccentric subject. When references to the everyday or to the slippage between media narrative and bodily disorder in turn destabilize even these new centers, we are likewise seeing an invocation of the ecstatic subject. The problem is that as soon as these shifts in perspective have been effected, as soon as the lives of those beside themselves or outside of the center have been reframed, there is an immediate return to the bounded, unitary subject or narrative. Reframing, that is, does no more than reinforce the notion that centrality and coherence are what make a disaster meaningful.

What I do in this book is make the case that if a frame exists at all in the politics of disaster, its purpose is to define what lies—and what will always lie—outside of the picture. I argue that the disaster comes into existence because of what is, and always will be, offstage. What I think needs to be considered in discussions of disaster is thus *not* that a disaster in *x* marginal space is just as meaningful as a disaster in *y* central space—*not* that destruction of *x* marginal population must be recognized as tragic in the same way that destruction of *y* central population is. Rather, I suggest that disasters are produced via reference to spaces and subjects that do not have—and never will have—*any* actual relationship to the destruction itself. What produces a disaster is the invocation of spaces and subjects so far offstage, in such a state of ecstasy, that they can never become central or bounded. What produces a disaster are fantasy Indians and undersea pirates thousands of imaginary miles from the space of destruction.

I conclude this chapter by citing one last influential work in the field of catastrophe studies—a work that makes this point better than I do. Near the end of his book, *Dead Cities*, Mike Davis states:

> last June (1998) *Science* published a short article about polar bears on the Arctic island of Spitzbergen in the Barents Sea. A team of Norwegian scientists has been systematically tranquilizing and tagging the animals in a long-term study of their population dynamics. They were shocked to discover that an anomalous number of the bears are hermaphrodites. They suspect that polychlorinated biphenyls (PCBs), which condense

> from the cold Arctic atmosphere and concentrate in the marine food chain, are the endocrine disputers responsible for the bizarre sex-change. Amid all the environmental tremors of the recent past, including Hemisphere-scale droughts and continent-size wildfires, it is the hermaphroditic polar bears that most haunt me.[48]

In a book devoted to every conceivable sort of destruction, from floods to tsunamis to toxic spills—in a book about countless populations starving, dying, and becoming ill—what makes disaster meaningful for Davis are intersexed bears in the arctic. What frightens him about disaster is the possible existence of bears of uncertain gender. The reason that I end this chapter with the above passage is that it highlights the logical conclusion to the reframing process that I discussed above. It is a hyperbolic variation on the theme of the ecstatic, eccentric subject of disaster. And I believe that it returns us in a strangely apt way to Braidotti's initial point—that gender and sexuality are in fact at the heart of any rhetoric of crisis.

The Gift of Life

Blood, Organs, and Viruses

Introduction

Rather than begin the first major chapter of this book with a shattered city, I begin it with a shattered body. In 1914, Benjamin Cardozo wrote one of his first opinions for the New York Court of Appeals, in a case brought by Mary Schloendorff against the Society of New York Hospital.[1] In this case, Schloendorff argued that the hospital had performed unnecessary and dangerous surgery on her without her consent. Cardozo's opinion in this case has been extraordinarily influential in the jurisprudence of bodily integrity in the United States,[2] but this is not why I bring it up. Instead, I want to look more carefully at the way in which Schloendorff's story was told. As Paul A. Lombardo has pointed out in an essay on the uncertain legacy of the case, one aspect of *Schloendorff v. Society of New York Hospital* that is almost never mentioned—especially given the valorization of the decision as the source of every United States citizen's right to bodily inviolability—is that Schloendorff herself lost both the case and the appeal. Moreover, as Lombardo continues, Schloendorff "had no ordinary tumor . . . [I]t was a fibroid mass in her uterus and the operation done against her will was a hysterectomy."[3]

All of this might seem like a strange place to start a discussion of disaster, ecstasy, and the gift of life that occurs at their intersection. There is, however, a backstory to Schloendorff's lawsuit that makes it relevant to this book: although the doctors cut Schloendorff's uterus out of her in New York, and although the case was heard in Cardozo's jurisdiction, the condition that led these doctors to their diagnosis had initially manifested itself shortly following Schloendorff's experiences in the 1906 San Francisco earthquake. Both the newspaper reports of the trial and the court transcripts dwell on this moment. In the newspaper, for example, she is, according to Lombardo, depicted as,

> an elegant and dignified lady on the witness stand. Having survived the San Francisco earthquake in 1906, she suffered from "nervous shock." After entering the hospital in January 1907 she was prepared to leave when "some of the medical staff suggested that she undergo an examination" to determine her "exact physical condition." Mrs. Schloendorff "had a lump in her side" for five years and "of which her nurses knew." A doctor suggested an "ether examination" saying that she was too nervous to examine otherwise. To this she also consented, but stipulated that there be no operation at that time. The surgeons called the lump a "phantom tumor" and gave her the impression that it might be due to nervousness. On recovery from the effects of the ether, Mrs. Schloendorff found that the surgeons had made incisions in her back and abdomen. In consequence, she testified, her fingers developed gangrene and she lost the use of her right arm.[4]

In the court transcript, Schloendorff's first words on the witness stand were: "I lived prior to November, 1906 in the City of San Francisco, California. I lived there nearly all my life . . . [M]y physical condition in the fall of 1906 was, I might say, perfect. The earthquake of San Francisco occurred on April 18, 1906. Well, I was greatly frightened and nervous, of course."[5] As Lombardo notes, "this admission of 'nervousness' following the great earthquake was reiterated by several later witnesses, not as the explanation for Schloendorff's stomach problems, but as the basis for arguing that she was noncompliant as a patient and unreliable as a witness."[6]

Embedded within the ignored story of Mary Schloendorff's forced dismemberment[7] and sterilization at the hands of the New York medico-legal establishment, in other words—a story that is in turn usually embedded within a triumphalist progress narrative of embodied rights and liberties—is an even quieter tale of the San Francisco earthquake. Before the earthquake, Schloendorff was in perfect health. After the earthquake, she became nervous and hysterical. As a result of this hysteria she was (1) incapable of having a real tumor or feeling real pain (but emphatically capable of having a phantom tumor and feeling phantom pain);[8] (2) incapable of granting or denying real consent to a medical operation (but, again, capable of granting or denying phantom consent); and (3) incapable, once the case came to trial, of giving real testimony (but capable of giving phantom testimony to the newspapers). The quietly central San Francisco earthquake, that is, became meaningful in this scenario only once the gory, violent ecstasy of one of its many subjects had been trotted out and displayed.

My point in starting with this vignette is not so much to highlight the various brutal conclusions that follow from the rhetoric of hysteria—although this case is obviously an excellent example of the logic of this rhetoric. Nor is it even to point out the sadism inherent in the common wisdom that linked the onset of hysteria to periods of crisis or disaster. Rather it is to repeat that—even here—the subject in ecstasy endowed the earthquake with meaning. And in particular, the gendered subject in ecstasy was invoked in these discussions—a gendered subject who had in fact been in the process of definition and narration many decades before Cardozo made her an object of law.[9]

In 1899, for example, a writer for a popular U.S. monthly wrote that "women are always more alarmed than men" during earthquakes, that "many of them have a feeling of sea-sickness," and that "I never yet saw a female otherwise than frightened out of her wits during an earthquake."[10] A decade earlier, a more professional medical journal differentiated between the postdisaster somatic effects produced by hysterical fear, and the postdisaster somatic effects produced by external physical stimuli. During the Charleston earthquakes, for example, there were,

> sundry sensations closely resembling those ordinarily produced by the shocks of electro-magnetic batteries, viz., prickling sensations, "needles and pins," feelings beginning in the fingers and toes and extending up the arms and legs. Many of these occurred in adult *males*, and in children of both sexes, too young for any "hysteroidal" element to prevail. I do not think that all these sensations should be ascribed to fear, or to purely nervous disturbances.[11]

Finally, by the early twentieth century, four years before Cardozo wrote the *Schloendorff* opinion (but when the case was already in the New York court system), these popular and medical interpretations of hysteria and disaster had become the basis for new political and legal analyses of rights and gender. As one scholar noted in a discussion of the "Effect of Earthquake on the Emotions," for instance,

> with the inhibition of man's reason, his instincts take its place, and it would seem that many of our instinctive actions are not much different from those of the brute . . .

> [O]ne phenomenon in this connection is almost embarrassing to mention, in view of the present growing sentiment in favor of women's rights and woman suffrage. It appears from the effects of the recent earthquake on the American people, that human reason is more readily inhibited in the gentler sex and in children than in men . . . [T]his distinction is implied in the wording of one report which states that "men were excited, women and children frightened" . . . [I]n no case is a man mentioned as having been specially afraid.[12]

Earthquakes, that is, affect women by terrifying them—and terrifying them so completely that they are dizzy and nauseated, out of their wits, and devoid of reason. This fear, moreover, is the result of internal hysteroidal stimuli, often bearing no relation to what is going on outside. Men, contrarily, are influenced solely by physical and measurable ("electro-magnetic") stimuli produced by natural phenomena. The response of men is not hysteroidal—it is in fact quite reasonable given that their bodies are being acted upon by external forces. Men are incapable of fear, of being out of their wits—and are motivated into useful action by a controlled excitement. *As a result*, the women's rights movement—the process by which women in the United States were articulating their political and legal identities[13]—is called into question. Earthquakes make women hysterical. Women are thus unfit political and legal subjects.

Again, my point in mentioning these three examples of what is by now a well-documented genre of law, medicine, and misogyny is not simply to provide one more example of the problematic foundations of political, legal, and medical structures in the United States. Instead, I am trying to resituate the *Schloendorff* case and to draw some provisional conclusions from it about the relationship between disaster and legal subjectivity. As I noted in Chapter One, there is an assumption in legal studies that law demands and insists upon a bounded, rational subject—and indeed the passage above, questioning "women's rights and woman suffrage," rests squarely upon that foundation. Here, however, we can see an example of just how fragile that assumption is.

No matter how rational Mary Schloendorff appeared to be—no matter how calmly she repeated her story and provided witnesses to back it up—the law asked that she be beside herself and devoid of reason. Her case, the doctrine of bodily integrity that derived from it, and above all the disaster that contextualized it in many ways could not make sense *unless* she was in ecstasy. Much like the metaphor of disaster that became concrete over the late nineteenth and early twentieth centuries, the ecstatic subject that defined this disaster became similarly concrete in the *Schloendorff* case. The subject of disaster law is in part a hysterical one—she is out of her mind. Not only *can* this subject be chopped into pieces, therefore, not only *can* she be made physically and concretely ecstatic,[14] but arguably she also *must* be. Rhetorically, this is what motivated the doctors who dismembered Mary Schloendorff, the victim of disaster, and—rhetorically—this is what motivated Cardozo, who turned these doctors into the heroes and defenders of every citizen's right to bodily integrity.

I suggest as well that this is likewise what has motivated the transfer and transplant of various bodily fluids and body parts during moments of disaster. This chapter is not actually about Mary Schloendorff and the right to bodily integrity. It is instead about giving blood, about donating organs, and about spreading disease during and after earthquakes. More particularly, it is about the legal and political narrative of this postcrisis rearrangement of what has been called "living matter." Throughout this chapter, therefore, I argue that when law is called upon to regulate the transfusion of blood, the transplant of organs, and the transmission of disease, the subject of this law is—quite concretely—in ecstasy and off-center. The subject is dismembered Mary Schloendorff. The disaster becomes intelligible when its legal and political subjects are quite physically beside themselves.

Ecstatic Life

I argued in Chapter One that the subject in ecstasy—although familiar to regimes of biopolitics—is in many ways the opposite of the biopolitical subject. Unlike *homo sacer*, the ecstatic subject is spiritually over determined, defined by anything but bare life. I must add now that the subject in ecstasy is likewise involved in a very distinct variation on the "gift of life"—a variation that is far removed from the biopolitical regulation of bare life and death. Indeed, I make the case in this chapter that blood transfusions and organ transplants, that milk distribution and disease control, are precisely the same thing that hysterectomies, gangrenous limbs, and hysteria control were in the *Schloendorff* case: the concrete realization of subjects beside themselves. In no way the endpoint to a politics of bare life, these processes are rather the starting point to a law and politics of ecstasy.

Most scholarly analyses of contemporary transfusions and transplants nonetheless ordinarily see them as paradigms par excellence of (1) the triumph of

Descartes' rational subjectivity or (2) the success of biopolitical power networks. What I do in this section, therefore, is first summarize a few examples of these analyses, and then explain how my interpretation of the postdisaster rearrangement of living matter engages with and diverges from them. With that in mind, I begin with Emiko Ohnuki-Tierney's 1994 discussion of organ transplant and brain death in Japan, the United States, and Europe. In this discussion, Ohnuki-Tierney argues, first of all, that "transplant technology leads to a series of transgressions of received categories in almost all cultures—life and death, animate and inanimate, human and non-human animal, self and other, and nature and culture."[15] At the same time, there is a definite disjuncture, she claims, between the "cultural meaning" of transplants in European countries and their cultural meaning in Japan—especially since the "need for donated organs" has led to the "construction of brain death" as a human being's final moment.[16] "The conceptual bedrock of brain death," according to Ohnuki-Tierney, is "the cherished principle of [European] culture, especially in the Enlightenment philosophy espoused by intellectuals since the seventeenth century . . . whereby *rationality* is the most important criterion for humanness. As a corollary the brain—the seat of rational thought—occupies the most prominent place among the body parts."[17] In Japan, contrarily, Ohnuki-Tierney argues that the inactive brain initially "represented a *prolongation of life* rather than, as it has come to be viewed in some Western countries, a *prolongation of the process of dying*."[18]

The result of the predominance of what Ohnuki-Tierney sees as the European model is thus the creation of a "hybrid human," a subject "whose identity is solely based on rationality located in the brain."[19] As both Ohnuki-Tierney and others have pointed out, however, this triumph of the rational subject—this privileging of the bounded, self-conscious, autonomous individual—rests squarely upon the complete disintegration of any *bodily* boundaries between the self and others. Margaret Locke, for example, has suggested that (rational) existence and non-existence have become infinitely complicated over the past decades "because there are now those patients whose dying and living become inextricably linked through serendipitous coincidental failure of their body parts."[20] Organ transplant, in other words, assumes first, the primacy of bounded, self-conscious, rational subjectivity—Cartesian existence in all its grandeur, and second, a series of blurred bodily borders that make this rational subjectivity possible. Rational subjects exist, that is, because their bodies have disintegrated.

This relationship between mind and body is something of a departure from Descartes' notion that the body must be curbed and controlled by the mind. The Cartesian subject, after all, enacted his rational will precisely on the unruly passions of his body. With the disappearance of the body altogether, this will becomes meaningless.[21] The absurdity of a Cartesian subject existing in the presence (or absence) of the modern and contemporary body became so pronounced throughout the late twentieth century, that a number of scholars—drawing on Foucault's theories of disciplinary power networks and, more so, biopower—tried to describe transplants and transfusions in a vocabulary of biopolitics rather than in a vocabulary of rational autonomy. These discussions relied in particular on Foucault's point that contemporary political structures take the population or species, rather than the individual, as their subject—and argued that organ transplants are thus much more about making populations live than they are about not letting individuals die. Braidotti, for instance, states that the notion of "organs without bodies,"

> marks a planetary transaction of living matter carefully invested to keep the species alive and healthy and white. In a perverse twist, the laws of unity of the "subject" result in the human being lending its organic components to many a prostitutional swap: the part for the whole. "Organs without bodies" marks the transplant of and experimentation with organs in a cynical, postindustrialist simulacrum of "the gift."[22]

Again, Braidotti's point is primarily a point about the medico-legal shift in focus toward the population—its life, its health, its racial purity—and away from the dispensable individual. At the same time, she also notes the "perverse" way in which the unity of the subject enters this new domain—the valorization of its wholeness leading to "many a prostitutional swap" of bodily parts.

What I suggest, however, is that although these critiques of the rational subject and its role in transfusion and transplant—these analyses of the biopolitical bad faith that motivates the transfer of living matter—are important ones, there is more going on here than simply biopower in high gear. First, the rational subject deprived completely of its body has been, I believe, insufficiently well theorized. What, after all, is a subject—"rational" or not, outside of its body, deprived of its body, linked, if anything, to a small pile of detached body parts—if not a subject in ecstasy? This is the very definition of bodily ecstasy. What I argue, therefore, is that although couched in a rhetoric of Cartesian boundedness, and ostensibly valorizing the self-conscious, rational individual of the Enlightenment, both the notion of brain death and the transplant regimes that have been built up around it assume above all ecstatic, eccentric subjects—subjects beside themselves.

Moreover, given that the assumption and invocation of these subjects *precede* the transplants and transfusions, the transplants and transfusions are arguably nothing more than concrete, physical manifestations of their subjects' ecstasy. It is not, in other words, that there is a perceived need for blood and organs to keep the population healthy or the subject sane, and that brain death is in turn invented to respond to this need. Rather it is that the subject in ecstasy is invented, and methods of reifying this subject—transplants and transfusions included—are in turn brought into play. This is, I believe, the only way to explain the massive outpouring (or "donating") of blood and organs that almost always follows disasters—often despite explicit statements on the part of political and medical authorities that they already have an excess of each.

If we turn to more general discussions of life, politics, transplants, and transfusions, we can see this process in action. Pheng Cheah, for instance, has discussed the rhetoric of the prosthesis—the transplant—in the context of neocolonial politics. Starting with Hegel's argument that survival—political or otherwise—involves "limiting the organism's relation to alterity," and that "life is thus the subject's power to overcome its other by containing it within itself as a contradiction that can be sublated,"[23] he makes the following point:

> the organic body remains self-supporting precisely because the prosthesis has been organized and made an integral part of its proper self. In contradistinction, a bad prosthesis acts as a conduit that makes the body vulnerable to hostile foreign elements. Instead of becoming an organic member of the body, it opens the body to external forces and even makes it dependent on them . . . [T]he neocolonial state is the deadly prosthesis par excellence.[24]

In a very different context, Butler paints a nonetheless similar picture of transplants, transfers, and prostheses. Addressing the counterintuitive rhetoric of the natural and the artificial in medical responses to intersexed individuals, she notes, first, that in the case of intersexed individuals "the norms [that] govern intelligible gender are those that can be forcibly imposed," and that "the malleability of gender construction . . . turns out to require forceful application."[25] At the same time, however, "the 'nature' that endocrinologists defend also needs a certain assistance through surgical and hormonal means," leading to a situation in which "nonnatural intervention in anatomy and biology is precisely what is mandated by nature."[26] As a result, she concludes, "malleability is . . . violently imposed. And naturalness is artificially induced."[27]

Although each of these passages is part of an argument that is in many ways quite distinct, each also highlights a key aspect of the relationship between transplants and subjectivity. In the universe that Cheah is describing, a good transplant results in the organism (the nation) overcoming the foreignness of the prosthesis (the state)—it results in the establishment or reestablishment of a self-contained, bounded whole. A bad transplant, contrarily, results in a tension, a deadly competition, between the foreign prosthesis (the state) and the organism (the nation). From the point of view of the organism, the foreign prosthesis becomes a conduit for further foreign invasion and for a further erasure of bodily and political boundaries. Put bluntly, a good transplant produces a rational subject (a healthy nation-state); a bad transplant produces a subject both physically and politically shattered, beside itself, in ecstasy (a neocolonial nation-state). More to the point, however, it is the bad transplant that is assumed and then created—like Mary Schloendorff's shattered body—by international legal systems.[28] It is thus once more the subject in ecstasy that becomes, quite physically, the subject of law and politics.

Similarly, the intersexed individuals invoked by Butler are above all subjects beside themselves. The very contradictions, the very illogic, inherent in making intersexed subjects potentially bounded subjects—the enforced malleability of gender, the artificially induced naturalness of sex—indeed emphasize the impossibility of them ever being bounded, self-conscious actors. The body parts added or removed from the intersexed individual remain foreign, impossible to overcome or to subsume into an identifiable whole—physical manifestations of a shattered subjectivity, even as this subject becomes the focus of (a quite relentless) law, politics, or medicine. Like the neocolonial nation-state, therefore, the intersexed individual is indicative of a complicated and fraught relationship between transfusions, transplants, and transfers on the one hand and the ecstatic subject of law on the other. I suggest throughout the remainder of this chapter that the gift of life—the transfer of fluids, body parts, and bacteria that follows on a crisis—is a means of making this subjectivity concrete. Both the donor and the recipient become ecstatic, and in their ecstasy produce the disaster's political meaning.

Bodily Fluids and Bodily Parts

The transfusion of blood and the donation of organs are very much twentieth-century phenomena—each becoming widespread or commonplace only in the 1930s and 1960s, respectively. Long before the turn of the twentieth century, however, the possibilities inherent in each motivated a great deal of scientific research—research which in turn set the foundation for the later field of physiology. The issues raised by nineteenth-century researchers into blood and organs continued to frame conversations about the nature, use, and moral value of bodily fluids and body parts well into the twentieth century. Key to their investigations were questions about which fluids or body parts were alive and which were dead, which could be transferred between humans and animals (or among nations and races) and which could not, and—as a direct corollary to these earlier questions—which processes were beneficial to individuals, nations, or states, and which were not.

Claude Bernard, for example—one of the founders of the modern field of physiology and a tireless investigator into the nature of organs and bodily fluids—was particularly interested both in their relative "life" and in their species-specific qualities. With regard to the first, he argued that blood constantly renews itself, that it is always young, but that one could no more rejuvenate organs via contact with young blood than one could rejuvenate an elderly person by feeding him a child's diet.[29] At the same time, however, Bernard continued that if the organs are sick, the blood will become sick, and that even if one were to remove this weak blood, one could never regenerate it.[30] With regard to the question of species-specific fluids, he notes that an animal whose blood has been removed will fall into a state resembling death, but that if the blood is reintroduced in time, the animal will revive—and that this is the birth of the transfusion.[31] Once again, however, he adds a caveat: although one can revivify the tissues of one animal using the blood of a different species, *transfusions* between different species of animal cannot be successful.[32]

In the Ottoman Empire, similar research was being carried out on the nature of blood, bodily fluid, organs, and their transferability. As early as 1836, for example, the bodies of criminals who had died in prison were being dissected in anatomy lessons,[33] and throughout the 1820s and 1830s discussions about the character and the life-giving or life-preserving potential of blood and other fluids were widespread. As one early nineteenth-century scientist, Şanizade Mehmet Ataullah, noted, blood is a flowing matter, it has the power to feed and revive (*ihya etmek*) every type of body, it is made up of two fundamental types—one resembling milky water and one dense and red—and under a microscope one can see that it is composed of globules (i.e., cells).[34] Later on, Ottoman researchers were talking more specifically about the feasibility of transfusions, and asking pointedly what differentiates a live organism from a dead one.[35] With regard to blood itself, for instance, Mehmet Şakir, a student of Claude Bernard, argued that it is entirely possible to move blood from one person's veins to another person's, that in a blood transfusion, one part of the fibrin (the clotting protein) is separated, and the part that remains is given to the recipient of the blood, and that if appropriate blood is not found for a transfusion, then pure water should be given in place of the blood that has been lost.[36]

In England, scientists were likewise engaged in research on the nature of blood as a living fluid. As an article in *Blackwood's Edinburgh Magazine* put it, the appropriate question to ask at the time was "what is meant by blood being alive"—especially given that so many physiologists had a difficult time conceiving of "a living liquid."[37] The answer, according to the article, was that "it is not the *liquid* which is alive, but the *cells* floating in that liquid, and these [one must] regard as organisms."[38] Again, these issues were being addressed in countless laboratories throughout the nineteenth and early twentieth centuries—and their conclusions have been analyzed by a number of historians of science. My particular interest in this early research on blood and blood transfusion is thus less its role in the broader narrative of modern scientific method and more its relationship to the elaboration of political and legal subjects. So I pause here to highlight the implications of these studies—especially to the extent that they demanded a reevaluation of the bounded, self-conscious, rational subject that had become, by this time, the assumed subject of modern law and politics.

Most fundamentally, nineteenth-century research on blood and its transferability raised the possibility of something (aside from a fetus)[39] that could be (1) a part of the body, (2) taken from the body, and (3) upon its escape from bodily borders remain both alive and self-contained. The "living fluid" dilemma raised by earlier scientists—the idea of something being both living and devoid of borders—was in fact resolved with the invention of cells as organisms, clotting mechanisms, and their relationship to the body from which they were derived. Second, and equally important, the science of transfusion redrew the lines that separated species, groups, and individuals. The fact that blood could *always* distinguish one species from another species, but that it only *sometimes* distinguished one human group from another—in one case linking individuals through the gift of life, and in another case separating them through "incompatibility"—raised questions about the national and racial categorizations that were already in place by the early nineteenth century. Having demonstrated that blood could be alive and self-contained, that it could rejuvenate and revivify, *and* that it could potentially serve as a means of distinguishing one (political) group from another (political) group, the research on transfusion made possible a situation in which blood itself could become more important to a nation or a state than the body that had contained it.

Almost immediately upon the development of blood typing and arm-to-arm transfusions in the first decades of the twentieth century,[40] for example, various anthropologists and social scientists attempted to link blood groups to preestablished "ethno-anthropological" categories. A Turkish dissertation published in 1946, for instance, sought to determine whether Turkish racial characteristics could be predicted by blood typing,[41] eventually coming to the disappointing conclusion that there was "no correlation" between "physical and racial traits" and blood groups in Turkey.[42] At the same time, the contradictory nature of blood—something that in its very ability to save life made it something worth killing for—was becoming quite obvious to minority groups and marginalized groups in various nation-states. As Luise White has argued in the context of late twentieth-century East African narratives of the gift of life,

> if blood is taken to be universal, then its power to terrify comes from that; if blood is taken to be a gendered bodily fluid, then the loss of blood is far more alarming to adult men than to adult women. But in either case, blood is the most ambiguous of bodily fluids; according to context it can signify life or death . . . [S]tories about blood-sucking firemen cover a wide geographic range, from the East African coast to eastern Zaire . . . [M]any of these narratives contain generic fire brigade vehicles; more often than not, captured people were put into a vehicle and taken away, sometimes to be kept in a pit in the local fire station, "the property of the local government."[43]

Here, in other words, blood in its universalizing capacity to join all members of humanity together is just as potentially violent as blood in its exclusionary capacity to draw distinctions—in this case gender distinctions as opposed to "ethno-anthropological" distinctions. It represents, as White notes, both life *and* death.

More to the point, it represents both the potential whole (humanity, the nation, the healthy individual) *and* the potential part (blood taken from the individual, transferred from one person to another for the sake of the nation or humanity). Finally, blood represents both the state's duty to provide bodily fluids to each and every citizen, and the threat inherent in that duty—the need to isolate certain citizens, certain bodies, as sources of that fluid. Both the Turkish dissertation and the African narratives of fire brigades as vampires[44] thus play up the twentieth-century potential of the nineteenth-century research on transfusion—the disintegration of isolated physical bodies in the name of an abstract whole, the concrete manifestation of the subject beside itself.

Narratives of organs and body parts removed, transplanted, or turned into prostheses were equally ambivalent. Again, organ transplants and blood transfusions were scientifically as well as politically bound up in one another—Bernard, for example, insisted on the mutual interdependence of healthy (young) blood and healthy (young) organs. More broadly, the question of living versus dead tissues and organisms—of which bodily fluids or body parts were "alive" with the power to rejuvenate, and which were "dead" with no power at all—remained a key one, central to the breaking down of bodily borders and boundaries in the apparent name of an abstract rational whole. Finally, body parts as well as blood could be accepted or rejected—could, in their exchange, play up simultaneously the universal commonality of the human species and the exclusionary lines drawn among individuals and groups.

At the same time, the removal and exchange of body parts and organs, almost more than the transfusion of blood, came to represent the subject in ecstasy in the early twentieth century. In an article written on the "aesthetics of dismemberment" in France following the First World War, for example, Amy Lyford has suggested that there was a direct connection between the destruction and construction of body parts and prostheses on the one hand and the politics of war and reconstruction on the other. In analyzing the Val-de-Grace hospital and museum of medicine, and its influence on the surrealist movement, for instance, she argues that "body parts had *already* been turned into aesthetic objects for national consumption by the early 1920s, although at Val-de-Grace the body-in-pieces symbolized France's regeneration rather than its destruction."[45] She continues that this artistic "emphasis on dismemberment suggests a proposal to recast the state's rhetoric of reconstruction in language that reasserted the carnal horror of war."[46]

With regard to more general themes of dismemberment, Lyford notes that in Max Ernst's collage, "Altar of the Fatherland,"

> historical memory emerges from an altar made of severed limbs, and the female figure kneeling at that altar pays homage to the leg before her as if it were a religious icon. As her lips caress the leg that juts from a wall above her, the woman presents herself as a dutiful, obedient subject. She worships at the altar of male mutilation and, in this way, Ernst's interpretation of French History [l'Autel de la Patrie] critically reinterprets the individual's relationship to the state . . . [T]hrough prose and gesture, the collage graphically underscores the weirdness of the State's implicit demand that trauma be lauded as if it were national triumph.[47]

Again, Lyford's starting point in both of these passages is that there is something strange or unexpected about associating healthy political systems with dismembered bodies or isolated body parts, that the state's insistence that body parts—the "carnal horror of war"—be valorized is contrary to notions of national triumph or reconstruction. I suggest, however, that what we are seeing here is simply one further manifestation of the ecstatic subject and its political potential.[48] In both representations, there is a distinct coming together of the science of transfusion and the politics of ecstasy. Indeed, these surrealist statements serve as a good jumping-off point for talking in more detail about further variations on the relationship between transplants or transfusions on the one hand, and the political subject in pieces on the other—this time explicitly in the context of natural disaster.

Before I turn to my case studies, I must mention that transfusion and transplant technologies only became widespread in the middle part of the twentieth century, and so my discussion will be limited for the most part to their role in the 1999 Istanbul earthquake. Nonetheless, I must contextualize this late twentieth-century narrative of blood, disaster, and body parts within two earlier accounts—the first a failed transfusion of sorts that followed the 1906 San Francisco earthquake, and the second a successful transplant of sorts that followed the 1922 Tokyo disaster. In the first, a "respectable" San Francisco citizen, A. W. Hussey,

> came to the station at the Hall of Justice and told how, at the direction of a policeman whom he did not know, but whose star number he gave as 615, he had cut the arteries in the wrists of a man pinioned under timbers at St. Katherine Hotel. According to the statement made by Hussey, the man was begging to be killed, and the policeman

> shot at him, but his aim was defective and the bullet went wide of the mark. The officer then handed Hussey a knife, with instructions to cut the veins in the suffering man's wrists, and Hussey obeyed orders. Chief of Police Dinan directed that Hussey be locked up. There was no opportunity to investigate his story, but police believe that the awful calamity rendered him insane, and that the incident reported to them had no existence excepting in his imagination.[49]

This incident clearly has little to do with the science of transfusion or with the gift of life. Even so, however, it is clearly a narrative very much embedded in the rhetoric of blood, law, and ecstatic subjectivity that I described above. There is, for example, first of all, the shifting aside of the formal, legal relationship between citizen and police officer in favor of an informal, biological relationship between citizens. When the police officer fails to maintain, via the bullet, an appropriate distance between himself and the trapped citizen, he hands the knife to Hussey and orders him to engage in a far more intimate political interaction. It is precisely the voice of the law, in other words, that demands the abandonment of any formal legal relationship.

As soon as this not-legal relationship is established, however, it is turned into fiction, into something unthinkable. Hussey, it turns out, was insane. What happened to him happened only in his imagination. Like Mary Schloendorff, that is, Hussey is ecstatic, not quite real. But also like Schloendorff's, Hussey's ecstasy and eccentricity by no means disqualified him from becoming the normative subject at the center of the disaster. Rather, the transformation of Hussey from respectable citizen to ecstatic madman, the transformation of the man pinioned under the timbers from citizen in need to figment of Hussey's disordered imagination, and the transformation of the letting of blood from act of pity to deranged fantasy were all necessary political transformations in the articulation of disaster law. They all began with the prototypical moment of political subject formation: the hail (real or imagined) of the police officer.[50] But far from initiating any rational process of subjection, far from reinforcing the relationship between law-giving officer and law-abiding citizen, this process *unraveled* Hussey's subjectivity. At the moment of the hail, Hussey became shattered, the man under the timbers became imaginary, and bloodletting became the only effective means of political interaction. The policeman's hail, that is, turned Hussey into an *ecstatic* subject, who in turn served as an explicit model for how the police might interact with other citizens struck by the "awful calamity."

Nearly fifteen years later, during the Tokyo earthquake of 1922, we can see similar narratives being created around the removal and transfer of body parts. Once again, I rely on only one anecdotal incident here, but this incident is indicative of a broader trend that will play out more obviously in the 1999 Istanbul earthquake. This story, like the story in San Francisco, is set following the fire that ripped through Tokyo after the first shocks of the earthquake had passed. In addition to destroying most of Tokyo's houses and businesses, this fire likewise trapped and killed thousands who were left in the wreckage, including 32,000 people who had taken refuge in a central part of the city. In photographs taken after the fire, bodies are described as "touching each other as far as the eye could see," and a monument was later "erected there of cement made from the ashes of the dead."[51] Prior to the construction of this monument,

> those who came over the ashes when the fires had exhausted their fury found in this field a solid mass of dead, with twenty thousand still standing on their feet, held up by the other dead around them . . . [I] visited this field of death two weeks later, when the last of the fifty thousand dead of Honjo were being thrown into the rough crematorium erected there . . . [B]efore these bins passed a row of mourners, dry-eyed, silent, and stony-faced. [They] . . . shuffled in wooden clogs over the cinders, each selecting indiscriminately from the bone heaps one or two small fragments which were placed ceremoniously upon wooden trays.[52]

Once again, this story has very little to do with the science of organ transplant or the technology of the prosthesis. Just as Hussey's bloodletting did, however, it can nonetheless tell us something important about the nature of body parts and subjectivity during and after moments of disaster. Again, what occurs in this story is a situation in which, first, the self-contained, bounded body is proved to have nothing to do with any sort of healthy, politically meaningful wholeness. The bodies left by the fire are separate enough to be distinguished by "touching each other," distinct enough to be still standing, but it is precisely the separate, self-contained nature of the burned bodies that makes them horrific. It is thus the duty of both the mourning families and the government, first, to break the bodies up into indistinguishable parts—"selecting indiscriminately" from the bone heaps—and, second, to join these bodies together into a politically meaningful whole. The monument made of cement from the ashes of the dead is a hyperbolic variation on the Ernst collage—it is simultaneously a physical expression of shattered subjectivity and, explicitly, a *monument*, the thing that produces the disaster's meaning.[53] The removal, replacement, and transfer of body parts—the erasure of *any* borders separating one body from another—serves unambiguously to commemorate subjects beside themselves and their role in making the earthquake and fire intelligible.

If we jump ahead to the end of the twentieth century, these themes play out much more obviously and are much more directly linked to actual blood transfusions and organ transplants. There are, in fact, two major aspects of the Turkish response to the 1999 disaster that I address here—the first is the decision of the Health Minister, Osman Durmuş, to refuse blood donations from Greek and Armenian donors, and the second is the fear of the "organ mafia" that appeared in the mass media. Each gets at a key aspect of disaster and subjectivity, and each forges a link between legal ecstasy and its concrete realization in the bodies of citizens. Both the fear of Greek and Armenian blood and the fear of bandits who might steal one's internal organs are motivated by a distinct legal and political regime focused above all on subjects beside themselves.

Osman Durmuş's decision to limit blood donations prompted almost immediate protest both within and outside Turkey. Durmuş himself, a member of the far right Nationalist Action Party (MHP), was reviled as a provincial racist, who in no way represented mainstream trends in Turkish politics, and was called upon to explain himself and, in some newspapers, to resign. Although Durmuş's reaction to the threat posed by foreign blood was, without question, radically nationalist, racist, misguided, and based in the worst sort of mid-century pseudoscience, however, I suggest that it is also a clear and logical conclusion to a century-long *transnational* politics of disaster. Indeed, in many ways Durmuş can be seen as the inheritor of the decision reached by that emphatic liberal, humanist, Judge Cardozo. A disaster had struck Turkey, tens of thousands of citizens had died, and Durmuş's response was to insist upon the realization of the subject in ecstasy, the threat of the bad prosthesis, and the ways in which each could make the earthquake politically intelligible.

If we consider, for example, Durmuş's initial statement together with the speeches he made in response to the criticism leveled at him, we can see a definite pattern developing. Less than a week after having turned away the offer of blood from the Greek and Armenian governments, Durmuş was attempting to rationalize his decision, first of all by arguing that he "could have been ignorant" of the importance of both giving and receiving blood, that it was "impossible for him to know everything," and that in any case this was "not the time to go looking for guilt."[54] He continues, however, by defending his initial statement, insisting that he was not against Greek and Armenian help per se, but that he remained critical of "unneeded help"—that "in place of material that we don't need," foreign governments should instead send help that is asked for.[55] In direct response to the accusations of racism, he stated:

> I don't discriminate against doctors according to their nationality. In the beginning, we needed surgeons, but now we don't. We don't need Greek blood—which is to say that we don't need any blood. Because blood can't be kept longer than 21 days. It's a waste and extravagance (*israf oluyor*). Thankfully, thousands of volunteers have donated blood. Right now, the need has passed. I'm saying this so that [the blood] doesn't go to waste. And this is my request: if one day I'm hurt and I need blood, give me blood from any nationality.[56]

In the months that followed, Durmuş continued to defend his position, turning the initial refusal of blood into a broader political point, while nonetheless declaring his friendship to the Greek and Armenian people. Accusing the Turkish press of launching a smear campaign against him and spreading "false news,"[57] Durmuş argued that "Marxists" in particular were using the "blood issue" to sow dissension.[58] In oblique response to Durmuş's declarations, the Greek government issued a statement a month later, following an earthquake that struck Athens: "We'll Take Turkish Blood." This statement was immediately juxtaposed in the Turkish press to Durmuş's unpopular decision.[59]

Again, the most obvious interpretation of this series of statements and events is that Durmuş is racist, that he tried and failed to rationalize his racism, and that the Greek government used the opportunity a month later to play up their own tolerance and cosmopolitanism. Unquestionably, all of these things are true. However, the incident is also more complicated than that—raising questions about blood, political identity, and the gift of life that for the most part remain unanswered. First, for example, we might ask why Durmuş preferred Turkish blood. Certainly he did prefer it—even when he explained his initial refusal of Greek and Armenian donations, his reason was that *Turkish* volunteers had already donated enough blood, and so *foreign* donation was unnecessary. The foreign blood would go to waste. Given the choice, therefore, Durmuş would always take Turkish blood before foreign blood. Why should this be?

Second, and perhaps more important, why should the response to the earthquake both within and outside Turkey be to give blood—indeed to give far more blood than was needed? Why do people want to give blood to victims of disaster in a way that they do not—as Durmuş pointed out—want to give food or money? Finally, why should there be such an outcry over the refusal of blood? If Durmuş had refused donations of food or money from the Greek and Armenian governments, there would undoubtedly have been some consternation, but his decision would never have become the international incident that his refusal of blood became. So in addition to asking why people immediately give blood, even when it is unnecessary, we might ask why people should be so offended when their blood is refused.

With regard to the first question, it is worthwhile to take Durmuş's statements about context, international friendship, and his personal beliefs at face value. Durmuş states, before anything else, that this is not the time to be allocating blame. He reminds the Turkish population that Istanbul is in a crisis situation, that the western part of Turkey is a disaster area, and that his decision should be judged according to this context. His position, in other words, is a product of the earthquake—and his unapologetic preference for Turkish blood is something directly related to the crisis situation. Indeed, he emphasizes the importance of context when he states later that *personally* he would be happy and grateful to receive a blood donation from an individual of any nationality. There is a difference, he is saying, between the widespread, general transfusions that occur following a disaster and a transfusion that might occur following a private accident. The former demands Turkish blood, the latter healthy blood of any provenance. And it is for this reason, he implies, that there is no contradiction between declaring his friendship to the Greek and Armenian people on the one hand and refusing to accept the gift of life from them on the other. As a private individual, he would be grateful for foreign blood. As a politician, he has nothing but respect for foreign governments. In a crisis situation, however, he uses his role as a public figure to keep the Turkish blood supply "pure."

My point here, again, is not that this position is any less racist than a straightforward declaration that all Greek and Armenian blood, no matter what the situation, is tainted. Neither is my point that Durmuş and his party did not take advantage of the crisis to try to push through policy that they would also be very happy to see operating in day-to-day circumstances. I do, however, think that there is an important assumption about the relationship among blood, disaster, and political subjectivity that underlies these statements, and that transcends both Nationalist Action Party policies and Turkish politics in general. People respond to disaster situations by opening their veins—by deliberately and self-consciously erasing the boundaries between their own bodies and the bodies of others. Politically responsible citizens, in other words, make sense of a disaster by becoming physical manifestations—on a mass scale—of the subject in ecstasy. Their ecstatic subjectivity makes the disaster meaningful—it brings the earthquake to life.

This is a very different process from the giving and receiving of blood on a private, individual level. If we think about what Durmuş was trying regulate in the days following the crisis, it was arguably less the purity of the blood supply—which in any case was already made up of donations from a variety of sources—and more the *process* of opening veins and erasing bodily boundaries. Durmuş was making a statement about which citizens could effectively destroy their bounded selves in the name of a common whole—which citizens had the right to blur their bodily borders and become physical manifestations of disaster law's norm—and which (noncitizens) could not and did not. It was for this reason that the excess foreign blood was both a waste and an extravagance. It bore no relation to the ecstatic subjectivity demanded by *Turkish* disaster law. If anything, it was a menace to this subjectivity: if the Turkish subject in ecstasy made the disaster meaningful on a national level, the foreign subject in ecstasy threatened to turn it over to international ownership. Durmuş was thus not so much protecting Turkish racial purity as he was protecting the independence of the Turkish legal and political system. If the subject in ecstasy was internationalized, so too would be the law and politics of disaster that took this subject as its starting point.

This entanglement of apparently abstract legal or political norms and concrete bodily processes can likewise explain the seemingly inexplicable insistence on giving blood—and excess blood—during crisis situations—and the intensity of the anger that we see when this blood is refused. Giving blood, I argue, is more than just a rational, self-conscious decision to make blood available to victims of disaster. If giving blood *were* only about supplying an existing need, then arguably donors would stop giving once it was clear that enough blood was available—and they would greet news of their blood's refusal with relative equanimity. But donors do not stop giving when news arrives that the need for blood has been met. And they do not meet news of the gift of life's refusal with anything approaching equanimity. Rather, this news is met with anger—anger verging on political hysteria.

The rhetoric of the gift of life in this situation thus very much represents an *abandonment* of rational subjectivity—an embracing of the subject in ecstasy and an attempt to make this subject concrete. What matters in this rhetoric of the gift of life is the process of breaking down bodily boundaries, of producing intermingled political and legal subjects, and of making the disaster intelligible. Like Longinus's subjects beside themselves, the blood donor becomes the normative subject of law and politics. When the gift of life is refused, therefore, so too, in part, is the donor's political existence—an insult quite definitely worthy of anger. Whereas it is true, in other words, that yes, giving blood is an act of humanitarian concern, it is also more than that. Understanding blood donations only in terms of this concern indeed begs the question as to why people *want* to give blood—and especially why they want to give blood more than they want to give, say, money or food.

Moreover, this attitude toward the mixing of living matter and political subjectivity has likewise incited the fear of and fascination for the "organ mafia" that operates during and after disasters. As one article in the Turkish press, titled "Warning: Organ Mafia in Search of Homeless Children," states,

> after the looters, after the opportunists, and after the sorrows of the catastrophe, now the organ mafia has begun work. In a statement from the Bolu Crisis Center, we are informed that a 30 person group has been kidnapping children in the disaster area for use in the organ trade. According to the statement, the group is operating in the areas most badly hit by the 17 August earthquake, targeting children without relatives or whose families were trapped under the wreckage . . . [T]he group's basic goal is to procure organs from homeless children, and according to the [government] statement: "citizens should be warned and act with care against people with this sort of bad intent."[60]

In a second, more personal, account published on the one-year anniversary of the earthquake, a woman shows a reporter a photograph of the son she lost in the disaster. The reporter then tells the harrowing story of the woman's unsuccessful search through over 400 hospitals—and then morgues—for her son. The article, however, ends on a "hopeful" note: "if my son didn't fall into the hands of the organ mafia, he is living."[61]

What makes the organ mafia particularly horrific, in other words, is not just that it harvests organs, but that it (1) targets children who have lost their families, (2) sells these organs on an illegal market, (3) bypasses political and legal structures, and (4) produces a political death far more horrific than any biological death that might land a body in a morgue. Rhetorically linked to looters and opportunists, the organ mafia represents the unthinkable moral depths to which an individual—and those whom that individual targets—might sink in a crisis situation.

Again, though, I pause to interrogate the fear and the horror that greet these stories of organ theft. Like looters,[62] the organ mafia takes advantage of the weak and the miserable—people who have already suffered far more than the average citizen ought. More than that, though, the work of the organ mafia plays up the fragility of political identity during moments of crisis. Children without families can disappear. And once they disappear, their body parts are worth more than their bodies as a whole. The victims of the organ mafia become like the bodies of those presumed kidnapped and held in the East African fire stations—the property of a group that values living matter more than it values life. Their dismemberment in turn serves no purpose in the broader politics of disaster, and thus bars these victims from both the reality of the crisis and the reality of political life during this crisis.

The organ mafia, that is, terrifies because it dismembers bodies for *rational* purposes—because it *does* understand the gift of life to be a self-conscious, understandable exchange. Unlike the transplants and transfusions that occur under the auspices of political and legal structures in crisis—transplants and transfusions that are predicated precisely upon an irrational and shattered subjectivity—the transplants undertaken by the organ mafia are about the transfer of living matter alone. Far from rendering concrete the ecstatic political subject and thereby endowing the disaster with meaning, the work of the organ mafia dissociates dismemberment from political and legal structures altogether. The rhetoric of organ transplant in this scenario, in other words, rests on two assumptions: the first is that appropriate organ transplant is the result of a politics of ecstasy; the second is that inappropriate organ transplant is the result of a politics of bounded rationality.

Viruses and Bacteria

A final, if less obvious, manifestation of the postdisaster gift of life is the spread of disease and infection that occurs at moments of crisis. Indeed, a case can be made that the transfer of viruses or bacteria is as key to the elaboration of disaster law as the transfusion and transplant of bodily fluids and body parts are—that the containment, control, and regulation of diseases are as productive of the subject in ecstasy as the regulation of blood and organs is. I suggest in this section that the law of disaster defines this particular variation on the rearrangement of living matter in precisely the way that it defined transplants and transfusions before: postearthquake disease control is, first, about creating concrete expressions of subjects beside themselves so that, second, the disaster can become intelligible. If we articulate disease control in the vocabulary of the *Schloendorff* case, we might say that all disease codes as hysteria during a disaster, and that in turn both the infected political subject and the political subject in danger of infection are hysterical, beside themselves, and thus produce the disaster's political meaning.

This relationship between earthquakes and disease has been a point of discussion among scientists and political theorists for at least the past two centuries. Not content with pointing out that epidemics often follow on the heels of disaster, for example, a number of nineteenth-century scholars and scientists posited a direct linkage between the "physical phenomenon" that was the former and the "physical phenomenon" that was the latter. As Noah Webster wrote in 1800,

> the comparative mildness and infrequency of pestilential epidemics in the more civilized parts of the world, in modern times, and the prevalence of the doctrine of the importance of contagion, has produced a degree of inattention amounting almost to forgetfulness of the principles which usually govern the course of such diseases.[63]

He continues by arguing, first, that there is a direct historical connection between "pestilential epidemics and sundry other phenomena of the physical world," second, that "the phenomenon most generally and closely associated with pestilence is an earthquake," and third, that it is indeed difficult to find "an instance of a considerable plague, in any country . . . which has not been immediately preceded or accompanied with convulsions of the earth."[64] In another article, a year later, he raises the example of the Lisbon earthquake and notes that "the great earthquake, which destroyed Lisbon in 1755, was followed by a distemper so fatal as to raise an alarm in England, and an order was issued by the government for all ships from Portugal to ride quarantine."[65] A contemporary memoir that includes personal anecdotes from the Lisbon disaster operates according to the same assumptions—the author remembering that he "contracted a fever" from the "intolerable stench from the dead bodies," and that as a result he "avoided passing near certain places, where the stench was so excessive that people began to dread an infection."[66]

None of these discussions of disease and disaster is particularly unique for the time—each is predicated on well-received doctrines of miasmas, pestilential space, and infection that I discuss in more detail in Chapter Four. For now, though, I highlight one key aspect of the relationship between the two that is elaborated here, and that sets up a framework for later nineteenth- and twentieth-century policies of postdisaster disease control. Both Webster and the anonymous memoirist produce what is at this point a familiar story of civilization, disaster, and in this case plague. According to Webster, "considerable plague" is (a) always the result of "convulsions of the earth," and (b) only occurs ("now") outside of "more civilized parts of the world." What we have here, in other words, is a situation in which *if* there is considerable plague in a certain region or among a certain population, there must *also* have been an earthquake that prompted that disease—an earthquake that in turn shifted the affected region or population to the margins of civilization.

Disease, that is, proves the existence of an earthquake even if there is no other indication that an earthquake actually happened. The diseased subject or the subject under threat of disease thus becomes simultaneously the subject of disaster law—in need of regulation and control—and also proof that the disaster struck in the first place. When boats from Portugal are quarantined to protect civilized spaces such as England, therefore, and when visitors to Lisbon avoid certain parts of the city to evade the stench and the threat of infection, more is going on than simple precautionary measures. Like the transfusions and transplants undertaken during crisis situations, disease control measures here are less about rational cost/benefit analyses and more about creating a certain type of political subject. The quarantined individual is a concrete manifestation of the eccentric subject—an enforced expression of the subject at the margins, offstage, not part of civilization. At the same time, the vaccinated individual is a concrete manifestation of this subject's ecstatic counterpart. Each is the norm of disaster law, each is a variation on Schloendorff in her hysteria, and each—eccentric and ecstatic—is proof that the disaster occurred.

The striking similarity in disease control measures effected by vastly different governments at the end of the nineteenth and the beginning of the twentieth centuries thus has less to do with common approaches to stopping the spread of infection and more to do with a common understanding of subjects beside themselves. Following the 1895 Istanbul earthquake, for example, the Ottoman government immediately took measures against the spread of cholera by, first, issuing a decree that only boiling water be used in hospitals and, second, subjecting all school children to health control.[67] In the days following the disaster, the Sultan issued a number of further decrees attempting to regulate the health and hygiene of those homeless citizens who were forced to sleep in open areas and gardens. Citing in particular the possibility that "last year's cholera microbe might reappear," the government insisted on special policies of "cleanliness," on the "disinfection and purification" of people as well as places, and on the sale of only clean and ripe food and drink.[68]

Ten years later, in San Francisco, the military regulations and decrees issued to halt the spread of disease were similar. As Major General Adolphus W. Greely, the commanding officer in charge of earthquake relief, noted later, "the conditions under which lived many, outside of the army camps, were often insanitary, and it was speedily evident that concentration into large camps under military supervision would best insure the public health."[69] Within the camps, "samples of water in common use were collected weekly and cultures made therefrom to determine its potable safeness," while "every resident of a camp who would consent was vaccinated. As to those refusing, it seemed best under the conditions of the public mind to defer compulsory vaccination until small pox should break out in some camp, which it did not."[70] Indeed, Greely insisted that these "precautions, along with lines recommended by the medical officers of the Army, served as preventives against the development of sporadic cases [of infection] into an epidemic."[71] In the "General Orders" issued in the days following the earthquake, the population of San Francisco was reminded that: "our greatest danger in the future may be expected from unavoidable insanitary conditions, and every person is cautioned that to violate in the slightest degree the instructions of the sanitary officers would be a crime that could have no adequate punishment."[72]

At the same time, there were those, according to journalist James Russell Wilson, who were already outside the realm of consent and punishment, and who were thus beyond the regulations of the military officers. In a personal account of his experiences during the earthquake, Wilson writes that,

> we went to Agnews . . . and found the asylum in ruins and 200 demented creatures buried there. It was a sight to transfix one with horror to see scores of mad men and

> women strapped to trees all over the grounds, crying, shrieking, and cursing. Ordinarily troublesome in their way, the excitement of the falling building made them mad indeed, and their uncanny looks and fiery eyes were terrible to behold. Nothing could be done for them, as there was no place to put them, and every sane man, woman, and child available was digging to release the other unfortunates buried in the ruins.[73]

Finally, the 1923 Tokyo-Yokohama earthquake prompted similar disease control responses, but effectively eradicated Wilson's neat division between the mentally capable who could be concentrated into camps, and the mentally incapable who remained scattered and disorganized throughout the shattered asylum grounds. In Japan, "homeless people over sixty years and those under sixty years who were imbecile, blind, or otherwise defective, or were invalids, were taken to the Tokyo Asylum for the Aged,"[74] along with "pregnant women," whom "the municipal authorities . . . promptly housed . . . in a temporary hospital."[75]

I talk in more detail in Chapter Four about the division of space into camps, hospitals, and asylums. For now, I look more closely at the rhetoric of infection itself and at the disaster law that developed around this rhetoric. First, we can see as early as the 1895 Istanbul earthquake that disease during a crisis situation takes on additional or alternate meanings—that postdisaster disease is not quite the same as disease in day-to-day circumstances. "Last year's cholera microbe," for example, is a different kind of threat now that disaster has struck—its potential destructive capacity deserving of more effective regulatory measures than its actual destructive capacity deserved the year before. Like the implied distinction between day-to-day blood transfusions and blood transfusions in crisis situations, there is a definite divide here between the familiarity of last year's cholera and its reappearance under the guise of a postearthquake plague. Moreover, the immediate targets of the emergency decrees are schoolchildren and the homeless—people ordinarily at the margins of legal and political discourse, or at least present only as silent, passive objects of the law. Indeed, it is precisely the marginal figure, the figure offstage, who is of particular interest to antiepidemic decrees—the eccentric subject who reveals the degree of the microbe's danger.[76]

As the military decrees following the San Francisco earthquake and the political responses to the Tokyo disaster make clear, however, even nonmarginal, nonvulnerable populations are gradually turned ecstatic in the days following the destruction. It is not, in other words, *just* that those figures ordinarily at the margins of legal discourse become suddenly of interest during moments of crisis. More than that, the law of disaster and the control of postdisaster epidemics is aimed at turning *all* political subjects into marginal figures, of making each and every citizen a child, a vagrant, or a hysteric. As Greely insisted in his discussion of military rule in San Francisco: (1) conditions outside of the camps were productive of disease, and (2) all individuals were thus threats to themselves and others until they became subject to camp protocol—until they submitted to what was essentially the regime of the hospital or the asylum. Even consent to medical treatment became the *fantasy* of consent to medical treatment that surrounds the child or the lunatic—Greely will "only" insist upon nonconsenting vaccination when he, as an authority figure, deems that such vaccination is necessary.

Likewise, in the statement issued directly to the population of San Francisco, the unhygienic citizen—in other words the citizen who does not submit to camp protocol—is effectively placed beyond the realm of law. Being unsanitary is described as a crime "that could have no adequate punishment," a crime that transcends notions of innocence and criminality, and a crime that therefore shifts its perpetrator to the realm of the insane. Like the lunatic, the unhygienic citizen simply cannot be defined by ordinary, day-to-day notions of punishment. Just as those within the camps are marginal figures, made children or vagrants by the intensity of the regulatory regime under which they live, those outside the camps likewise become marginal because they are "insanitary"—and for all intents and purposes insane. And as a result, the insane themselves—those "poor demented creatures"—become in many ways irrelevant. Mary Schloendorff is hysterical. A. W. Hussey is hysterical. The respectable citizens of the city are all hysterical—and thus the hysterics themselves have literally *no space* to be insane. They have become identical to the general population—a situation made all the more explicit by the Japanese government's decision two decades later to focus above all on the homeless, the elderly, the pregnant, and the imbeciles as the new eccentric subjects of antiepidemic law.

By the end of the twentieth century, this postdisaster tendency toward the creation of marginal, eccentric subjects had become far more pronounced. Following the 1999 Istanbul earthquake, for example, the Turkish media, in response to government warnings, was quick to point out that the "greatest danger" to earthquake victims was inadequate health protection, and that it was of the utmost importance that citizens therefore know and make use of government information about the prevention of infection. Among other measures adopted to protect the health of Turkish citizens and to stop the spread of hepatitis A, dysentery, and typhus, the government decided to "empty" dangerous areas and construct hygienic camps to shelter the victims.[77] Within these camps, citizens might avoid such threats as kidney failure resulting from toxins in untreated water,[78] and be given inoculations against diseases carried by rats frequenting the city centers.[79]

At the same time, the camps—like those in San Francisco—could not prevent the more psychological manifestations of postdisaster plague and infection. The "psychic trauma" experienced by children in the days and weeks following the earthquake, for example, became a medical condition in and of itself—deserving of special treatment, particularly to the extent that these sleepless and depressed children refused to return home:

> if there is no risk, the decision should be taken to return home. Children may not want to enter their houses. This can pose a big problem for families. It's necessary to re-introduce our children to their homes. This should be limited to five to ten minutes. Repeat this a number of times during the day. Then extend the time to one to two hours.[80]

Women likewise experienced frightening psychosomatic illnesses, resulting in an overall "decline in male births." Citing the work of British, Danish, and American specialists, a number of Turkish newspapers noted that "great stress raises the number of female births and lowers the number of male births," that if a woman experiences a natural disaster such as a fire, flood, or earthquake before conception or in the first few days of pregnancy, the likelihood that she will have a boy diminishes, and that, according to at least one researcher, "psychological shock will effect sexual activity, fertility, and hormone production, will cause a decline in sperm quality, and will increase the likelihood of miscarrying a male embryo."[81]

In this late twentieth-century take on the prevention of postearthquake infection, in other words, we can see precisely the emphasis on the eccentric subject—precisely the insistence on mobilizing law to create the eccentric subject—that we saw before. The center—be it the city center, the center of the disaster area, or the domestic center—was either actually dangerous or perceived to be so. Illnesses—viral, bacterial, mental, or otherwise—afflicted those who remained on the scene. If one refused to leave the scene, to go offstage, the result was the ecstasy of infection, the blurring and breaking down of bodily borders. On the one hand, therefore, citizens were encouraged to marginalize themselves, to enter camps, to be subject to regulation as simultaneously threatened and threatening beings. On the other hand, children especially had to be reintroduced to their homes. Traumatized and hysterical, these children were eccentric to themselves, frightened of the very spaces that should be the center of their lives. Their refusal to enter their homes and the medical advice on reintroducing them thus revealed the paradoxical centrality of the off-center subject and the role of this subject.

More so, however, the disease that afflicts women in crisis, and afflicts them such that they can give birth only to girls, turns both these women and their daughters into the normative subjects of disaster law. Like Webster's "pestilential epidemics," the decline in male births in this analysis is—above all—scientific proof that a disaster occurred. Even without any other indication of shock, illness, or hysteria on the part of the mother, the birth of a girl in a disaster area will now always be suspect—will always be possible evidence of a more pernicious, widespread trend toward nervous mothers and miscarried male embryos. Women who give birth to girls following an earthquake are therefore in many ways concrete expressions of the turn to the "feminine," as the eccentric, in times of crisis—they are the marginal, unknowable subjects analyzed by Braidotti who, in their very marginality and hysteria, prove that the disaster occurred. Scientifically, these women and their daughters become the eccentric, fantasy subjects who prove that the disaster happened (even in the absence of any other evidence).

Conclusion

The widespread success of blood transfusions, organ transplants, and disease control is ordinarily held up as evidence of the twentieth-century triumph of the rational, bounded subject. Judge Cardozo's decision in *Schloendorff v. Society of New York Hospital* is likewise usually analyzed as the prototypical twentieth-century decision, a decision that privileges above all the self-conscious, thinking citizen and his[82] inviolate bodily borders. Each in a different way has been seen as a validation of the Cartesian universe—each a political or legal confirmation of the sane, lucid individual's ability to control his disorderly, disruptive body.

What I have done in this chapter is challenge these interpretations of transplants, transfusions, and the legal narratives that surround them. Without necessarily throwing out the rational subject altogether, I tried to complicate the progress story—to link blood transfusions, organ transplants, and disease control to blood letting, dismemberment, and failed prostheses—to suggest that these transfers of living matter and these gifts of life are not as clearly connected to the bounded, self-conscious individual as they might initially appear to be. Especially to the extent that they are defined by the law of disaster, these processes are quite definitely playing multiple roles—providing necessary relief to the suffering while also providing countless concrete expressions of the ecstatic, eccentric, subject of disaster, the subject whose unintelligibility makes the disaster in turn intelligible.

Indeed, the contradiction between Cardozo's opinion—the vindication of every citizen's right to bodily integrity—and Mary Schloendorff's actual—gory—fate is possible *only* given this more complicated reading of the gift of life. It was precisely the San Francisco earthquake that made Schloendorff's dismemberment possible—and that in turn allowed this dismemberment to be read as the triumph of a humane, rational legal system. And arguably, Cardozo's opinion *did* represent the triumph of a humane, rational legal system. It was the triumph of a legal system, however, that took as its normative subjects those subjects in pieces, in ecstasy, hysterical, and beside themselves.

If we turn, for example, to a second, equally influential opinion written by Cardozo a decade later, we can see this same tendency toward valorizing the ecstatic, shattered subject as the legal and political norm. Indeed, we can see in this case the beginning of a distinct overlap between the apparently unique, ad hoc world of the disaster and the apparently continuous, well-formulated world of ordinary law. Cardozo's 1928 decision in *Palsgraf v. Long Island Railroad* is usually read as a foundational discussion of negligence in the same way that his decision in *Schloendorff* is read as a foundational discussion of the right to bodily integrity. In it, Cardozo reverses a lower court's decision to grant Helen Palsgraf damages for injuries she sustained after an explosion occurred on the Long Island Railroad track.

In concluding this chapter, however, I discuss *Palsgraf* less as an example of U.S. tort law in action and more as an example of the interconnectedness of disaster law and everyday law. The details of the case make clear, as do the details of *Schloendorff*, that Cardozo was not a judge particularly impressed with women's claims that they should remain free from bodily harm.[83] Whereas the lower court recognized in the Long Island Railroad accident a distinct act of negligence, Cardozo emphatically did not. As far as he was concerned, Palsgraf had not demonstrated effectively that her rights[84] had been violated during the explosion, and thus she did not merit damages.

More important to my own argument, though, is the *language* in which Cardozo and his fellow judges expressed their opinions of Palsgraf's claim. It is indeed worth pointing out that despite the fact that *Palsgraf* is now quite literally a textbook case in torts classes in the United States, and despite the fact that the usual lesson to be learned from studying the case is a lesson about intent, cause, proximate cause, and effect, Cardozo himself rarely uses an explicit vocabulary of negligence in his opinion. It is instead in Judge William Andrews' *dissent* that most of the talk of intent, cause, effect, and general negligence occurs. Cardozo, rather, speaks a strange, if now familiar, language of "bodily security."

Whereas Andrews, for instance, argues that negligence is "a wrong not only to those who happen to be within the radius of danger but to all who might have been there—a wrong to the public at large,"[85] Cardozo argues that "the plaintiff as she stood upon the platform of the station might claim to be protected against intentional invasion of her bodily security. Such invasion is not charged."[86] Whereas Andrews emphasizes the inherent "illogic" of trying to delimit "proximate cause"—the extent to which "because of convenience, of public policy, of a rough sense of justice, the law arbitrarily declines to trace a series of events beyond a certain point," and the extent to which "this is not logic. It is practical politics"[87]—Cardozo emphasizes the "futility" of tracing a violation of bodily integrity rights to a separate violation of property rights.[88] Finally, Andrews states specifically of Palsgraf's claim:

> the only intervening cause was that instead of blowing her to the ground the concussion smashed the weighing machine which in turn fell upon her. There was no remoteness in time, little in space. And surely, given such an explosion as here it needed no great foresight to predict that the natural result would be to injure one on the platform at no greater distance from its scene than was the plaintiff . . . [U]nder these circumstances I cannot say as a matter of law that the plaintiff's injuries were not the proximate result of the negligence. That is all we have before us.[89]

Cardozo, meanwhile, in what is again a perhaps unexpected echo of his *Schloendorff* opinion, stated:

> negligence is not a tort unless it results in the commission of a wrong, and the commission of a wrong imports the violation of a right, in this case, we are told, the right to be protected against interference with one's bodily security. But bodily security is protected, not against all forms of interference or aggression, but only against some.[90]

While Andrews, in other words, talks about time and space (cause, effect, proximate, and not proximate), Cardozo remains immersed in his vocabulary of bodily security, bodily boundaries, and the ways in which these boundaries might or might not be violated. This disjuncture in language is indeed so great that at times reading the decision together with the dissent is like reading responses to two completely separate fact patterns.

And yet, neither Cardozo nor Andrews seems bothered by this discrepancy in vocabulary. Although they disagree vehemently with one another, each refers to the opinion of the other in his own opinion, and each presents himself as arguing an opposing point based, nonetheless, on identical terms, givens, and assumptions. The fact that they appear to be speaking completely different languages does not enter the picture.

It is for this reason that I conclude this chapter with an examination of Helen Palsgraf's claim. The assumption in *Palsgraf* that a discussion of "proximate cause" is no different from a discussion of "bodily security" is arguably as odd as the assumption in *Schloendorff* that the right to bodily integrity can best be exercised via its violation. I suggest, however, that just as the contradiction in *Schloendorff* was resolved—if rendered no less disturbing—when we recognized the normative function of the subject in ecstasy and the quiet centrality of the San Francisco earthquake, so too this discrepancy in *Palsgraf* is resolved when we consider the possibility that both Cardozo and Andrews are once again attempting to articulate a *Schloendorff* style political subjectivity. Both *Schloendorff* and *Palsgraf* point to a distinct collapse of disaster law and everyday law—and a collapse most clearly manifested by the subjects that each case takes as its norm.

If we think about what precisely disturbed Andrews, for example, it was first and foremost the irrationality of trying to describe accidents in the language of law. Andrews recognized that as soon as law admitted these limitations of rational language—even if only in the apparently narrow field of tort law—there came into existence a much more general arena, known to exist but unintelligible, that was likewise inexpressible. In his extended definition of proximate cause, he was thus arguing in a quite universal way that there is a point, an illogical, arbitrary, inexpressible point, at which cause and effect can no longer (legally) operate. There is a point at which the field of the intelligible is separated from the not-field of the unintelligible. And in the particular case that he was hearing, Helen Palsgraf occupied that point.[91] Even as Andrews attempted to extend the boundary of the intelligible to include Palsgraf, therefore, he was forced to recognize that this extension was arbitrary and subject to failure—that Palsgraf was effectively excluded from the universe of the rational, offstage, and eccentric to herself.

That Cardozo then reinforces Palsgraf's eccentricity not via Andrews's vocabulary of time and space but rather via a vocabulary of bodies beside themselves simply plays up the simultaneity of this physical, spatial, and temporal existence. Cardozo and Andrews were *in fact* speaking the same language—a language, however, not of cause and effect, not of rational systems of rights, but of ecstatic and eccentric subjectivity. Indeed, the primary difference between the two was that whereas Andrews recognized the irrational endpoint to legal rationality, Cardozo chose to ignore this endpoint and to displace the hysteria onto his shattered women plaintiffs. Just as in *Schloendorff*, however, in *Palsgraf* too, this move was ineffective. Far from placing the rational, autonomous, self-conscious figure at the center of law and politics, *Palsgraf*, like *Schloendorff*, demonstrates the relentlessly normative function of the unbounded subject, the subject in ecstasy. Just as Schloendorff's shattered body became the paradoxical centerpiece of Cardozo's articulation of the right to bodily integrity, Palsgraf's shattered body became the paradoxical foundation upon which twentieth-century U.S. narratives of public safety and negligence were built.

When I say, therefore, that disaster law and ordinary or everyday law have gradually become identical—and that *Palsgraf* is an ideal example of this process—I am making a quite specific claim. It is not just that accidents are like small catastrophes—each demanding a legal response but each at heart irrational, unintelligible, and incapable of legal articulation. Nor is it just that in foundational cases like *Schloendorff*, there is often a disaster, the San Francisco earthquake, lurking the background. Nor is it even that the gift of life in its various manifestations is both something that occurs every day, under ordinary circumstances, and something that demands a future accident or catastrophe. More so, it is that as disaster law and everyday law are elaborated alongside one another—each producing and assuming the same ecstatic, eccentric political subject—each requires the existence of Mary Schloendorff and Helen Palsgraf.

Respect in Death

Ghouls and Corpses

Introduction

I started the previous chapter with a discussion of Mary Schloendorff's phantom tumor and the political and legal regime that created it. This chapter begins with a ghost of a different sort—far more active than Schloendorff's tumor and central to the following three anecdotes.

In the first, a young German woman, Miss Trauer, becomes engaged to a lieutenant in the Nazi army, whom she then marries in September 1940, three months after he is killed in the north of France. As Edouard Conte and Cornelia Essner put it in their *La Quête de la Race*, "by the grace of the Fuhrer and the Chancellor of the Reich, death could not separate [the fiancés]."[1] According to Conte and Essner, the dead German soldier could even divorce his widow if she was unfaithful to, or behaved in an undignified manner toward, his memory or the German people.[2]

The second anecdote concerns the publication of the Italian fascist criminal code, which went into effect in 1930. In this code, the chapter on "Crimes Against Respect Due to the Dead" becomes gradually more central to Italian law in general—the dead body an object of intense scrutiny on the part of the state, regulated in detail, and protected above all from any living individual who might "commit upon it acts of brutality or obscenity."[3]

The third story arises out of the U.S. military's 2003 invasion and occupation of Iraq. In this story, dead American soldiers become the most recognizable subjects of the Geneva Conventions, their bodies maintaining their legal rights and their legal form even as their biological form gradually disintegrates. At the same time, live Iraqi prisoners, occupying the same geographical space, are shifted into a legal and political vacuum, their biological existence intact even while their legal existence dissolves into nothing.

What connects each of these three anecdotal stories is their unapologetically ghostly or ghoulish[4] nature. In each, the dead individual—or, in the second two vignettes, the dead body—is more politically and legally real than the live individual. In the language of liberalism, the dead body or dead citizen has inalienable rights that the live body emphatically does not. Not only can Miss Trauner's dead fiancé invoke the German civil code and marry his true love, but he can invoke the criminal code later on—in a way that his widow cannot—when this true love turns sour. Likewise, not only does the respectable Italian corpse possess a right to bodily integrity that surpasses any similar right protecting its live counterparts, but this right to bodily integrity is juxtaposed to the bodily trespasses undergone by the criminal who takes advantage of the corpse, and who then ends up in penal servitude. Finally, and perhaps most unequivocally, the dead American soldier is protected by all of the apparently ambiguous, contingent, and fragile rights of the Geneva Conventions, whereas the live Iraqi citizen is not. In each of these stories, in other words, the extension of systems of rights and the elaboration of rights rhetoric serves above all to define, protect, and preserve the dead. In each, rights are extended and elaborated on behalf of the dead—and in each, these rights are likewise extended against those who remain alive.

My purpose in this chapter is not to engage in a critique of rights or to question the use or validity of rights rhetoric. Rather, I argue that in times of disaster or crisis, the dead become exaggerated rights bearers, while the living are gradually deprived of their rights. I argue, in other words, that the dead become political subjects in a way that the living cannot. Moreover, I suggest that this is the case because the dead body, more than any other body—more than the dismembered body or the hysterical body—is an expression of the subject in ecstasy. The dead body, as it dissolves and disintegrates, arguably provides the clearest and most obvious physical proof that bodily borders and that bounded self-consciousness are meaningless concepts and pointless desires. Disaster law, that is, endows dead people with rights precisely because dead people, more than anyone else, are manifestations of the subject in ecstasy.

Ecstatic Death

In many ways, this shifting of rights rhetoric, this reimagining of bodies, bodily borders, and biological matter, smacks of regimes of biopolitics. As I noted in Chapter One, the ecstatic subject that I describe in these chapters is very much a product of the biopower critiqued by Foucault, Braidotti, and Agamben. As I also argue in Chapter One, however, the ecstatic subject is in some respects quite different from the biopolitical subject. The question, therefore, is how respectable corpses become ecstatic subjects of law—and how in particular these rights-bearing dead bodies have engaged with biopolitical structures and how they have escaped from them.

I begin with a series of familiar passages from Foucault's 1975–1976 lectures, in which he develops his theory of biopolitics against the backdrop of the "juridical model of sovereignty." According to Foucault, this juridical model of sovereignty is based on the "classical" right of the sovereign either to "have people put to death or let them live," and that, indeed, "in terms of his relationship with the sovereign, the subject is, by rights, neither dead nor alive."[5] Contrarily, biopolitical right—the right that eventually joined together with and overshadowed this juridical right—was a sovereign right "to make live and to let die."[6] Less interested in ending life or allowing it to continue, modern biopolitics concerns itself with preserving life and allowing it to end. Foucault elaborates on the nature of biopower by contextualizing it within a discussion of disciplinary power. "Disciplines," he argues, "dealt with individuals and their bodies in practical terms . . . [B]iopolitics deals with the population, with the population as a political problem, as a problem that is at once scientific and political, as a biological problem and as power's problem."[7] With regard to the role of *death* in these systems, it is "beyond the reach of power," "power literally ignores death."[8]

Again, the ecstatic subject of disaster law is in many ways a product of these biopolitical systems—and if we look at responses to disaster such as the early twentieth-century American Red Cross reports, their biopolitical starting point is obvious. In a 1920 report, for instance, the "Average American" is chided for considering "health a private affair" rather than "a public asset," especially when "the public learned in the stress of war that one-third of its men between the ages of eighteen and thirty-five were physically unfit for active military duty, [and] that during the war ten babies died in America for every American soldier that was killed in France."[9] In a report a year earlier, the relationship between military and economic strength on the one hand, and the health of the population on the other was a similarly central concern, once again manifested in a discussion of live soldiers abroad and dead babies at home:

> As the United States faced toward reconstruction, the statistics brought out by the war revealed the fact that while the wealth of the United States is greater than that of any nation, it spends only twenty-seven cents per capita upon the health of its citizens. One-third of the young men of the Army draft were rejected on account of minor physical defects; one out of every 7 babies dies in its first year; 150,000 die annually of tuberculosis; 500,000 died during the influenza epidemic.[10]

In both of these reports, the population is quite clearly a political problem, a biological problem, and power's problem. In each, the health and well-being of the American population is as public and as important to national well-being as any other natural resource. The state's sovereign right to protect, preserve, and prolong the life of its citizens, to make live and let die, is overt in this formulation—the biological existence of each and every individual directly connected to the military defense of the state writ large.

Again, though, I depart in this chapter from such straightforward biopolitical analyses. Rather than tracing the marginalization of the rights-bearing citizen whose life is predicated on the juridical sovereign's will, that is—rather than looking at the gradually sharpening focus on healthy populations of bodies whose death is determined by sovereign power—I look instead at the conjunction of the two, at the ways in which the rights-bearing individual and the healthy population *together* give rise to dead people with rights. My interest in this chapter, in other words, is what sort of legal and political regime composes a healthy population out of an explicitly dead citizenry. I suggest that the subject of disaster law, in its ecstasy and eccentricity, can be so easily manifested in the respected dead precisely because of this shift in biopolitics—of this reintroduction of death as a focus of power during moments of crisis.

What I describe in this chapter is thus not biopolitics per se—not the normal, functional regulation of populations. Nor is it the eighteenth-century rights-based juridical model of sovereignty. It is instead something else—a politics of ecstasy. Whereas the juridical model dealt with the rights-bearing individual and society, and biopolitics dealt with biologically defined populations, here we will see biopolitical statistical mechanisms like the death toll mobilized as a means of defining the rights of the citizen, as a means of turning the corpse into a political subject. Likewise, whereas the juridical model assumed its subjects to be simultaneously alive and dead, and the biopolitical model assumed its subjects to be always alive, the politics of ecstasy assumes that its subjects are dead, if nonetheless active.

This extension of rights to corpses and dead bodies is certainly nothing new in the history of modern political identity. Rather, it is arguably part of what has become an increasingly vigorous process of endowing things not ordinarily conceived of as part of the eighteenth-century social contract—animals being the most obvious example[11]—with the duties and privileges of citizens. Endowing a dead body with rights should therefore not seem in and of itself strange. Holding up the dead body as the *normative* subject, however—as the ecstatic figure to which everything else must conform in order to be recognized legally and politically—is relatively unique. Even so, what I show in this chapter is that this is precisely the political relationship at the heart of disaster law. A physical manifestation of the ecstatic subject in every conceivable way, the respectable corpse eventually becomes the only bearer of rights, the primary focus of the sovereign's interest. The assumption of disaster law, therefore, is that citizens are dead—or about to be so—and that death is thus the means by which law endows the disaster with meaning.

Another way to think about this phenomenon is within the more literary framework of mourning and melancholy. Slavoj Zizek, for instance, paraphrasing the work of Agamben, notes that "'melancholia offers the paradox of an intention to mourn that precedes and anticipates the loss of the object . . .' [the lovers] perceive their current pleasures under the aegis of the catastrophe (separation) to come."[12] In the legal and political formulation that I describe here, the state-citizen-population relationship is likewise melancholic—the citizen may be currently alive, the population may be currently healthy, but both life and health are perceived "under the aegis of the catastrophe to come." The assumption is that at some point in the not too distant future, state, citizen, and population will be dead.

In a very different context, Karen Sanchez-Eppler has described a nonetheless similar interpretation of death and subjectivity in the work of Wordsworth on English burials and epitaphs. Addressing Wordsworth's description of death and intimacy in the poem, "We are seven,"[13] she argues that "for [the girl] presence is more a function of locality than vitality . . . her cheerful intimacy with her dead play mates suggests that the grave marks not loss but presence,"[14] while for Wordsworth this confusion between being dead but nearby on the one hand, and alive but far away on the other, marks "the permeability of the boundary between the living and the dead."[15] Here, in other words, it is the physical proximity of the grave or the corpse that makes an individual knowable. Living people, contrarily, are much less comforting: they may be biologically alive, but, in the context of disaster law, they are less real politically and legally than those quite definitely dead and close at hand.

What I suggest over the rest of this chapter is that these melancholic, if cheerful, interpretations of death and subjectivity are what drive the slightly shifted biopolitics of disaster law. In a juridical analysis, the purpose of declaring an individual dead is to bring that individual's political life to a close; in a biopolitical analysis the purpose of compiling a death toll is to construct one further statistical tool in population management. In the law of disaster and the politics of ecstasy, both the declaration of death and the compilation of the death toll are a means of making the dead body the normative subject of law. Likewise, in both juridical and biopolitical analyses, the decomposition of bodies is irrelevant to politics, while the disinterment of bodies is unthinkable. In the politics of ecstasy, however, decomposing bodies are the building blocks of democracy,[16] their disinterment a necessary precursor to political subject formation. Finally, in juridical analyses, looting is an assault on a citizen's privacy rights; in biopolitical analyses, looting narratives serve as antecedents to the concentration and regulation of unruly postdisaster populations. In the politics of ecstasy, looting narratives serve one essential purpose: to distinguish the political existence of dead property holders from the political nonexistence of their live, but ghostly, counterparts.

Death Tolls and Declaring the Dead

Disasters are not the only moments at which the dead must be declared. The juridical and biopolitical structures of contemporary daily life require constant assertions of death or life on the part of citizen and political subject. As Christine Quigley has shown in her history of the corpse, for example, making a dead body "official" in any functional modern state involves a cumbersome bureaucratic process that in many ways mirrors the gradual, lifelong process of becoming politically alive. "A corpse," she states,

> becomes official when a death certificate is completed by the attending physician, coroner, or medical examiner and filed with the local government. In the United States, a death certificate is required for all deaths except those of fetuses weighing less than 500 grams, which are considered medical specimens . . . [T]he regular death certificate, which is rejected if not filled out in black ink, varies from state to state, but usually requires the following information about the deceased: name, sex, race, and citizenship; date and place of death or date and place the body was found; date and place of birth (if known), age or approximation, and social security number; marital status, name of surviving spouse, and parents' names; occupation and residence; cause of death and contributing factors, manner of death (natural, accident, suicide, homicide, or undetermined), and time of death; whether an autopsy was performed; method of bodily disposition; name and address of the funeral home and cemetery or crematory and signature of the certifier.[17]

Again, at one level this seems like a ghoulish mockery of the procedure involved in endowing an individual with political life. The corpse is no longer living: why this almost fetishistic detail about the various relationships and biological states that together produce a political status? I think the answer to this question is that more than simply *ending* a citizen's political life, the death certificate and its attendant procedure are also *creating* a new and different political life. It is not that death has ended the citizen's existence. It is that death is a different, slightly shifted, alternative form of existence.[18] What I suggest in this section is that although the processes and procedures are truncated to some extent, declarations of death during moments of disaster are even more intent on the production of this new status of "citizen" than their day-to-day counterparts are. Postdisaster declarations of death and death tolls are—more than anything else—a means of constructing and then counting an increasingly normative collection of political subjects, a collection of subjects that makes the disaster intelligible, and a collection of subjects absolutely essential to the elaboration of disaster law. Declarations of death and death tolls are the first step in a lengthy process of making corpses respectable, ecstatic citizens, and in this way fulfilling the promise of the melancholic postcrisis political relationship.

Various nineteenth- and early twentieth-century discussions of death in disaster, of counting corpses, and of declaring their status, in fact make clear the political stakes involved in defining and regulating death during crisis situations. An 1843 article on postearthquake "presumptions of survivorship," for instance—while definitely concerned with the question of what survivorship means for those still living—is almost more interested in the legal and political status of the dead *for their own sake*. It is true that the article begins in a familiar and self-consciously rational manner, stating that "the presumption of survivorship may arise . . . when many persons perish at the same time, as under the ruins of a falling building, or in a sand pit, or by an earthquake"—that "the first inquiry is as to the cause of death, whether by suffocation, hunger, thirst, or wounds, [along with] the age, condition of the body, sex, and the position of the dead."[19] The author then, however, moves on to a much more complicated analysis of survivorship in the days following, in this case, a major earthquake in Calabria, Italy.

In addition to noting that "the state of the lungs" is a key element in deciding who has outlived whom under the rubble, for example, and that practitioners should beware that "although the external wounds may not appear severe, yet on dissection, we shall find the large blood vessels and the heart itself lacerated," the author assures his readers of the following:

> should we find such persons in various situations and positions . . . in which it is evident that the deceased could not have been placed after death, as with the extremities drawn from the body, the arms upraised, or resting like the feet on the ground, or if we find under the fingernails, sand etc., as if the sufferer had endeavoured to extricate himself, or if some of these foreign substances are seen in the mouth and windpipe, it is beyond a question that such a one must have survived another, on whom these marks were not found. It was remarked of those who were entombed by the earthquake in Calabria, that the last position at the moment of death, of males, was an exertion of all muscles in apparent struggling; while that of the female sex exhibited marks of the wildest despair. The latter, particularly, had their hands clasped above their heads. But when there were any children with the mother, she evidently thought only of protecting them, and with her own body endeavoured to ward off the danger. The father, on the contrary, seized his child and then opposed himself to it.[20]

The presumption of survivorship, in other words, involves, first, determining the cause and thus the probable time of death; it involves a clarification—for the benefit of the living—of lines of inheritance or custody. Indeed, the status of the dead body, what the dead body can tell us, supersedes any possible claim that the living may have on property or surviving children. Presumption of survivorship is, therefore, the deciding factor in the fate of those who remain alive.

However, presumption of survivorship also involves determining the likely emotional and psychological state of the recently dead; it involves raising the possibility that the dead body screamed or struggled to escape the debris; and above all it involves reinforcing the certainty that, even in death, men and women will play their appropriate gender roles. Presumption of survivorship is based fundamentally on the ongoing *attitude* of the corpse. If, for example, a female corpse does not play its proper gender role—if it is *not* found, for instance, wrapped around its dead baby or in the depths of despair—then it does not exhibit signs of having outlived its counterparts, and its legal claims become invalid. Presumption of survivorship, in other words, both privileges the discursive power of the corpse as a political subject *and* requires the corpse—like any subject—to conform to certain roles if it is to maintain its political rights.

The gendered nature of the respectable dead citizen is made clear in the countless, repetitive stories—at all times and in every region—of female corpses found in attitudes of wifely or maternal anguish.[21] The national and civilizational characteristics of the rights-bearing corpse, however, are almost equally prominent in these narratives—almost equally indicative of its political centrality in the realm of disaster law. As a mid-nineteenth-century English analysis of the 1755 Lisbon earthquake (counterintuitively) put it: "some conception of native mortality may be formed from that of the English: of the comparatively small number of whom were resident at that time in Lisbon, no less than twenty-eight men and fifty women were among the sufferers."[22]

Similarly, various discussions of late nineteenth- and early twentieth-century earthquakes in the south of Italy brought together nationalist rhetoric, statistical findings, and scientific hypotheses in the nascent field of seismology, all of which together produced variations on the normative rights-bearing corpse, and thus the political meaning of the disaster. One analysis of an 1857 earthquake near Naples, Italy, for instance, states that although "the extent of the catastrophe was not nearly as great as that of many of the South American earthquakes,"

> it happened in a highly civilized country, and at a time when men like Sir William Hamilton and Dolomien were at hand to investigate the results . . . [H]earsay and traditions were therefore not included in the history of the earthquake, but careful and trained observers noted and delineated the phenomenon. The loss of life was not less than that of 40,000 individuals, and at least 20,000 died subsequently from the results of injuries, fright, and exposure. By far the greater number were buried under the ruins of their houses.[23]

In a second discussion of the same disaster, we learn likewise that independent observations during and after the destruction yielded the population

> of the different communes in the province of Basilicata, and the loss of life in each due to the shock; and from these figures we can find the percentage of deaths at nearly every place of importance. As will be seen from Fig. 10, it varies from seventy-one at Montemono and fifty at Saponora to less than one at all places marked to which figures are not attached . . . [I]t seems clear that one focus was situated not far from Montemono.[24]

These late nineteenth- and early twentieth-century discussions of the 1857 death tolls in turn provided a vocabulary for addressing one of the most destructive earthquakes to hit the Sicily and Calabria region in centuries—the 1908 disaster that destroyed the city of Messina and produced "a larger total [of deaths] than has ever yet been due to a single earthquake.[25] At the same time, although "3/5" of the population of Messina, or "sixty thousand people" were killed, the city itself had revived "in less than five years": "the number of inhabitants, which in 1908 exceeded 160,000 . . . has already risen again to 130,000."[26]

Each of these anecdotal accounts of disasters and death tolls is built around similar assumptions concerning the political identity of the corpse and its role in making the disaster intelligible. In the first, it is precisely the number of *English* corpses that makes the "native mortality" during the Lisbon earthquake understandable. This is not the case because there were no numbers or estimates as to the total casualties, undifferentiated by nationality, in the 1755 quake—indeed quite a few observers published such statistics. Rather, it is because, for the readers of *Blackwood's Edinburgh Magazine*, English corpses have meaning. English corpses indeed have a distinct, understandable, political identity. English corpses are differentiated and possessed of rights. And as a result, the way to know the "native" mortality, the way to make the Lisbon earthquake meaningful, is to count not the total dead, but the total English dead. Corpses *must* have a recognizable political status.

This relationship between the rights-bearing corpse—the disintegrating ecstatic subject of disaster law—and these increasingly scientific narratives of the disaster becomes far more pronounced in the analyses of the Italian earthquakes. Not only must cool, rational, scientific thinkers be on hand to measure the earthquake—to remove it from the realm of "hearsay and tradition"—but their particular role is to count dead bodies. Moreover, once the dead bodies have been tallied, they are linked *directly* to the likewise cool and rational determinations of the epicenter of the quake. Montemono had statistically the highest number of deaths; therefore the earthquake occurred in Montemono. This is not a determination based on waves or seismic force or physical measurements; it is a determination based—like the presumption of survivorship—squarely on the attitude of the dead body.

I must be clear about the position of the rational, self-conscious, thinking subject here—about the role of the doctor dissecting the corpse or of the seismologist counting the dead. These rational subjects are completely secondary. What tells the story of the earthquake, what serves as a focus of the laws and regulations that follow the earthquake, is the shattered, crushed, and scattered corpse. It is the corpse, in ecstasy, that is the subject of both the disaster and its law—even to the extent that when Messina "revives" and its living population revives with it, it is in relation to the postdisaster *death* toll that these changes makes sense.

By the time, therefore, that we get to the end of the nineteenth century and the first of my case studies, there is already a framework in place for endowing the dead body with rights and a political identity. Thirty-five years before the 1894 disaster hit Istanbul, the Ottoman government was already well versed in declaring the dead, postcrisis. Following an 1859 earthquake in the Anatolian city of Erzurum, for example, "official returns" compiled by the governor produced a death toll of "460 Musulmans; 11 Gregorian Armenian Christians; 1 Catholic Armenian Christian; [and] 2 Greek Christians."[27]

After the 1894 disaster, state officials were less successful in establishing an exact and immediate death toll. Moreover, this apparent failure on their part—along with the unofficial estimates published by the press—produced much popular and political anxiety.[28] The government indeed issued repeated warnings to the press to stop printing what it called unsubstantiated statistics, stating that the newspapers were spreading terror among the people,[29] that the "unfounded and trifling" reports were stirring up public opinion, and that if it continued, the media would be further censored.[30] Eventually, citing the need for "the truth"—rather than "complete exaggeration" and "untruths"—to reach the provinces and foreign embassies, the government closed much of the telegraph system and clamped down on what printing presses it could.[31] When the official death toll *was* finally established, there remained disturbing gaps—including, for instance, the number of dead on the Princess Islands in the Marmara Sea (which were populated at that point primarily by Christians and Jews).[32] As these gaps were filled in, the government maintained a tight hold on the official number of dead, insisting that the death toll never rose above 200 and publicly sending out experts and officials to verify that such was the case.[33]

A similar story unfolded in San Francisco a decade later. The death toll remained uncertain throughout the disaster, and there was thus a great deal of competition among various organizations and individuals as to who could officially (1) declare the dead, (2) declare the various *categories* of the dead, and (3) in turn compile official statistics. As James Russell Wilson, put it, "when chaos came again, and all the channels of familiar life were closed, and human anguish grew to be intolerable, compilation of statistics was impossible, even if it were not repugnant to the feelings."[34] Wilson nonetheless had no difficulty overcoming his feelings of repugnance long enough to note that "since 1137, when the first reliable records apparently were made of such disasters, 1,096,000 persons have lost their lives by earthquakes,"[35] and that,

> the total number of bodies recovered up to Sunday night and either buried or burned was 500. No complete record could be had, as many bodies were buried without permits from the Coroner and the Board of Health. The searchers of the Coroner's department and the Board of Heath found twenty bodies during the day. Whenever a body was found it was buried immediately, without any formality, and these burials were made at widely separated points.[36]

Far more disturbing to Wilson than this, however, was the probability that many of the bodies buried in the rubble were in an indeterminate state between life and death, that "under the smoking mounds" there were "hundreds and hundreds of dead, and some . . . still living, but buried beyond finding and absolutely doomed."[37] *Less* disturbing to Wilson, but equally productive of official uncertainty, was the destruction of San Francisco's Chinatown, where "no one will ever know how many lives were lost," given the "moral certainty that men overcome with opium, slave women in their dungeons, and many a hapless wretch, unconscious from morphine, were killed when the tremor of the earth toppled the buildings."[38] According to Wilson, it was "improbable that any attempt [would] be made to reach the bodies of the Chinese victims."[39]

By the time declarations of death and official death tolls were being produced and compiled in Tokyo, the legal and political narrative structures supporting them were thus quite well established. First of all, just as in Istanbul, in Tokyo as well, the press with its "wild rumors" and unofficial statistics was immediately censored.[40] Nonetheless, one French journalist observing the city in the months after the earthquake did manage to play up to his audience the uncertainty surrounding the dead, noting that what particularly struck the "impartial" visitor was the "contrast between the living ruins of Tokyo and the dead ruins of Yokohama," the way in which living and dead collapsed into one another, and the difficulty in distinguishing what was alive and what was dead.[41] Likewise, Otis Manchester Poole, a memoirist writing on the Tokyo earthquake in the style of Wilson above, commented on the uncertain status of the dead. After first invoking his colleague's experiences at Gallipoli during the First World War—being "one of thirty-eight survivors of the South Australian Light Horse"—in order to explain this man's ability to "churn ahead" through the mud and the piles of dead bodies,[42] Poole then turns to a discussion of the bodies themselves: "one felt that somehow the multitudes of creatures under that wreckage must surely give a mighty heave and emerge alive in their hundreds. But all was silent; only here and there a shriek from the depths, or encouraging shouts for some frantically digging group."[43]

Again, however, more disturbing to Poole than the confused status of the bodies under the rubble was the possible ethnic or political miscategorization of bodies both alive and dead. In addition to praising the work of the American destroyer, *Smith Thomson,* as it "picked up all the foreigners" from the shore, for instance,[44] he tells the harrowing story of "Aunt Mabel"—missing still when "nearly all foreigners had been taken off," but then found miraculously by "an officer of the last *Dongola* lifeboat," who was "searching through the throng and shouting for any foreigners left," and who "came upon her . . . alone in the mob . . . scorched but otherwise unhurt."[45] Despite Aunt Mabel's narrow escape, however, "of the 3000 foreigners who were in Yokohama at the time, approximately one-half perished."[46]

Throughout each of these accounts of late nineteenth- and early twentieth-century disasters, in other words, there run a number of common themes. In all three, for instance, there is a fear verging on paranoia of unofficial death tolls. In the Ottoman Empire and Japan, the governments go so far as to pass decrees criminalizing the broadcasting of unofficial statistics. Meanwhile, in San Francisco, there is a distinct and mounting frustration voiced by the Coroner's office that official paperwork cannot be filed—and numbers cannot be compiled—when bodies are being buried or destroyed by any average citizen.

At the same time, there is a seemingly contradictory trend toward, first, categorizing the dead, and, second, designating certain categories uncountable. In the mid-nineteenth-century Ottoman Empire, the death toll was easily divided according to religious belief because an individual's religious community determined his or her political identity. Citizenship was a function of religious identity. By the late nineteenth century, however, this easy process of categorization had become confused in the face of separatist national movements and attempts on the part of the government to create an overarching Ottoman citizenship that would transcend religious identity. Although the death toll remained both officially and unofficially divided along religious lines, therefore, certain segments of the population—most notably the minority communities on the islands—became gradually less subject to counting.

In San Francisco, likewise, the Chinese remained an uncountable mass[47]—a group whose death toll was immeasurable not because compiling statistics was repugnant, but because doing so was simply impossible and unthinkable in Chinatown. Finally, in Tokyo, an inverted process seemed to happen—at least from the perspective of the expatriate community. The precise number of "foreign" (i.e., white) dead was well known—live foreigners and dead foreigners separated instantly from "the mob" and taken to boats offshore or to other parts of the city—while the number of Japanese or Korean dead was impossible to determine.

Finally, there is the repetitive theme of the body beneath the rubble, suspended between life and death, but also knowable via recourse to some unexpected and seemingly extraneous reference point. Wilson is particularly disturbed by the thought of live bodies, never to be discovered, expiring beneath the wreckage,[48] and invokes an apparently random statistic—the number of dead in earthquakes since 1137—in order to bring this issue home. Likewise, Poole is disturbed by the individuals, simultaneously living and dead, buried beneath the ruins of Tokyo. But he makes his point clear via reference to Anzac soldiers at the battle of Gallipoli.

The persistence of each of these themes thus raises a number of questions. First, for instance, why is the death toll such a key aspect of modern disaster law, and why is such political ire directed at those who attempt to appropriate it—at those who compile and spread unofficial, alternative statistics? Second, why should some populations lend themselves to exact—fetishistically exact—death tolls and some be simply impossible to count? Finally, why should not dead bodies, not live bodies, but bodies of *unknown status* cause particular panic in postdisaster observers, and why should this panic be manifested in the invocation of some strangely irrelevant bit of information about other people, at a different time, possibly dying elsewhere?

I think the answer to these questions, again, can be found in the particular role that the dead body plays in the law and politics of disaster. Each question pinpoints in a different way the political status of the dead body; its continuing role as a rights-bearing citizen; and its particular ecstatic, eccentric potential to make the crisis intelligible. The intense anxiety about the compilation of unofficial statistics exhibited by government officials in Istanbul, San Francisco, and Tokyo is arguably the result of what these statistics represent—is linked to the possibility that these statistics determine something beyond immediate infrastructural need. It is true that the stated purpose of censoring the press and its "untrue" reporting is to curb panic among the postdisaster population. But this explanation begs the question as to why precisely an incorrect death toll—or simply an *unofficial* death toll—should, in the eyes of the government, produce this panic.

Again, if we engage with the possibility that dead bodies are the real citizens, that the respectable rights bearers are also corpses, then this (assumption of) panic makes a great deal of sense. Death tolls are not about determining how many political lives have ended, but about determining how many political lives must now be created. They are about citizenship *formation*. And if an organization or institution outside of the government—if a private or unofficial group—suddenly takes on the role of determining who may be a citizen and who may not, then the government itself loses its meaning and purpose. The panic produced by the unofficial death toll is thus a panic that makes some sense—a panic that ignores individual existence or nonexistence to focus instead on collective existence or nonexistence. If unofficial death tolls are unofficial lists of potentially normative citizens, then they are very much worthy of the political responses that they provoked in Istanbul, San Francisco, and Tokyo.

That the death toll is not just a list or compilation of those who no longer exist becomes even more credible when we turn, first, to the various populations that elude proper counting and, second, to the living/dead bodies under the rubble that cause such concern to those above it. The populations whose dead cannot be counted are composed of those minorities (or, from the perspective of expatriate communities in Japan, those "natives") who—when living—are not quite complete or effective citizens. At an intuitive level, it makes sense, therefore, that the dead members of these communities should be of less interest to the state than the dead members of more politically viable communities. Once again, though, this differentiation among the dead of different communities raises the question of what the purpose of the death toll is. If the purpose of the death toll is simply to count the dead, then the formerly living individual's political existence or lack thereof would be irrelevant. There would be no question of determining prior political status, no question of any ongoing interest in the previous ethnicity, biology, or social relationships possessed by the now dead body. If, however, the purpose of the death toll is to form a new citizen out of the corpse, then the dead body's former community, its ethnicity, its biology, and its prior position within social and political structures, remains of the utmost interest. The dead body's prior political affiliation is of interest because it can indicate, above all what sort of citizen this same body will be in the future.

Whether the body is dead or alive thus becomes of key importance—and the simultaneously living and dead individual, unreachable under the rubble, very much a source of much anxiety. The body in this indeterminate state represents not just the biological horror of suspended existence, but the political horror of nonexistence. The simultaneously living and dead body possesses neither the rights of the live citizen nor the rights of the dead one. It is quite emphatically *nothing* in a way that a corpse would never be.[49] It is indeed the *political* implications of being buried alive—of being treated as politically dead despite biological survival—that lends these stories their gothic force. It is, in other words, the *political* confusion produced by the rightsless body—the body that cannot be honored as a respectable corpse and cannot be regulated as one of the unhygienic living—that causes such unease to those who describe it.

The recourse to the apparently irrelevant in such narratives—to death tolls in the year 1137, or to the experiences of the Anzac soldiers at Gallipoli—is a means of transforming these indeterminate bodies into proper citizens. A hyperbolic invocation of the eccentric and the offstage—a reference to the irrelevant—contextualizes the bodies under the rubble within the broader scope of disaster law. Like the medieval population of Constantinople or the Anzac soldiers at Gallipoli, the bodies under the rubble are unknowable, impossible to determine—but in this way they are also now a reference point for endowing the disaster with meaning. The definitely dead are in ecstasy and serving a normative function. The possibly dead are in turn made eccentric and can perform the same task.

If we turn to the late twentieth century, we can see further variations on these processes of declaring the dead, determining the death toll, and rendering corpses normative citizens. Immediately following the 1999 Istanbul earthquake, the number and type of citizens who would be constituting the respectable dead became a key element in many government and media reports. In the mass daily, *Hürriyet*, for instance, there was particular focus in one article, titled "A Burial Every Minute,"[50] on the number of burials (per hour) in Avcılar, one of the most badly hit neighborhoods: "on the first day close to 100 funerals took place," and "on the second day 150 new graves were opened to the side of the cemetery because there was no longer room within it."[51] The article continues by noting that the "Ministry of Cemeteries" would help families to bury the dead, that even the largest cemeteries were proving too small for the earthquake stricken, and that volunteers were working as hard as they could to bury everyone without "excessive waiting."[52]

A second article published the day after the disaster drew particular attention to *soldiers* trapped under the rubble (and assumed to be simultaneously living and dead). Describing the condition of two major barracks in the town of Gölcük—near the epicenter of the earthquake—the article notes that precisely 43 soldiers had been rescued from the fallen buildings, while 187 soldiers were still trapped and "awaiting rescue."[53] It then moves on to the losses suffered by the naval forces—250 people under the rubble—and states that among those still in the ruins were retired and highly ranked personnel.[54]

Finally, an article published three weeks after the disaster invoked the Princess Islands again. The article, "The Islands Have Emptied,"[55] analyzes the rhetoric of the Islands during and after the 1894 earthquake, and explains how this rhetoric continued to influence attitudes to the area one hundred years later: "rumors . . . have emptied the Islands. Because the four Princess Islands are very close to the North Anatolian fault line, and because of rumors that the Islands vanished under the water during the earthquake one hundred years ago, summer tourists have begun to flee the region."[56] The streets, it continues, are "completely empty," only year-round residents have stayed, and the head district official of the region is feeling "anxiety" at the mass departure: according to the head district official, "the rumors that the Islands will sink into the Marmara Sea are simply untrue—and that is why we're so sad at the people leaving. The rumors are absurd . . . [T]he Islands are safe."[57]

By 1999, the Princess Islands were no longer so heavily settled by—or associated with—minority populations. This lingering insistence, however, that they were subject to additional, unthinkable seismic devastation—the fear that they were liable to disappear completely, to sink into the sea—arguably does hint at the unthinkable disappearance of uncounted members of minority groups during the earthquake one hundred years before.[58] It forges a link, that is, between the late nineteenth-century rhetoric of the death toll and its late twentieth-century counterpart. It was clear, for example, that the Islands did not in fact sink into the sea in 1894; they were very much present and visible one hundred years later. But the idea that they could (have) cease(d) to exist was nonetheless a widespread one—apparently indicating some alternative interpretation of "non-existence." The partial physical existence of the Princess Islands during this twentieth-century moment of crisis, in other words, gestures toward the partial political existence enjoyed by those who inhabited them one hundred years before.

I suggest that in each of these accounts—the burials in the badly hit neighborhood of Avcılar, the various soldiers "awaiting rescue" under the fallen barracks, and the empty streets of the Princess Islands—there are distinct and meaningful methods of counting that are often identical to the methods we saw at the end of the nineteenth century. Moreover, these methods of counting in some ways quite explicitly play up the peculiar political force wielded by the earthquake *dead*. In the first story, for example, there is a continuing slippage between what the dead want and what the living families want—the harried Ministry of Cemeteries attempting somehow to serve both. By the end of the article, however, it is not entirely clear whether the frustrated people whom the volunteers are trying not to keep "waiting" are the live people seeking closure or the dead people seeking burial.[59]

The second article repeatedly reminds us of the importance of political status to the newly respectable dead. In it, each earthquake victim is identified according to his rank, role, and position within the army—and each of these political designations follows the body even into its grave. Moreover, for those "awaiting rescue," this process of assigning rank and position becomes even more insistent. Seeking to rescue these simultaneously living and dead bodies from the threat of complete political nonexistence, the military assigns these "soldiers" (rather than bodies) under the wreckage every political designation at its command.

Finally, there are the empty, sinking Princess Islands. Once again, the Islands did not sink in 1894 and—as the head district official made clear in his exasperated statement—they were unlikely to sink in 1999. Nonetheless, the Islands occupied an uncomfortable rhetorical position in the broader narrative of the earthquake. In 1894, the (minority) population that had inhabited them was uncountable—the dead members of this population never effectively making it onto the death toll and thus never effectively sharing in the politics of disaster. As of 1999, the composition of the Princess Islands' population had changed, but the inhabitants were nonetheless not taking any chances. Rather than staying in a place that was known to exist only partially during moments of crisis—its population uncounted, its land prone to "sinking"—they preferred a return to the city, where the dead were known, counted, registered, and declared. Better than nonexistent death *or* life on the Islands was the very real possibility of existent death on the mainland, among majority populations. The dead body—its political identity, its respectability, and its emphatically inalienable rights—in this way determined not just the layout of the impromptu cemeteries, but the movement of living populations within the shattered city and its suburbs.

Decomposition, Disinterment, and Democracy

In the previous section I made the case that death tolls are more than simply an accounting of bodies—that decisions about who should be counted and who should not, about the means of counting, and about what qualities constituted death all serve to produce a unique, and uniquely normative, dead political status. I showed that determining and declaring the death toll is a key precursor to defining the respectable corpse-citizen. What I do now is talk in more detail about the nature of this citizen—about what *sort* of rights a disaster-stricken corpse possesses, and what sort of politics these rights in turn determine. My particular interest is the relationship between decomposition and disinterment on the one hand—the gradual rather than sudden production of ecstatic subjectivity—and the peculiar type of democracy defined by these processes on the other. I argue, in other words, that the politics of disaster are a distinctly democratic politics, predicated, however, upon the disinterment and decomposition of masses of dead individuals.

To begin my discussion, I turn to Sophocles' *Antigone*—which is without doubt one of the most recognizable and widely read texts on rights and political identity (and decomposition and disinterment). As one scholar has noted, "the conflict between individual morality and the laws of the state is . . . the long accepted theme of *Antigone*"—and a theme that has reappeared in countless discussions of the play, especially in late nineteenth- and early twentieth-century Europe.[60] Slavoj Zizek has likewise pointed out that the morality presented in the play is in many ways an antiliberal morality—the rights that underpin it irrational, transcendent, and true for no other reason than that they are true: "is Antigone not the anti-Habermas par excellence?" he asks. "No dialogue, no attempt to convince Creon of the good reasons for her acts through rational argumentation, but just the blind insistence of her right."[61]

Martha Nussbaum has similarly highlighted (and criticized) the absence of a liberal ethic in both Creon's and Antigone's world views—analyzing and condemning the relative "radicalism" of each,[62] and arguing that "Antigone, like Creon, has engaged in a ruthless simplification of the world of value which effectively eliminates conflicting obligations. Like Creon, she can be blamed for a refusal of vision."[63] Nussbaum, however, argues that there are "important differences" between the two that suggest "that this criticism of Antigone is not incompatible with the judgment that she is morally superior to Creon."[64] Among these differences, the following is one of the most salient to my argument: "Creon's attitude towards others is like necrophilia: he aspires to possess the inert and unresisting. Antigone's subservience to duty is, finally, the ambition to be a *nekros*, a corpse beloved of corpses."[65]

The question of death, disinterment, or the state of the corpse is a question that is frequently passed over in analyses of the text—except, perhaps, among classicists interested in Greek burial traditions per se. I emphasize, therefore, both Nussbaum's point and its implications: in the play, Creon has not only decreed that Antigone's brother, Polyneices, may not be buried, but he has repeatedly had the body disinterred when Antigone herself covers it up—to the extent that the guards watching the body comment on the "stench" of the "rotting corpse."[66] The point of contention between Antigone and Creon is thus, yes, Antigone's moral right to bury the body—a right held up against Creon's political right to have it exposed—but more than that, it is Polyneices' right himself to be interred. This is in many ways an argument about the dead body's political status—about the relationship between the decomposing corpse and, in more recent interpretations of the text, the construction of a democratic state. I suggest, in fact, that when we turn to the eighteenth, nineteenth, and twentieth centuries, the elaboration of democratic systems during moments of disaster is predicated precisely on the disinterment and decomposition of various dead bodies—and therefore predicated likewise on Antigone's "morally superior" desire to be dead and beloved by the dead.

This relationship between democracy and decomposition is particularly obvious in late eighteenth- and early nineteenth-century revolutionary and post-revolutionary writing and activism. In July 1793, for example, in the early years of the new French Republic, "the tombs and mausoleums of the former kings [were] destroyed . . . to celebrate the first anniversary of the monarchy's overthrow (August 10)."[67] In the process, the "lead coffins and metal artifacts [were] recast as arms against insurgents," and "bodily remains [were] transferred to 'a common trench dug for that purpose of sufficient depth and width.'"[68] After the disinterment was complete, the French government published its findings as follows: "Most of the bodies were putrefied. They emitted a thick black vapor with an intense odor that was checked with vinegar and burnt saltpeter, but not before workers succumbed to diarrhea and mild fever."[69] The relationship between decomposition and democracy, in other words, is made quite clear in the government reports. Democracy, and especially liberal revolutionary democracy, cannot happen without bodily and biological disintegration; the disinterred and/or decomposing dead body is central to the articulation of the rights-based liberal democratic state.

In the early years of the American Republic, Ralph Waldo Emerson evoked similar sentiments in a somewhat different context "by characterizing decomposition as a kind of irresistible democracy, fusing politics with biology."[70] As one scholar has written, paraphrasing Emerson, "it is against nature for the citizens of a democracy to cling to the image of a preserved past. Like the natural process by which a body returns to the soil, true democracy bears us ceaselessly away from the past and toward a new incarnation of life."[71] In this alternative interpretation of the relationship between decomposition and democracy, then, the progress narrative underlying liberal democratic systems is made manifest in the body's disintegration. In Emerson's political universe, the decomposing citizen's body quite explicitly represents a movement toward a brighter, egalitarian future.

It is true that this is a slight shift away from the universe of the French revolutionaries—a universe in which it was the decomposed *aristocrat's* body that represented progress toward equal rights and citizenship. In both, however, it is clear that the dead body *as* a dead body both possesses and guarantees certain rights—above all the right to be interred or disinterred. Like the right to bodily integrity, however—a right, as Cardozo made clear,[72] that leads *both* to the preservation of bodily borders *and* to their invasion—the right to be interred or disinterred is in many ways more a matter of political status than it is a matter of actual freedom from coercion. Citizens have the right to be interred. Aristocrats have the right to be disinterred. But *both* sets of rights mean progress toward decomposition as democracy—both sets of rights are inalienable, constituting the citizen as a political subject.

By the time we reach the early twentieth century, this relationship between decomposition and democracy had indeed become quite fixed. In the years following the First World War, organizations like the American Red Cross and the War Graves Commission, for instance, were expending almost more time on interring and disinterring various bodies and body parts than they were on alleviating the illnesses of living victims. In what was called "an effort to restore dignity," for example, "the War Graves Commission employed 15,000 men to exhume and re-inter the bodies of the dead. In the desire to recover as many bodies as possible, the whole battlefield area in France and Flanders was searched six times, some parts as many as 29 times."[73] Meanwhile, "the Red Cross in France [was] taking photographs of American graves and sending them back to the relatives of men who lost their lives on French battlefields."[74] This was a task undertaken in concert with the "Graves Registration Bureau of the Army," so that the film might be "sent to Washington to be developed," and thus "remain the property of the United States Government."[75]

By the time we reach the late twentieth century, this relationship between disinterred dead bodies and democratic state-citizen interaction was being subverted by "mothers" especially, who questioned the validity of this particular variation on rights rhetoric. As Carol Acton has argued,

> refusing to relinquish [their sons'] bodies, the mothers have "undone" the military funeral and burial, and exhumed their dead sons to reveal their mutilation. This public act of grieving, in which the mother is reunited with her dead son and holds him physically, as she had done in infancy, challenges the military ownership of the son, and subverts the military attempts to offer platitudes in place of the dead son. Even while the military returns the body of the son to the mother in America, it at the same time seeks to disown the presence of injury in the literal and metaphorical act of covering the body with the flag.[76]

Each of these interpretations of the decomposition/democracy relationship—even the subversive last example—thus rests upon the same unquestioned assumptions about the political status of the dead body that motivated the eighteenth-century revolutionaries. The dead body first of all has a right to be interred—a right, however, that can manifest itself in *dis*interment under certain politically fraught circumstances. Second, in possessing this right, the dead body is constituting a specifically *democratic* state-citizen interaction, a relationship that valorizes the (potential) political equality of every citizen in reference to the state. Finally, the dead body most clearly invokes this right and constitutes this interaction when the ecstatic process—or *progress*—of decomposition is well underway. These assumptions indeed are most obviously in force in the last passage—an inversion of the Antigone story—where the mothers reveal the *disintegrated* bodies of their beloved sons[77]—in all of their quite literal unwholesomeness—as a means of demonstrating their sons' right to be free, not to be owned by anyone, including the military.[78] In this situation, the decomposed body becomes in many ways the hyperbolically free, liberated subject of the liberal, democratic system.

I also suggest that when we see the decomposition/democracy relationship playing out in disaster situations, these rights possessed by the dead body become even more insistent—eventually overriding any possible rights that the live, whole body might possess. Following the 1894 Istanbul earthquake, for instance, the "widows and orphans" of those "heads of families" who had died in the earthquake were the subject of far more concern, and the recipients of far more aid, than those who could not claim a respectable corpse—the dead body here once again serving as the privileged citizen.[79]

In a much more overt way, the military government that oversaw disaster relief in San Francisco repeatedly privileged the rights of the dead—and particularly the decomposing dead—over the rights of the living. Whereas on the one hand, there was horror that "buried bodies had been churned up by the disaster, which was scattering putrid corpses among those seeking safety in cemeteries,"[80] on the other hand, there was the question of the precise relationship between these corpses and those "seeking safety." As Wilson stated,

> the soldiers were needed for other work, so, at the points of rifles, the citizens were compelled to take up the work of burying the dead. Some objected at first, but the troops tolerated no trifling, and every man who came within reach was forced to work at least an hour. Wealthy men, unused to physical exertion, labored by the side of

> working men, digging trenches in which to bury the dead. Many remained unburied and the soldiers were still pressing men into service.[81]

It goes without saying that the principal motivation for the burial and reburial of these corpses was the fear of miasmas and disease. Even more, however, the relentlessness with which the rights and liberties of the living were suspended—at the quite explicit "points of rifles"—in the name of the rights of the dead points to more going on here. Indeed, in many ways this is once again a variation on themes from *Antigone*. The rights of the dead are transcendent, ecstatic. They brook no compromise—no discussion. And thus the "soldiers" *compel* the "citizens"—many of them "wealthy men" implicitly used to rational discussion rather than "physical exertion"—to see to it that these rights are upheld. The "putrid corpses," yes, do pose a threat to those who seek safety in cemeteries. But this threat is more closely linked to the rotting body of Polyneices than it might initially appear—this is the threat posed by the ecstatic subject, the subject whose rights override any bounded, self-conscious, rational exchange, the corpse beloved of corpses.

If we turn to the interment and disinterment of the respectable dead in Tokyo, we see similar assumptions about the relationship between decomposition and democracy playing out. I address just one example here, and that is the memorial designed and created in 1931 to commemorate the earthquake victims. As a photo caption in *The Illuminated London News* put it,

> the Government printing works produced a white Japanese paper of very fine quality on which the names of the victims were carefully inscribed in Chinese ink. As containers for these scrolls, jars of fused quartz crystal were constructed by melting the finest Brazilian crystals in an electric furnace in the form of rods, which were then placed side by side . . . [I]f they can be protected from the prying hands of the archaeologists and sightseers among future generations, the records, it seems, may well lie inviolate and unaffected by decay or the action of any element, fire, earth or water for untold ages . . . [T]he innermost of a nest of containers [is] designed to preserve records of the names of victims of the Japanese Earthquake of 1923 for 10,000 years.[82]

Here, in other words, the logic of the death toll and the logic of interment come together and reach their conclusion. Provided no archaeologist or sightseer "pries into" the jars, thereby undermining the rights of the dead, the death toll will remain inviolate forever. The bodies of the victims of the earthquake have been burned, have disintegrated altogether, and in this ecstatic destruction of their biological borders and boundaries, their political subjectivity—enshrined in the death toll—becomes eternal. Their bodies have disintegrated, their names have been compiled into a single mass, devoid of any distinction, and this death toll has been preserved via burial in the ground.[83] The process of producing the respectable corpse is in this sense complete.

I pause here to emphasize, first, the way in which each of these examples points to the dead body as, above all, a rights bearer, and second, the way in which each situates the dead body within a relentlessly democratic system. Again, I understand "democracy" broadly, as Agamben does, as a system in which "man as a living being presents himself no longer as an *object* but as the *subject* of political power."[84] I understand *modern* democracy as a system that likewise "is constantly trying to transform its own bare life into a way of life and to find, so to speak, the *bios* [political life] of *zoē* [bare life]."[85] In a schematic way, modern *liberal* democracy is thus a system in which it is via the articulation or rhetoric of rights that individuals become subjects of political power and that bare life is gradually made politically relevant.

How, though, does this play out in these various stories of disaster response? First, the dead body is immediately granted "dignity." It is dignity that the War Graves Commission is seeking to restore with its photographs, and it is likewise dignity that the Japanese government is seeking to restore with its earthquake monument. That this is moreover a particularly *political* dignity—an attribute that shifts the body from the realm of political objecthood to the realm of political subjecthood—is made clear by the government "ownership" of both the photographs of the graves and the list of the earthquake dead. The government, that is, seeks not only to endow the dead with personal dignity, but also with the political dignity attached to democratic political subjects.

Second, the way in which this dignity will be preserved is via the extension of rights to the dead body. Not only will the dead body be buried, not only should it be buried, but it has a *right* to be buried. There is an explicit threat to the dignity of the corpse as political subject—namely, looters, ghouls, and archaeologists. And then there is the extension of political protection over the dead body's right to burial as a means of eliminating this threat. The fact that this protection is part of a system of rights rhetoric in particular is evident in the dual nature of postdisaster burial practices. Like the live body's abstract right to bodily integrity, the dead body's abstract right to burial is frequently articulated via a concrete violation of this right. It is not simply that the body has a right to buried and will be buried. More often than not, the body becomes political, achieves its status as dignified, rights-bearing political subject, at the moment that it is disinterred, moved, exposed, burned, or revealed to have decayed.

Finally, the fact that the corpse as a rights-bearing citizen becomes, in disaster law, the *normative* rights-bearing citizen is made clear when we compare the strength of the dead body's rights to the strength of the live body's rights. Like the normative citizen of any other system, corpses possess rights that, during crisis situations, supersede those of their fellow, less valuable citizens. This becomes most obvious in San Francisco, where live citizens are explicitly deprived of their freedom of movement, labor, and livelihood in order to preserve and maintain the dead bodies' right to burial. But it is also apparent after the Istanbul earthquake, where a relationship with a dead body gave living bodies more leverage with the government and more access to food and housing. In each situation, the dead body becomes a political subject, the dead body becomes possessed of rights, these rights supersede the rights of less normative subjects, and political life in turn subsumes bare life completely.

These processes had become relatively commonplace by the end of the twentieth century. In Istanbul, for instance, one of the first issues that the government had to deal with was the "insufficiency" of the morgues and the hygienic issues that this insufficiency raised. The government thus called on more and more "volunteers" to help bury the dead.[86] This problematic relationship between the living and the dead became increasingly fraught, however, until countless volunteers were brought in to see to it that the right to be disinterred and reburied was respected. Now it is true that the voluntary activity of the living in Istanbul was quite different from the compulsory activity of the living in San Francisco, but each in a different way nonetheless emphasized aspects of the decomposition/democracy relationship. In each, it was precisely the burial of dead bodies that produced cohesive political interactions and social contracts—more liberal in the Turkish case and more authoritarian in the U.S. case. And in each, the ecstatic state of the decomposing body turned this body into the normative citizen—the hyperbolic rights bearer—par excellence.

Ghouls and Ghosts: Assaulting the Rights of the Dead

In concluding this chapter, I turn to a final exaggerated expression of the dead body with rights: the corpse that is victimized by the living "ghost" or "ghoul." In general, what follows in this section are examples of living individuals who are accused of undermining the dead body's rights and political status—and who are thus themselves *turned* dead, made ghostly or ghoulish in the eyes of the state. For the most part, it is looters who are treated in this way—living citizens who assault the dead body's right to property, and whose right to life becomes in turn less valid than the property rights of the corpse. As we shall see, however, the relationship between the politically living corpse and the politically dead ghoul transcends property disputes and becomes one of the most clear articulations of the ecstatic dead body's normative role. In each of these cases, the corpse in fact becomes *so* central, so key to the formulation of disaster law, that the live body disappears altogether.

We can see hints of this inversely proportional relationship between the rights-bearing dead body and the fading, ghoulish looter as early as the 1755 Lisbon earthquake, when all victims of the disaster were prohibited "from leaving the city without a passport," to prevent "those who had robbed the people,[87] or plundered the church plate . . . from escaping to the country."[88] Here an early manifestation of the refugee's political death[89]—the absence of papers or passport—is visited upon those foolish enough to remain living and suspect in the disaster area. Moreover, the political identity of the living is withheld precisely in the name of those citizens whose right to property transcended even the grave.

It took a century and a half, however, for this nascent dead/living relationship to reach its logical conclusion. In San Francisco, for example, the military government became gradually more insistent that the decaying dead body be possessed of ineradicable political rights. According to Wilson, U.S. soldiers "formed guards about the collapsed Valerian Hotel and other buildings where the dead were lying. In their rifles they carried death for the ghouls that might try to prowl among the dead victims of the catastrophe."[90] In a caption under a photograph entitled "Man Killed in Market Street," Wilson continues: "this is a ghoul, or robber, who was shot by soldiers for robbing a victim of the earthquake. The body of the robber was afterwards burned, and only fragments of his bones were left."[91] The property rights of the respectable dead thus override the right to life of the ghoulish living.

In Tokyo, likewise, the living were, first, accused of assaulting the rights of the dead before, second, being rendered politically ghostly to nonexistent. In an analysis of postdisaster violence quite similar to Wilson's, a memoirist, R. O. Matheson, spins the story of the massacre of hundreds of Korean civilians in such a way that it supports, above all, the unshakable status of the dead:

> through these suburbs ghouls were prowling, at first believed to be escaped convicts from the big Yokohama penitentiary, later known to be fanatical anarchists . . . [T]hese ruffians were looting, outraging women and girls, and destroying property. The first few caught and promptly executed were found to be Koreans . . . [T]he populace generally went mad after the earthquake, and many of the young defenders of hearth and home against the Korean invasion . . . slashed at the bodies of the earthquake dead. The bodies of some few foreigners were treated this way, resulting in a report among foreign refugees that Japanese were murdering foreigners on shore.[92]

Whereas in Wilson's account it is simply the criminal, the looter—the violator of the dead citizen's property rights—who loses his effective political identity, and in turn becomes a ghoul, far more dead than the corpse, here there are a number of different types of ghosts who all work together to emphasize the dead body's normative political status. It is in fact only "at first" that the ghouls were thought to be criminals from the penitentiary. Upon more careful consideration, however, it became clear that the ghouls were in fact anarchists, Koreans, and—in some unfortunate situations—hysterical Japanese "defenders of hearth and home" who had been driven mad by the earthquake, the chaos, and the "Korean invasion."[93]

These are people, in other words, who are in many ways already politically dead—subject *already* to various forms of biopolitical violence. All it takes is the victimized dead body—deprived of its right to property by the looter and, more so, its right to bodily integrity by the crazed, slashing defender of domestic space—to highlight the ghostly fragility of these living citizens' political status. All it takes is one unhappy or disrespected corpse to make clear the fact that the law of disaster (a) takes the dead body as its normative subject and (b) requires in turn that every living body conform to this sepulchral norm.

By the late twentieth century, the insistent quality of the dead body's rights—the extent to which the dead citizen demanded that living citizens likewise become ghosts or ghouls—had become more apparent. In the case of the 1999 Istanbul earthquake, it became particularly clear in the discourse of ghostly looters and monstrous contractors responsible for widespread death and destruction. The contractors especially were seen as the true ghouls of the earthquake—their badly built structures the product of bribe-taking inspectors, and the collapse of these structures the cause of death for tens of thousands of innocent civilians.

A number of articles and editorials in the mass daily *Hürriyet*, for example, addressed appropriate (and inappropriate) ways of dealing with the "killer contractors" and their "looting" counterparts. In the days immediately following the earthquake, it appeared that the contractors would be tried and convicted according to straightforward criminal procedure. One article, for instance, told the story of a contractor, Haşim Güngörsü, who had not only built a weak structure that collapsed on ninety-six people, but also the vacation home of the former Turkish President, Kenan Evren. In this article, a local official is quoted to the effect that "we are looking into the matter. We've applied to the police so that the contractor Haşim Güngörsü might be apprehended."[94]

Soon, however, it became clear that the ghoulish contractors were to be addressed in a much less transparent way. Two weeks after the earthquake, the Turkish government granted an amnesty to over 26,000 prisoners—ostensibly as a means of appealing to the sensibilities of the European Union. In addition to pardoning political prisoners of various kinds, the president, Parliament, and Justice Ministry granted amnesty to gang members, torturers, celebrities, assassins, and contractors. In an article titled, "Encouragement to Gangs and Amnesty to Contractors," *Hürriyet* noted that the contractors were forgiven because the deaths they caused had been deemed "providential," and that they, along with "grave robbers,"[95] torturers, and gang members had been pardoned. Among those *not* granted amnesty were traitors, corrupt bureaucrats, drug dealers, those who destroyed forest lands, and those who attacked the memory of Atatürk.[96]

The fate of the killer contractors pardoned in Istanbul and the fate of the ghoulish looters gunned down on the streets in San Francisco could not seem more different. If nothing else, the contractors evaded public vengeance, drawing on the protection of the state, and remained—above all—living. The looters, meanwhile, were defined by both the police forces and the government as looming threats and legitimate targets. Nonetheless, the looters in San Francisco, the contractors in Istanbul—and the "anarchist Koreans" in Tokyo—were all arguably operating in much the same political and legal framework.

All three assaulted the rights of respectable corpses—the right to property, the right to bodily integrity, and, paradoxically, the right to life—and as a result, all three were placed outside of the day-to-day legal system, and made subject to pardon, amnesty, and/or summary execution. All three were shifted into the realm of the sovereign decision—into a universe governed by the opposite of the rule of law. The only difference was that whereas the decision vis-à-vis the looters was biological death, the decision vis-à-vis the contractors was biological life.

The contractors, as much as the looters, that is, were linked to a form of "lawful lawlessness."[97] Pardoned regardless of any trial, they entered into precisely the indistinct space of the exception. They may have *benefited* from the deprivation of their legal identity, but this deprivation was nonetheless still a deprivation. Having assaulted the rights of the respectable dead homeowner, they were made politically dead themselves—even if this political death did not automatically lead to their biological death as it did for their counterparts in San Francisco and Tokyo.

Conclusion

The granting of rights to dead bodies is not ordinarily studied as a form of legal or political subject formation. Nonetheless, over the course of this chapter I have described various processes—the compilation of death tolls, the disinterment of decomposing bodies, the designation of the living as ghouls and ghosts—by which rights structures transform the dead body into the normative subject of disaster law. It is true that the obvious or commonsense explanations for each of these processes remain compelling. The death toll is necessary for infrastructural purposes or for population control; the disinterment and reburial of decomposing bodies preserves health and hygiene; and the emergency crackdown on looters maintains long-term law and order. But these explanations, although reasonable, cannot effectively account for the fears and fixations that surround so many of these issues—they do not explain, for example, the terror of the unofficial death toll, the obsession with citizens digging up bodies and then reinterring these bodies elsewhere, or the fact that the right to property or bodily integrity *explicitly* overrides the right to life when the living disaster victim confronts a corpse.

I have therefore argued in this chapter that in addition to their more commonly accepted goals, these responses to disaster also serve a number of additional purposes. The death toll, for example, can in many ways be read as a list of *new* citizens rather than as a list of citizens now gone. It can be read as a roster of newly political bodies that must never be left in private, unprofessional, or unofficial hands. These decomposing dead bodies can in turn serve as excellent expressions of Antigone's classically tragic point or of Ralph Waldo Emerson's liberal-democratic one: that the rights of the corpse are beyond argument, that these rights more than any others fly in the face of tyranny, and that these rights override the rights of anyone selfishly left living after the crisis has occurred. Finally, the attitude toward the living ghosts, ghouls, and killer contractors in the aftermath of disaster makes sense only given an already present political respect for the mass of dead and decomposing citizens. The dead body is in ecstasy, it is beyond reason or bodily borders, it has incontrovertible rights, and it is at the center of the legal and political system. As a result, anyone—living or dead—who remains within that system must conform to the ghoulish norm that this respectable corpse has established.

However, just as the postdisaster gift of life was gradually regularized within the universe of tort and accident law, so too the ecstatic rights-bearing corpse has become a figure by no means unique to crisis situations. I therefore conclude this chapter by bringing disaster law once more into the realm of the everyday—this time by situating it within the ordinary sphere of death penalty law in Turkey, Europe, and the United States. Just as Cardozo's decision in *Palsgraf* emphasized the simultaneity of disaster law and tort law so too, I suggest, Turkish and U.S. death penalty cases have highlighted the simultaneity of disaster law and criminal law. Just as *Palsgraf* represented an ordinary, everyday manifestation of the postdisaster gift of life, so too, I argue, does capital punishment in Turkey and the United States represent an ordinary, everyday manifestation of postdisaster respect in death.

It is true that the legal and political rhetoric surrounding the death penalty differs significantly in the United States and Turkey. In the United States—despite popular, political, and scholarly criticism—capital punishment remains common. Hundreds of executions have been carried out since 1976, and thousands of inmates await execution on death row. Turkey, contrarily, abolished the death penalty in 2002, and even before that, capital punishment was not a topic of much debate—the government having halted (if not legally abolished) the practice in 1984.[98] Nonetheless, in 1999—the year of the Istanbul/Marmara earthquake—the Turkish courts tried a case that brought the death penalty to the forefront of public discussion.

This case, brought against Abdullah Öcalan, a Kurdish political figure accused of terrorism and separatism,[99] split Turkish public opinion both when the courts initially heard it in 1999, and in 2002, when Öcalan's sentence was commuted to life imprisonment. The rhetoric surrounding the Öcalan case was in many ways identical to the rhetoric surrounding a similarly fraught case tried in the United States in 2003—in which it was decided that Charles Singleton, a mentally incompetent prisoner, could be involuntarily medicated in order to make him fit for execution.[100] In the aftermath of both decisions, agonizing questions were raised in both Turkey and the United States concerning the relationship among national identity, civilization, and capital punishment—about what role, if any, legal execution could play in a self-consciously modern, democratic, and rights-based nation-state.

In concluding this chapter, I do not address these broad—and ongoing—questions. Rather, I focus more narrowly on the type of political subjects produced and assumed by each case—suggesting that the (dead) subject at the center of the Turkish, European, and U.S. rhetoric of capital punishment is in fact no different from the (dead) subject at the center of disaster law. This is not, however, simply because death penalty law is necessarily concerned with dead bodies and their rights. More than that, it is because capital punishment in the United States and Turkey is nothing more nor less than an ordinary, everyday manifestation of disaster law: a means of transforming the living traitor, terrorist, or murderer into a respectable, reputable dead citizen.

In Singleton's hearing, for example, one of the key means of deciding on the prisoner's competence for execution was his preexisting relationship to life and death. According to expert testimony, what made Singleton "psychotic" and unfit for execution when he was off his medication—and what the court then sought to remedy—was his inappropriate understanding of what it meant to be alive and what it meant to be dead. When off his medication, Singleton "became paranoid and delusional, and believed that he had already been executed."[101] He "talked about . . . an execution just being stopping breathing and then you start up again somewhere else . . . that . . . execution correctional officers stop you from breathing and then the judge can do something to start it up again."[102] The most fundamental problem facing Singleton's execution, that is, was that he thought he was *already* dead. The role of the judge, as Singleton saw it, was not to decide on a prisoner's life or death, but rather to accentuate the arbitrariness of both states—to start a prisoner breathing again, on a whim, once the guards had already killed him.

The point of medicating Singleton, therefore, was above all to force him to recognize the political permanence of death—to make him realize that as a dead citizen, he would finally be stable and respectable. The narrative that the court developed around Singleton thus overlapped clearly with the narrative repeatedly developed around the subjects of disaster law. The court's desire to transform Singleton from a psychotic, ephemeral living prisoner—incapable of exercising even his right to punishment[103]—to a sane, normative dead body was simply a variation on the transition undergone by rightsless, ephemeral living ghouls or looters to rights-bearing, normative dead bodies. Both narratives assume the political and legal centrality, *stability*, and normativity of the disintegrating corpse: the one, however, in the context of ordinary day-to-day law and the other in the context of exceptional disaster law.

If we turn to the trial of Abdullah Öcalan, we can see a similar narrative developing—although in this case the controversy surrounded not the mutability of the prisoner's mental state, but rather the mutability of Turkish law and politics. To begin with, the Ankara State Security Court sentenced Öcalan to death in June 1999. Various European Union officials voiced an immediate protest, but this protest fell by the wayside after the earthquake struck in August 1999. By October and November, however, the protest had renewed itself, prompting responses on the part of the Turkish government and media to the effect that there is a great deal of difference between *sentencing* a prisoner to death and actually *carrying out* the sentence.[104]

In 2002, after the abolition of the death penalty, the question seemed to have been resolved. But by May 2005, the European Court of Human Rights had revived it with their decision in "Öcalan v. Turkey"—a decision in which it was precisely the inconsistency of Turkey's former death penalty law that now represented a violation of Öcalan's human rights. In addition to determining the trial as a whole "unfair," the court also went on at length about the ambiguity of the punishment:

> In the Court's view, to impose a death sentence on a person after an unfair trial is to subject that person wrongfully to the fear that he will be executed . . . [T]hat is, despite the Turkish moratorium on the death penalty, the applicant . . . could reasonably fear the implementation of his death sentence until that sentence was actually commuted.[105]

Here the disjuncture between sentencing and execution—between being legally dead and being biologically dead—was not a source of reassurance to human rights advocates, but rather a source of concern and apprehension. Indeed, the European Court of Human Rights was voicing the same apprehension with regard to Öcalan in 2002 that the Eighth Circuit Court in the United States was voicing with regard to Singleton a year later.

It is true that in Singleton's case, it was the prisoner's apparent mental instability that provoked the legal response, whereas in Öcalan's case it was Turkey's apparent legal instability that did so. But in both cases, the court was decrying an inappropriately blurry line between life and death—and in both cases, the court was demanding that death be recognized as a permanent, ongoing, stable state. Singleton's belief that he could remain politically alive (the judge starting him breathing again) even after his biological death was just as unacceptable as the Turkish government's belief that Öcalan could remain biologically alive (the sentence never actually carried out) even after his political death. Taking a page from the law and politics of disaster, both the European Court of Human Rights and the U.S. Eighth Circuit Court were using as their starting point the paradoxical political coherence of the corpse. It is against the corpse—the stable, immutable norm—that Singleton must be defined as sane or insane, capable of execution or not. Likewise, it is against the corpse—the stable, immutable norm—that Öcalan's status as legitimate prisoner of a democratic state or illegitimate captive of an antidemocratic state can be decided. In both cases, legal and political processes maintained their intelligibility only against the backdrop of the stable, respectable dead body.

Just as disaster law transforms the disintegrating corpse—a subject almost proverbially in ecstasy—into the respectable, neutral citizen at the center of politics, so too does the ordinary, everyday rhetoric surrounding the death penalty. It is by granting rights, privileges, and political force to that most unintelligible of subjects—the decaying body—that death penalty law makes the relationship between national identity and capital punishment itself intelligible. Put another way, when the dead body is the starting point rather than the ending point of legal process—as it is in both disaster law and death penalty law—both legal execution *and* the shooting of ghouls do in fact make a great deal of sense.

There is indeed a distinct continuity between the anecdotes with which I started this chapter and the cases with which I have concluded it—a continuity, moreover, that maps directly onto this continuity between disaster law and day-to-day law. The dead Nazi soldiers who maintained their rights to marriage and divorce, the dead Italian citizens who maintained their rights to dignity and honor, and the dead U.S. soldiers who maintained their rights to bodily integrity—both during wartime and during peacetime—were all arguably precursors and predecessors not only to Öcalan and Singleton, but to the hundreds of thousands of bodies populating twentieth-century disaster areas. Each was involved in a relentless variation on the social contract—not only possessed of rights and privileges, but representative of healthy state function; not only hyperbolically respectable citizens, but respectable citizens who could and would determine the fates of their less respectable, and decreasingly intelligible, living counterparts.

CHAPTER FIVE

Seismic Space

Camps, Cemeteries, Squares, and Monuments

Introduction

Chapters Three and Four addressed variations on the embodied and disembodied subject. Ecstasy was a state experienced by, or manifested through, diseased, decomposing, dismembered, or dead people. Ecstasy produced subjects beside themselves. What I do in this chapter is examine the space that surrounds this subject. Rather than addressing ecstatic citizens and bodies, I address ecstatic space, the type of space demanded by the politics of disaster—and I connect this space to the shattered legal subjects who operate within it. My interest in this chapter, therefore, is both the spaces that are born in the immediate aftermath of the disaster—the camp being the most obvious example—and the spaces that take on new meaning—public squares and cemeteries, for instance—when they are reconfigured on behalf of political subjects in ecstasy.

To get at the nature of ecstatic or seismic space, I return to the nineteenth-century geologist John Milne's analysis of civilizations (in decline) as civilizations likewise susceptible to earthquake. Recall that Milne's two major points were, first, that "in all earthquake countries" there is a certain "light hearted carelessness and disregard for the morrow," and second, that if, for example, "the seismic force of South America were turned loose in England or Germany, it . . . might result in sinking Germans and Englishmen to the lowest level in the ranks of civilization."[1] I brought up Milne's analysis at the beginning of this book to underscore the process by which seventeenth- and eighteenth-century metaphors of states and systems in crisis became nineteenth- and twentieth-century realities. Without losing sight of this particular aspect of his discussion, I turn now to another theme that Milne invokes in this analysis: the *space* that he categorizes as the "earthquake country."

Again, it is relatively obvious that the earthquake country in Milne's universe is first and foremost a space in which seismic activity leads to civilizational decay—a space in which geological knowledge reflects imperial reality. The study of seismology in the earthquake country is fundamentally a study of the civilizing mission and how to go about enforcing it. The earthquake-prone or disaster-prone area as an area that is (or should be) rhetorically (if not actually) colonized is in many ways a familiar trope at this point. As I noted in Chapter Two, there continues to exist an influential geography of disaster that seeks out "defenseless spaces" and "spaces of vulnerability," and that characterizes these spaces as "regions of misrule, where a population's vulnerability is enhanced by the operation of despotic or illegitimate governments."[2] Like the colony caught in a constant state of emergency, vulnerable because by definition it lacks sovereignty, lacking sovereignty because by definition it is subject to despotism, and above all impermanent—except to the extent that it is permanently unstable—the disaster area in Milne's analysis is crying out for a guiding hand.

This comparison between the colony and the disaster area is just as problematic as it is tempting. It is tempting, again, because more often than not the crisis that is the modern disaster has been defined, approached, and resolved in the same civilizational vocabulary as the crisis that is the modern colony. It is tempting because the emergency measures that modern states have put into effect to prevent or to respond to disasters have in many ways been identical to the emergency measures that modern states have put into effect to control colonies.[3] But it is problematic for the same reasons—and although the immediate similarities between the rhetoric surrounding the colony and the rhetoric surrounding the disaster area may be striking, they are also misleading.

What I do in this chapter, therefore, is first look in some detail at colonial or postcolonial space as ecstatic space—as space beside itself—and second, address the similarities and differences between this space and what I call seismic space. To describe these different spaces, I rely heavily on the work of three writers. The first is Achille Mbembe and his discussion of necropolitics and the postcolony. The second is Antony Anghie and his discussion of the colonial foundations of international law. The third is Henri Lefebvre and his theorization of space in capitalist Europe.[4] Although these three writers at first glance do not seem to have a lot in common, each in fact describes a type of space beside itself—in many ways a shifting and destabilized space—and a space that is therefore quite relevant to the politics of disaster and productive of the subject in ecstasy.

Ecstatic Space

With that in mind, I begin by thinking in a very basic way about political borders and political space in the modern, colonial period. As Anghie points out early on in his study of international law and colonialism, by the nineteenth century, "whatever the extent to which an entity may have satisfied other criteria of statehood, a failure to occupy territory would preclude that entity from being treated as sovereign."[5] This point may seem like an obvious one—or at least one limited in relevance to territoryless groups like eighteenth-century pirates or twenty-first-century terrorists. But it is likewise a fundamental one. Sovereignty—a state's political identity—is wed to territory and, more broadly, to space. In the absence of space, there can be no sovereignty. As we shall see, one of the defining characteristics of nonsovereign entities—of colonies, postcolonies, and neocolonies, for example—is the instability of space within or around them.

If we compare the sovereign political spaces described by Lefebvre to the colonial or postcolonial political spaces described by Mbembe, for example, there is a distinct tension or disjuncture between the definite—if oppressive—area analyzed by the former and the indefinite area analyzed by the latter. Lefebvre, for instance, argues that "walls, enclosures, and façades seem to define both a *scene* (where something takes place) and an *obscene* area to which everything that cannot or may not happen on the scene is relegated: whatever is inadmissible, be it malefic or forbidden, this has its own hidden space on the near or far side of a frontier."[6] Again, this point seems obvious. Walls, enclosures, and façades divide the scene from the obscene, they divide the knowable from the unknowable, and they differentiate the bounded from the ecstatic. The scene exists in visible space, the obscene in hidden space. If we resituate the scene and the obscene to Mbembe's analysis of the postcolony, however, the divisions between the two—the role that walls, enclosures, and façades play in defining them—become much less clear. As Mbembe has argued, "the grotesque and the obscene are two essential characteristics that identify postcolonial regimes of domination," and although writers such as Bakhtin claim that "the grotesque and the obscene are, above all, the province of ordinary people (la plèbe), . . . parodies that undermine officialdom by showing how arbitrary and vulnerable is officialese," in fact the grotesque and the obscene are used by the postcolonial state to "dramatiz[e] its own magnificence," and to "mak[e] manifest its majesty."[7]

In the postcolony, in other words, the obscene *is* the scene. The inadmissible and the forbidden are not outside of space; they are not beyond the frontiers of space; they are not even the "province of ordinary people." Rather, they are the basis and the foundation for narratives of sovereignty. The wall, the enclosure, and the façade thus also take on more complex meanings, representing both the self-consciously rational categorization and compartmentalization that define the colony or the postcolony, and the unbounded spatial instability that likewise defines them. Space in the colony is space beside itself. As Mbembe argues in another essay, space is

> the raw material of sovereignty and the violence it carried with it. Sovereignty meant occupation, and occupation relegated the colonized into a third zone between subjecthood and objecthood . . . [F]rantz Fanon describes the spatialization of colonial occupation in vivid terms. For him, colonial occupation entails first and foremost a division of space into compartments. It involves the setting of boundaries and internal frontiers epitomized by the barracks and police stations.[8]

Colonial space in this scenario is relentlessly compartmentalized. It is defined almost exclusively by the wall, the enclosure, and the façade. It is an arena of barracks and police stations. But the result of this compartmentalization, this throwing up of walls and enclosures, is not the production of rational, logical, spatial meaning but rather the explosion of any logic at all. The walls do not and cannot separate the scene from the obscene, the normal from the grotesque. They instead create a "third zone," space beside itself, the inhabitants of which hover, indeterminate, without a backdrop against which their existence might make *rational* political sense. When sovereignty is made synonymous with occupation, in other words, what actually occurs is an *opposition* between divisions within space and bounded spatial meaning. Colonial occupation immediately constructs the walls and divisions so fundamental to sovereign relations. But these walls serve no purpose other than to reinforce the dichotomy between rational sovereign space and ecstatic colonial space.

If we return to Lefebvre's analysis of the former, we can see that each type of sovereign space has its bounded place and its logical—if, again, oppressive—purpose. There is, for example, "abstract space," space that is reliant upon "exchange and interchangeability, on reproducibility, on homogeneity"—a relentlessly rational and normative space that "reduces differences to induced differences . . . to differences internally acceptable to a set of 'systems' which are planned as such, prefabricated as such."[9] At the same time there is "horizontal space," which "symbolizes submission," there is "vertical space," which symbolizes "power," and finally there is "subterranean space," which symbolizes "death."[10] Death, in particular, "has a 'location,'" in his analysis, "below or above appropriated social space; death is relegated to the infinite realm so as to disenthrall (or pacify) the finiteness in which social practice occurs, in which the law that that practice has established holds sway."[11] Finally, in Lefebvre's universe, there is also "strategic space"—space that "makes it possible simultaneously to force worrisome groups, the workers among others, out toward the periphery; to make available spaces near the center scarce, so increasing their value; to organize the center as locus of decision, wealth, power, and information."[12]

Again, each of these types of space is without question oppressive, especially to marginalized groups within the sovereign state. But each is also relentlessly rational. Each is definable, knowable, and makes good sense. In the colony, however, this easily definable space quickly becomes nonspace, quasi space, or ecstatic space. The divisions and differences within colonial space are systematic, but they are also meaningless. The spatial distinctions that Lefebvre describes so easily and rationally in sovereign space become fuzzy or chaotic in colonial space. As Mbembe notes, there *is* a sort of "vertical sovereignty" at work in sites of colonial occupation. But this vertical sovereignty leads not to the neat divisions of meaning described by Lefebvre. Rather it leads "to a proliferation of the sites of violence," it erases any "continuity between the ground and the sky," and it transforms "the underground as well as the airspace . . . into conflict zones."[13] In the colony, that is, death exists in the air as well as underground. The horizontal is a site of power in places where occupation more often than not involves "holding land." And finally, the law defined by "social practice" becomes subterranean, explicitly *underground*, as the sky becomes the new site of death.

There are, in other words, definite, incontrovertible, and indeed relentless divisions among vertical space, horizontal space, and subterranean space in the colony. Ignoring these divisions can imperil life. But these divisions exist only for themselves; their broader meaning is in constant flux. There can be, for example, no single "social space," no single "abstract space," and no single "political space" in a colony, a neocolony, or a postcolony. Even the coercive function of "strategic space"—the process by which it pushes "worrisome groups" away from the implicitly public "center"—is destabilized, reimagined, and redeployed in the colony. As Mbembe argues, "the postcolony is made up not of one 'public space,' but of several, each having its own logic yet liable to be entangled with other logics when operating in certain contexts."[14]

Space is thus divided in the colony, but these divisions shatter rather than reinforce spatial meaning. To the extent that walls, façades, and divisions exist only for themselves, they in fact aid in turning the obscene into the scene, the eccentric into the central, and the ecstatic into the potentially normative. If admissible space on one side of the wall is identical to inadmissible space on the other, the normal and the grotesque collapse into one another. If death is as much a defining characteristic of the air as it is of the underground, then the infinite and the finite, the permanent and the temporary become one and the same thing. Space in the colony, the postcolony, and the neocolony is something by definition indefinable, it is something shifting and in flux, and it is something that—under most circumstances—eludes rather than reinforces sovereignty.

This elusive nature of sovereignty in colonial and postcolonial space is usually cited as an implicit or explicit backdrop to discussions of colonial exceptionalism. The colony, in other words, is often described as a lawless space—and it is a lawless space precisely because *as* a space, it is indefinable. Mbembe, for instance, argues that "in modern political thought and European political practice and imagining, the colony represents the site where sovereignty consists fundamentally of the exercise of a power outside the law (*ab legibus solutus*)."[15] Most overtly, in Mbembe's analysis, life, death, and warfare operate outside of legal boundaries, "the sovereign right to kill," in particular, is "not subject to any rule in the colonies. In the colonies, the sovereign might kill at any time, or in any manner. Colonial warfare is not subject to legal and institutional rules. It is not a legally codified activity. Instead, colonial terror constantly intertwines with colonially generated fantasies of wilderness and death and fictions that create the effect of the real."[16] In the colony, Mbembe continues, "the fiction of a distinction between 'the ends of war' and the 'means of war' collapses; so does the fiction that war functions as a rule-governed contest, as opposed to a pure slaughter without risk or instrumental justification."[17]

Anghie's analysis is similar, tracing the development of "international" (European) law from its colonial origins to its present neocolonial and postcolonial manifestations. Imagined in the late nineteenth century as "a struggle against chaos that could only be won by . . . establishing and maintaining the taxonomies and principles that existed in fixed relations to each other,"[18] international law became increasingly indebted to the imperial classification systems and the civilizational hierarchies on which these taxonomies relied.[19] In consequence, Anghie argues:

> it was simply and massively asserted that only the practice of European states was decisive and could create international law. Any European law counted as law. Non-European states were excluded from the realm of law, now identified as being the exclusive preserve of European states, as a result of which they lacked both membership and the ability to assert any rights recognizable as legal.[20]

It was thus not just the administration and management of violence *within* the colony that rested upon the assumption of absent law, but also the international systems that regulated colonial relations. Colonies operated in a state of exception. In many ways they were the prototype for the state of exception. Colonial violence was in turn, almost by definition, exceptional violence.

What I do now, however, is challenge this discourse of colonial exceptionalism. Over the next few pages, I suggest that law is very much present in this shattered, chaotic, indefinable space—it is simply that this is a law that takes the ecstatic rather than bounded subject as its norm. Moreover, unlike sovereign space or the sovereign state of exception, colonial space or the colonial state of exception is defined by the hyperactivity of law—a clamorous law that moves the subjects and spaces it takes as its focus into states of irrational, unbounded ecstasy.

Mbembe, for instance, implicitly demonstrates this relationship among hyperactive law, spatial ecstasy, and exceptional violence when he describes the tendency toward excess or "vulgarity" that characterizes postcolonial sovereignty. "The postcolony," he argues "is characterized by a distinctive style of political improvisation, by a tendency to excess and lack of proportion," while "also made up of a series of corporate institutions and a political machine that, once in place, constitutes a distinctive regime of violence."[21] That the excessive, the obscene, or the vulgar are intentional and calculated stances in the postcolony is obvious, according to Mbembe, in that "the production of vulgarity . . . needs to be understood as a deliberately cynical operation. It is political in the sense . . .

that every polity is governed by 'master fictions' little by little accepted into the domain of the indisputable."[22]

It is, then, precisely the obscene, the vulgar, the loud, the excessive, the ecstatic, and the emphatically *not* silent that here become the foundation for colonial or postcolonial variations on political space—for the construction of the unquestioned "master fictions" that eventually become common sense.[23] The tacit, "indisputable" nonaggression pacts and contracts lauded by liberal theorists, and critiqued by Lefebvre, that is, are here loud, "vulgar," and the subject of constant, calculated manipulation. Just as, spatially, the obscene becomes the scene and ecstasy becomes the norm, in other words, legally and politically, the totalizing "rational" and "reasonable" become the excessive and the grotesque. Common sense, the "master fiction"—the foundation for both liberal politics and the exceptionalism embedded in liberal politics—become by definition not common, out of proportion, and bizarre when resituated within the colony or postcolony.

Although the biopolitical, thanatopolitical, and eventually necropolitical violence that characterizes the colony and postcolony is very much exceptional, therefore, this exceptionalism is wed, I argue, not to the sovereign decision that is ordinarily associated with the state of exception. In the colony or postcolony, exceptionalism has little to do with the suspension of law or legality in favor of legitimacy. Rather, law operates in the colony and the postcolony in the same way that walls, enclosures, and façades do. It exists. It divides, categorizes, and compartmentalizes. In fact, it divides, categorizes, and compartmentalizes far more emphatically in the colony than it does in the sovereign state. But its purpose, like the walls and the façades, is not to reinforce the silent legitimacy of sovereign power, but to destabilize and to blur it, to saturate the colony or postcolony with violence that, by definition, transcends any meaningful, rational borders or boundaries. It is exceptional, in other words, to the extent that legal and political rights do indeed exist in suspension, as a means of creating subjects and citizens. But the subjects and citizens who are created are unbounded and in ecstasy.

As Mbembe notes, one fundamental characteristic of the citizen of a postcolonial state is his or her relationship to a law that is simultaneously in effect, indefinable, destabilizing, and relentlessly totalizing. "What defines the postcolonized subject," he says, "is the ability to engage in baroque practices fundamentally ambiguous, fluid, and modifiable even when there are clear, written, and precise rules."[24] For the postcolonized subject, that is to say, law is on the one hand present and precise, and on the other ambiguous, fluid, and without boundaries. This positioning of law produces a situation in which violence is without question exceptional, but in which the sovereign who decides on the state of exception is neither indisputable nor invisible. Far from tacit and depoliticized, legal norms are vulgar, excessive, and grotesque, and the relationship between sovereign and citizen serves to highlight not democracy's silent legitimacy, but its clamorous legality. As Mbembe concludes, "the search for majesty and prestige [in the postcolony] contains within it elements of crudeness and the bizarre that the official order tries hard to hide, but that ordinary people bring to its attention, often unwittingly."[25]

The Environment: Nature and Wilderness

I begin now the transition from space, law, and subjectivity in the colony or postcolony to space, law, and subjectivity in the disaster area. To do so, I focus on one final aspect of colonial space that will become indispensable when we move to the disaster area—the role of the environment, or nature. The relevance of nature to any discussion of disaster is obvious—it is, after all, the apparent presence or absence of nature that deprives or endows a crisis with political meaning.[26] More than that, in both the colony and in the disaster area, nature serves in many ways to determine, fundamentally, what law is. The question of what constitutes nature in the colony has received almost as much attention as the question of what constitutes law—discussions of colonial nature or wilderness often shifting seamlessly—and suspiciously—into discussions of colonial law.

What I do in this section, therefore, is address nature in the same way that I addressed legal ecstasy above. First, I discuss the rhetoric of nature as it is articulated in sovereign space of the sort critiqued by Lefebvre. Second, I turn to the rhetoric of nature as it is articulated in the colonized or postcolonial space described by Mbembe. Finally, I suggest that although nature is crucial to discussions of colonies, and particularly colonial frontiers, it is crucial—perhaps counterintuitively—precisely because it *is* political.

Lefebvre spends quite of bit of time in his *Production of Space* discussing nature, natural space, and its relationship to social space. These passages of his book are the most overtly indebted to Marxist theory—framed almost exclusively in an analysis of work, labor, capital, and production. While acknowledging this analytical framework, however, what I do now is highlight three other aspects of Lefebvre's "nature" and its relationship to sovereign space. The first is the extent to which the natural serves in his analysis as a foundation for the social and the political. The second is the extent to which a concrete "nature" is frequently held up in opposition to an abstract "social" or political. The third is the extent to which nature is seen as "particularizing," whereas the social and the political are seen as unifying. What I suggest in this section is that this interpretation of nature is very much linked to *sovereign* space, and that when resituated within colonial space, it undergoes a distinct transformation.

Early in his discussion of social space, Lefebvre makes the point that "every social space has a history, one invariably grounded in nature, in natural conditions that are at once primordial and unique in the sense that they are always and everywhere endowed with specific characteristics (site, climate, etc.)."[27] This point is a relatively simple one. In essence, Lefebvre is arguing that there is some concrete, nonartificial groundwork, called nature, on which all social or political space is eventually mapped. It is a point that likewise rests on two assumptions that will become vital when we shift to colonized or postcolonial space: first, it assumes that the natural *is* more concrete (and less "artificial") than the social or the political. Second, it leads almost immediately to a further assumption that the natural is under threat of destruction or extinction at the hands of the social or the political. As he argues later in his study, "the initial basis or foundation of social space is nature—natural or physical space. Upon this basis are superimposed—in ways that transfer, supplant, or even threaten to destroy it—successive stratified and tangled networks which, though always material in form, nevertheless have an existence beyond their materiality."[28] The natural is thus both foundational *and* in constant danger of elimination by the elusive, the *more* than material, social.

Lefebvre indeed dwells at some length on the concrete materiality of nature, and how this both stands in opposition to, and is on the verge of obliteration by, the abstract and artificial social or political. Nature, he argues,

> is violent, generous, niggardly, bountiful, and above all open. Nature's space is not staged. To ask why this is so is a strictly meaningless question . . . [I]f we are to believe the word "nature," with its ancient metaphysical and theological credentials, what is essential occurs in the depths. To say "natural" is to say spontaneous. But today nature is drawing away from us, to say the very least. It is becoming impossible to escape the notion that nature is being murdered by "anti-nature"—by abstraction, by signs and images, by discourse, as also by labour and its products.[29]

Nature, in other words, is not only irrational (i.e., violent/generous, niggardly/bountiful, not subject to the question "why") and spontaneous, but associated with the "depths"—the space of death and the infinite according to Lefebvre's earlier analysis. Nature is timeless and it is fundamental. But it is also being slowly removed or destroyed by its apparent inverse—the abstract, the discursive, and the social. Indeed, Lefebvre argues later in this section that (1) "the more a space partakes of nature, the less it enters into the social relations of production," (2) "the once-prevalent characteristic 'natural' has grown indistinct and become a subordinate feature," and (3) "the social character of space—those social relations that it implies, contains, and dissimulates—has begun *visibly* to dominate."[30]

Set up as almost binary opposites, then, the natural (or natural space) and the social or political (or social or political space) are nonetheless linked to one another. Nature serves as a concrete, timeless, irrational, and fragile *basis* for the political, which is an abstract, imagined, discursive, and overwhelming *product*. Nature is real, but on the verge of extinction. The political is artificial, but about to triumph. As a corollary, the effects of political or social space gradually overwhelm the effects of natural space. "Natural space," Lefebvre argues, "juxtaposes—and thus disperses: it puts places and that which occupies them side by side. It particularizes. By contrast, social space implies actual or potential assembly at a single point, or around that point."[31]

As social space displaces natural space, in other words, the particularizing character of the natural is replaced by the unifying character of the social. It is not just that the concrete and the material are eventually dominated by the abstract and the discursive. It is also that the concrete and the material are specific and scattered—ecstatic, one might say—whereas the abstract and the discursive are general and unified. Taken one step further, the natural represents the irrational, discrete, unruly physicality that is the biological body in the Cartesian imagination, whereas the social represents the rational, unified abstraction that is the citizen. What Lefebvre is describing in his analysis of nature is indeed a very basic (if uniquely spatial) variation on one narrative of the liberal state-citizen relationship.

Again, however, Lefebvre is situating this narrative within the borders of a *sovereign* state. In sovereign space, Lefebvre is suggesting, the relationship between nature and politics is the following: the concrete, discrete, scattered thing that is nature serves as a basis or foundation for the abstract, general, unified thing that is politics. As the political develops, this basis is eventually destroyed—destroyed in fact by containment, by boundedness—and what remains is a functional, modern state composed of abstract, equal, and rational citizens. Because Lefebvre is not a liberal, he is of course very much aware of the oppression inherent in this narrative, and details it especially in his discussion of "abstract space" per se. Moreover, since his focus is on the spatial manifestations of the narrative, his particular interest is the way in which *spaces* are constructed (or produced) in aid of this process.

For the most part, though, Lefebvre does *not* consider the way in which this narrative plays out in areas that are not sovereign. It is true that he does step outside of urban European space at one point, in his analysis of what he calls "peasant dwellings." But this analysis is for the most part indebted to old and recognizable imperial themes. "Peasant dwellings" indeed serve a rather traditional, transitional role in his argument, marking the indistinct space between developed and undeveloped, between European and not-European. For example, "what can be said," Lefebvre asks,

> of a peasant dwelling? . . . [N]o matter how prosperous or humble such a dwelling may be . . . it remains, to a greater or lesser degree, part of nature. It is an object intermediate between work and product, between nature and labour, between the realm of symbols and the realm of signs. Does it engender a space? Yes. Is that space natural or cultural? Is it immediate or mediated—and, if the latter, mediated by whom and to what purpose? Is it a given or is it artificial? The answer to such questions must be: "Both."[32]

Lefebvre's easy assumption that the peasant exists in a space somewhere between "the natural" and "the cultural"—that the peasant dwelling represents both the concrete, the timeless, and the particular on the one hand, and the abstract, the mediated, or the universal on the other—is the product of a very modernist understanding of what constitutes the political, and what therefore constitutes the not political. It is likewise a key aspect of the similarly easy linkage that many modernists have made between peasants in Europe and colonized populations outside of Europe. Very basically, Lefebvre is arguing that peasants—productive of the half political/half natural space that is the "peasant dwelling"—are in a sort of intermediate quasi space not dissimilar from the colony. They are blurry and indistinct. They are "part of nature"—and thus unable to represent or be represented in the political realm of signs.

As I argue below, however, this rhetorical relationship between nature and politics is in fact inverted in a much more complicated way in colonies and postcolonies than modernist writers like Lefebvre suggest. In the rhetoric of the colony, postcolony, and neocolony, it is indeed arguably *not* nature that is concrete, particular, and ecstatic—it is *not* nature that serves as a basis for an abstract, unifying, rational politics. Rather, it is the political that is concrete, particular, and ecstatic in the colony—and the political that serves as the basis for an abstract, unifying, and eventually destructive and all-containing nature. Compare, for example, Lefebvre's discussion of the peasant and the space in which he or she lives, to Mbembe's discussion of colonized space. Framed within an analysis of Hannah Arendt's analysis of rights, Mbembe notes that,

> according to Arendt, what makes savages different from other human beings is less the color of their skin than the fear that they behave like a part of nature, that they treat nature as their undisputed master. Nature thus remains, in all its majesty, an overwhelming reality compared to which they appear to be phantoms, unreal, and ghostlike. The savages are, as it were, "natural" human beings who lack the specifically human character, the specifically human reality, "so that when European men massacred them they somehow were not aware that they had committed murder."[33]

This is not a situation, in other words, in which, like the peasant, the savage occupies an indeterminate space, neither natural nor cultural—in which the labor or dwelling (to use Lefebvre's vocabulary) of the savage is a part of nature, excluded from the realm of politics. This is a not a situation at the beginning of an implicit—if oppressive—progress narrative, in which the peasant dwelling is the starting point, the moment at which the natural starts to be displaced and represented by the social and political. This is not a situation that suggests the eventual triumph of abstract political universalism over concrete natural particularism. Rather, this is a situation in which nature exists simultaneously with—indeed as a result of—politics in the colony. Far from articulating a universalizing politics and a particularizing nature as the peasant dwelling does, colonial space instead articulates a universalizing nature and a particularizing politics that are completely contrary to the liberal progress narrative.

As Mbembe argues, for example, it is precisely *nature* that universalizes in the colony. It is nature, not politics, culture, or society, that produces the abstract norm that is the "savage." It is nature that defines the population in the colony. And it is natural space that serves as what Lefebvre calls abstract space—the space that unifies, generalizes, signifies, and represents—in the colony or postcolony. The general or abstract act that is murder, for instance, becomes an emphatically *particular* one in the colony. There is no abstract political concept called "murder" against which certain concrete behaviors can be measured. Instead, each act of political violence is ad hoc, a product of discrete circumstances, and operates in precisely the same way that natural violence operates in the sovereign state. Far from serving as the concrete foundation for an abstract political structure or space, nature is itself an abstraction of politics. The concept, "savage," with all of its natural connotations is the universal concept. Meanwhile, the concept "killing," with all of its political connotations is the particular one.[34] Within the framework of Lefebvre's analysis, that is, the concrete, ecstatic political serves as the basis for the idealized, rational natural in the colony.

It is nature that is the universalizing principle in colonial space. It is nature—as an actor—that is rational, nature—as an actor—that generalizes. And as a result, politics and political expressions like law take on the discrete, particularizing, ecstatic qualities that in sovereign space define nature. What I suggest now is that this model of colonial and postcolonial space, of colonial and postcolonial political violence, and of colonial and postcolonial natural violence has served in many ways as a template for the law and politics of disaster. The space defined by the politics of disaster is ecstatic space—space that can effectively serve as a backdrop for the construction of the ecstatic subject. Law is thus likewise ecstatic law—it is a loud, clamorous, hyperactive law that insists upon the grotesque and the obscene. The major difference between colonial space and the disaster area, therefore, is arguably less that ecstatic space in the former does not look like ecstatic space in the latter. More, it is that the construction of this space in the colony plays up the falsity of the colonial relationship, whereas its construction following upon disaster endows the crisis with political meaning.

The Camp

Like the colony and postcolony, the disaster area is a space defined first of all by its walls, façades, and enclosures—by divisions that exist, on the one hand, to categorize and compartmentalize but, on the other, to mingle the scene with the obscene. Just as in the colony, in the disaster area too, vertical sovereignty is confused, and death inhabits the air and the ground as well as the subterranean depths. In the disaster area too, space becomes ecstatic precisely as law becomes hyperactive. Law indeed operates in the disaster area just as it does in the colony and postcolony. It divides, categorizes, and compartmentalizes, but it exists purely to blur or explode meaning. Finally, just as in the colony, in the disaster area too, the relationship between natural space and social or political space is inverted, reimagined, and serves an alternative political truth.

One of the most overt manifestations of law at work in the disaster area, for example, is the frantic regulation or reregulation of space that follows upon a crisis. In a liberal state, the vocabulary surrounding this domination and rearticulation of space—the transformation of the sports stadium into a camp or public square into a military hospital, for example—is usually a vocabulary of rights. The disaster deprived a mass of citizens of their basic rights (to life, to sustenance, to personal security, etc.), and the sovereign is now reorganizing space such that these rights are reinstated. It goes without saying that in the process, the biopolitical, positive nature of even the most apparently negative liberal rights becomes gradually more obvious. In their spatial manifestations, these rights do not free the citizens inhabiting the disaster area from coercion; instead, they grant the citizen the dignity of constant intervention. The disrupted and then reinstated right to, say, personal security, for instance, is not about walls enclosing something called private space in which one is free from attack; it is about walls enclosing something called public space in which one is disciplined from attacking.

I suggest in this section that the walls and enclosures that appear so quickly in the days and weeks following a disaster serve a very distinct, quasi-colonial purpose. They operate to divide, to categorize, and to compartmentalize—but they do so not in the service of liberal freedoms, not as a means of restoring some notion of rationality, but rather in order to produce ecstatic space and to make the disaster intelligible. The camp—refugee, concentration, work, or otherwise—is the most obvious example of this destabilized space. But I want to look also at the definition, redefinition, and regulation of roads and schools. Each of these, I argue, is an example of colonial-style compartments erected in aid of ecstatic space.

The camp, as an invention of the late nineteenth century and a defining characteristic of the twentieth century, has received a great deal of attention over the past fifty years. According to Agamben, the camp indeed replaced the city quite early on as the paradigmatic political space of the modern period—the relationship between biopolitical sovereign and subject that characterized the camp far more meaningful than the relationship between liberal state and citizen that characterized the city.[35] More recently, there has been a growing interest in the intimate relationship between the *colony* and the camp as well, especially to the extent that each has come to be seen in different ways as the space par excellence of the modern biopolitical subject.[36] To this extent, it is the refugee/death camp in particular that has been the most frequently addressed.

The camps constructed following natural disasters have received less attention. They are, however, nonetheless excellent examples of modern political space—and in particular, modern space in ecstasy. One peculiarity of these camps is that rights rhetoric remains in effect—in fact, in hyperbolic effect—within their boundaries. Though, as I emphasize later, the camps defined by disaster law are also characterized less by what rights the population within their walls may or may not have, and more by the walls themselves.

The camp in the disaster area is above all an arena that slices up space. But, like the compartmentalization of colonial space, this carving out of enclosures and this throwing up of divisions serve no purpose in the camp except categorization for its own sake. And the result, just as it is in the colony, is to destabilize spatial meaning, to turn *all* space—both within the enclosure and beyond it, on one side of the façade as well as on the other—into an indistinct and ecstatic third zone. It is not that the population within the camp possesses or does not possess certain rights, whereas the population beyond it possesses or does not possess different ones. Rather, it is that the camp divides and disperses space itself, confuses spatial meaning, and turns the disaster area in its *entirety* into an arena beside itself.

If we look, for example, at one of the most self-conscious applications of the postdisaster concentration camp—its institution by the U.S. military following the 1906 San Francisco earthquake—we can see precisely this approach to space playing out. In both the published "internal" report that Greely wrote in the midst of his deployment in San Francisco and in the "general orders" issued to the population of the city by his subordinates, it is clear that, first, the redistribution and redefinition of space is of primary importance to the military and, second, that this redistribution of space serves above all to turn the disaster area in its entirety into something indistinct, indefinable, and in flux. With regard to the former, Greely writes that,

> as to the inmates of the camps, there were no restrictions on personal conduct or liberty save for three purposes—those of decency, order, and cleanliness . . . [T]he camps are made attractive by first assuring order, cleanliness, and also by giving the occupants for a time coffee and sugar in addition to the three components of the ration issued elsewhere, namely bread, potatoes, and meat. Gradually, methods of general messing were introduced, which had a tendency to cause those with money or credit to purchase their food and rely upon the Government only for shelter and bedding.[37]

With regard to the specific orders themselves, they included the following:

> all persons sheltered in permanent camps will render prompt and implicit obedience to the camp commander in regard to matters of decency, order, and sanitation. Anyone failing to comply with such orders will be ejected from the camp. Any person ejected from a camp under military control for failure to obey proper orders of the camp commander will not be admitted to any other military camp. The names of ejected persons will be reported to the commander of permanent camps.[38]

In each of these passages, there is an emphasis, first of all, on maintaining decency, order, and cleanliness or sanitation. Moreover, according to Greely, this emphasis in no way contradicts the assertions of liberty and freedom from coercion enjoyed by the camp's inhabitants. Aside from behaviors that might threaten decency, order, and cleanliness, everything is licit—there are "no restrictions on . . . liberty," except those having to do with indecent, disorderly, or unhygienic behaviors.

It quickly becomes clear, however, that in fact decency, order, and cleanliness are less about articulating rights or freedoms and more about legitimizing surveillance and discipline. In the second passage, for example, the point is not that the inhabitants of the camps have complete liberty except in certain, specific, hygiene- and order-related circumstances; rather, it is that the inhabitants of the camps must render complete obedience except in certain, specific, hygiene- and order-related circumstances. In the first, coercion is the exception; in the second, liberty is the exception. But this movement from liberal rights to authoritarian duties, articulated as it is in a vocabulary of order, decency, and cleanliness, should not be particularly surprising, and is not my primary interest in these passages. Instead, I emphasize the extent to which—even when invoking rights rhetoric as Greely does—each of these discussions of the camp focuses far more on space than it does on individuals and their rights.

In Greely's analysis, for example, order and cleanliness—although without question important to defining the rights of the inhabitants of the camps—are primarily a means of making the space bounded by the camp walls "attractive."[39] If it were not for the maintenance of decency, order, and cleanliness (along with the extra food rations), Greely implies, the space within the camp would be uninviting—and this is undesirable. Basically, that is, Greely imagines the camp enclosure as something that repels, and he seeks to correct this situation.

In the second passage—although there is a much more explicit emphasis on space (and very little interest at all in rights)—this space is characterized quite differently. On the one hand, the order rests, like Greely's discussion, on the assumption that the space within the camp is different from the space outside of it. There are things that happen on one side of the camp walls that do not happen on the other side—and if such things do happen on the wrong side of these walls, corrective action must be taken. But on the other hand, there is also the assumption that, first, being ejected from a camp, and second, being prevented from entering any other camp are effective deterrents to inappropriate behavior. Unlike the first passage, in other words, the second passage assumes the camp enclosure to be something that already attracts, and far from drawing the outside inward, the purpose of the regulations is to expel the interior out.[40]

All of this may seem obvious—the passages are seeking simultaneously to legitimize and to regulate the use of the camps, and so there are necessarily some contradictions in them. Both passages describe the camp walls as barriers between the scene and the obscene. Within the camp is a space of decency, order, and cleanliness (the scene); outside of the camp is a space of indecency, chaos, and dirt (the obscene). But the tension between Greely's discussion of the enclosure—a free space that must attract the outside—and the enclosure as it is expressed in the general orders—a regulated space that must expel the inside—emphasizes the failure of these divisions.

Without question, that is, the space within the camp walls is *categorized* as the scene. But the admission on the part of Greely that there remains some scene beyond the walls that needs to be brought within them, and its collision with the admission on the part of the general orders that there exists something obscene within the walls that needs to be pushed out, makes clear the extent to which there is no *actual* difference between the two. The scene and the obscene exist side by side both within the camp walls and outside of them, just as complete freedom and complete regulation do.

The role of the wall and the enclosure is thus arguably to divide space purely for the sake of division. There is a constant process of categorization and compartmentalization occurring, but all this process effects is a situation in which the disaster area as a whole—within the camp walls and beyond them—has no spatial meaning. This is not a situation in which, say, the scene that is the public square is briefly contaminated by the obscene behavior of an individual—by the sporadic and aberrant entry of something that should be hidden suddenly making an appearance. Rather it is the nature of the area *itself* that is uncertain, that is in flux, beside itself, and that in fact makes individual behavior itself irrelevant.

This process of categorization, compartmentalization, and resulting spatial disarray indeed becomes particularly apparent in the discussions of the separate concentration camps set up for the city's Chinese population. In describing these enclosures, Greely notes that,

> it is gratifying to report that neither in San Francisco nor in Oakland has any relief committee shown discrimination against the Chinese, and this line of action of the civilian organization has been consistently followed by the Army . . . [I]t was the consensus of opinion that the Chinese could be best cared for in separate camps; this policy was followed in San Francisco and in Oakland. An excellently arranged camp was constructed at Fort Winfield Scott on the Presidio grounds, the only objection thereto being its distance from the inhabited parts of the city, [but] as practically none of the Chinese are day laborers, no special hardship has resulted therefrom . . . [T]he agent of the Six Companies stated that many of them were living better than ever before . . . [L]ater, as mentioned under Oakland relief operations, the care of the Chinese was assumed by the Chinese minister.[41]

He then continues by discussing the situation in Oakland specifically, where

> the Chinese, in a camp established independently on Lake Meritt, were cared for in the same systematic and satisfactory manner as were the occupants at Adams Point. Under a Chinese superintendent, the camp was maintained in excellent condition, its occupants never causing trouble, and although located in the resident portion of the city, it was so admirably handled that its presence was never a cause of complaint.[42]

At first glance—leaving aside the obvious contradiction between the "absence of discrimination" and the establishment of a separate camp for the Chinese[43]—Greely's analysis seems similar to the one above. He begins by emphasizing rights—in this case the right of the Chinese to be (a) tolerated and (b) cared for—and then immediately moves on to a detailed discussion of space, how this space was arranged, where it was situated, and what sort of living conditions it promised.

However, a number of key issues from the earlier passages are missing from this latter discussion. There is, for example, no mention of decency, order, or cleanliness and sanitation in the description of the Chinese camp. Likewise, the focus on attracting populations from the outside or expelling populations from within is absent. Rather, Greely describes first, the relationship between the camp and the "inhabited" or "residential" parts of the city beyond it, second, the conditions in the camp compared to those enjoyed by the Chinese prior to the earthquake, and third, the extent to which the occupants of the camp caused no trouble or complaint in the bordering area. Unlike the rhetoric that surrounded the non-Chinese camps, in other words, a rhetoric that defined the space enclosed by the camp walls as the scene—and the space beyond those walls (indecent, disordered, unclean) as the threatening, lurking obscene—the rhetoric surrounding the Chinese camps defined the space within the walls as the obscene, and the space outside (residential, excellent, inhabited) as under threat. The discussion of the non-Chinese camps implied a chaotic exterior pushing against the walls from without; the discussion of the Chinese camps implies a chaotic interior pushing against the walls from within.

The Chinese, in other words, described, for example, by Wilson as coming "out of their underground burrows like rats and tumbl[ing] into the square, beating such gongs and playing such noisy instruments as they had snatched up,"[44] were by definition grotesque—they necessarily inhabited obscene space. Any space in which they were collected was a space that needed to be prevented from contaminating the scene beyond it. The Chinese camps were thus mirror images of the non-Chinese camps—enclosing what could not be mentioned, rather than preventing what could not be mentioned from getting in. The "camp" itself, therefore, quickly became a spatially meaningless concept. Again, without question, it categorized relentlessly, threw up insurmountable barriers, and established incontestable divisions. But these barriers and divisions existed only for themselves. The enclosed space was both scene and obscene—while both scene and obscene existed outside. The enclosed space both attracted and repelled—while the attractive and repellent likewise both existed outside. Finally, the enclosed space was both a space of complete liberty and a space of complete regulation—each of which simultaneously existed outside.

This spatial confusion surrounding the postdisaster camp was not a phenomenon unique to San Francisco or to the beginning of the twentieth century. There was a strikingly similar redefinition of space, for example, at the end of the century and on the other side of the world, after the 1999 Istanbul/Marmara earthquake. Immediately following the 1999 disaster, both the Turkish military and independent aid organizations rushed (and often competed) to reorganize and redefine space in an effort to make services available to those who had lost their homes. Just as in 1906, this reorganization of space and accentuation or erection of walls was often couched in a vocabulary of rights and security. But, also just as in 1906, the walls themselves very quickly supplanted in narrative importance the populations they enclosed or excluded.

For the purposes of this analysis, I focus on two discussions of the camps and the tent cities that arose in the weeks following the disaster, each from an article that appeared in the mass daily *Hürriyet* in the summer of 1999. The first of these is a straightforward statement that military camps were being opened for the victims of the earthquake. The second criticizes the activities of the Turkish Red Crescent Organization by suggesting that its aid policies were the product of a nineteenth-century mentality. Each, although for quite different purposes, gradually comes to emphasize the politics of space, and to highlight the extent to which postcrisis divisions of space—although relentless—were also responsible for complete disarray, for space beside itself, in the earthquake zone. The first article notes, for example, that the "Turkish Armed Forces" opened two military camps to meet "the health and sustenance needs of homeless citizens." The camps, the article continues, were "ordinarily used to train military students," but were now "emptied" so that the "earthquake stricken might be transferred" to them once sufficient tents were set up.[45]

The second, titled "The Tents are the Same Tents," begins with a description of an oil painting called "Privates Drilling" (*Talim Yapan Erler*) by the nineteenth-century military artist Şeker Ahmet Ali Paşa and compares it to a photograph of the earthquake-stricken areas of the Marmara region. It then continues by noting that,

> there is over one hundred years difference between the scenes reflected on the canvas and in the photograph . . . [D]espite this, for those looking carefully at both Şeker Ahmet Ali Paşa's painting "Privates Drilling" . . . and the earthquake photographs . . . there is an important similarity. This similarity is that the tents used by the privates at the end of the nineteenth century to pass the night, and the Red Crescent tents used by the earthquake victims following this late twentieth century disaster, are essentially the same . . . [T]his seemingly small, but really quite important similarity shows

> that the criticism of the Red Crescent . . . is valid . . . [a]nd that the Red Crescent is slowly losing the trust of every citizen whose needs are not being met.[46]

Once again, both of these discussions focus initially on the *inhabitants* of the camps and the tent cities, the rights possessed or lost by these inhabitants, and their living conditions. In the first, the military is concerned first and foremost with preserving the rights to health and sustenance enjoyed by Turkish "citizens." In the second, the Red Crescent Organization is criticized for failing to provide the services upon which the trust of these same "citizens" has been built—for failing, that is, to uphold a variation on the liberal social contract.

It is likewise clear that in both passages the real discomfort or confusion arises from space—and in particular military and civilian space—in flux. The issue at stake in each of these articles is not the civilian/soldier dichotomy or the citizen/trooper relationship per se. Rather it is the sudden disintegration of the lines differentiating the *space* designated "military" and the *space* designated "civilian" within the Turkish nation-state. In the first passage, for example, there is an explicit attempt to maintain the military space/civilian space dichotomy—the camps are military camps, the earthquake stricken are, repeatedly, civilians and citizens (at one point even "civilian citizens"), and the camps are "emptied" of the military element before civilians can enter them. Throughout the article, however, there is a discomfort with these sudden shifts from military to civilian and back again. Indeed, the very conflation of "earthquake stricken" with "civilian" (and, implicitly, nonearthquake stricken with military) renders both concepts ambiguous. If the area beyond the walls, when civilian, is "earthquake stricken," whereas the area within the walls, when military, is not, then as soon as the reversal takes place—as soon as the military empties out beyond the walls and the civilian is contained within them—all actual spatial distinction disappears. Both the civilian/earthquake stricken and the military/nonearthquake stricken exist on either side of the camp walls, destabilizing completely the original meaning of both spaces.

The criticism of the Red Crescent Organization operates in a similar manner. Whereas it is true that the condemnation of Red Crescent policy is couched more overtly in concerns over the passage of time than it is in concerns over the destabilization of space—the tents used at the end of the twentieth century are the same tents that were used at the end of the nineteenth century—there is also a distinct emphasis on this same military/civilian distinction. The fact that these tents are *military* tents is repeatedly highlighted both in the discussion of Şeker Ahmet Ali Paşa and in the historical vignette with which the article begins. It is not just that the Red Crescent Organization is inappropriately ignoring the passage of time; it is that they are also inappropriately allowing for the collapse of space. In the nineteenth century, the tents signified well-organized military space. In the twentieth century the same tents signified disorganized civilian space. The painting is a representation of the former, and the photographs are representations of the latter. And the lesson to be learned from both is that this disregard of spatial and temporal meaning, this emphasis on categorization without any actual spatial differentiation, leads to a gradual erosion of the social contract and thus the trust of the citizens.

This relationship between the waning trust of a nation's citizens and the steady disintegration of spatial meaning becomes even more apparent when we turn to the divisions embodied in roads and virtual roads—walls almost as important as those enclosing camps. The freeway, for example—that dividing line between the modern and the not modern, "slicing through space," and simultaneously linking and separating urban centers[47]—underwent a distinct transformation following the 1999 earthquake. Rather than serving as an obvious marker of the apparently modern city's "domination" over the apparently traditional countryside,[48] it upset this easy modern/traditional spatial and temporal dichotomy. Likewise, rather than slicing through space, it operated as a highly effective spatial *barrier*,[49] and far from linking urban centers even while it maintained their distinctive character, it irrevocably separated them even while rendering them indistinguishable.

If we look at four articles that appeared in *Hürriyet* on August 18, 19, 20, and 22, 1999, for example, we can see the road, the freeway, and the highway in precisely this state of spatial flux. The earliest of these articles, printed the day after the earthquake, merely states that first, the highway between the cities of İzmit and Istanbul is now toll-free, second, that vehicles can pass through the turnstiles on the highway between Adapazar, İzmit, and Gölcük without stopping, and third, that the bridges over the Bosporus still require tolls.[50] The second article is a self-described "highway guide," and goes into more detail. After first noting that the roads damaged in the earthquake are closed, it continues that these roads may be used only by aid vehicles and vehicles engaged in transporting the wounded. It then lists the roads that are closed except to official traffic, suggests alternative routes to those "wishing to approach the earthquake regions," and links cities and regions that might be visited in the following manner: "Düzce-Akçakoca-Karasu-Kandıra-Şile-Istanbul."[51] The third article describes traffic in one of the earthquake-stricken towns, Avcılar, as "paralyzed," continues that vehicles are bumper to bumper on the highway surrounding it, and notes that ambulances are having difficulty getting through.[52] Finally, on August 22, the same newspaper reported that a Health Ministry official made a statement in Istanbul that the town of Gölcük was under quarantine, that no one would be permitted to visit the area, but that nonetheless "people worried about those near to them and people hurrying to help [were] trying to enter the district using local roads rather than the main ones."[53]

After first describing the roads in a state of nearly complete effectiveness—not only open, but unimpeded by tolls and turnstiles—the newspaper gradually comes to represent them as ineffective, confused, and the source of nothing more than spatial disarray. The roads no longer represent the domination of the city over the countryside—now the city is engulfed and entrapped by the countryside, "paralyzed" by the very arteries with which it once brutalized the space surrounding it. The roads no longer slice and connect—they act as barriers. The initial freedom of movement announced in the first article is slowly circumscribed, until the roads—either damaged by virtue of natural violence, or closed by virtue of political violence—become a source of stagnation, an obstacle to overcome.

What became a far more exaggerated and overt trope in the images of, for example, the destruction of New Orleans following Hurricane Katrina—roads serving as spaces on which to camp and barriers against escape—is prefigured in these discussions of the 1999 Marmara earthquake. The roads explicitly *do not* link urban centers. They no longer serve as lines connecting distinct entities. Rather, the absence of a linkage turns Düzce into Akçakoca into Karasu into Kandıra into Şile into Istanbul, while Gölcük is explicitly imprisoned by them. Just as the walls enclosing the camp served to conflate the space surrounding it and the space within it, that is, the roads that once opened up the city now serve both to connect it to the world and to sever any connection. Just as the walls in the camp relentlessly and rhetorically categorized—military and civilian, decent and indecent, scene and obscene—while nonetheless undermining any actual spatial meaning, the roads surrounding the cities did the same, the main arteries "official," the local roads "unofficial," and both simultaneously forging connections and blocking connections within space in ecstasy.[54]

But how do these various spaces in ecstasy endow the disaster with meaning? How is space beside itself likewise space that brings the disaster home? Can the camp walls that serve no purpose but to divide, and the freeways and throughways that alienate the isolated city produce political truth? I suggest that they can—and that they can precisely by shifting the narrative of disaster from the realm of rational, empirical observation and analysis to the realm of ecstatic, unbounded understanding. Like subjects beside themselves, the scene turned obscene plays a specific role in making the disaster intelligible. It is not just that earthquakes shatter space and spread death and destruction. It is that the disaster, the earthquake, or the crisis reveals shattered spaces to be the norm—and to always have been the norm.

It is worth pointing out that this postdisaster spatial ecstasy, these regions, spaces, lines, walls, and façades that erupt in the days following the earthquake, are emphatically *not* caused by the disaster. They are made, created, and constructed by political and legal entities. They are like Mary Schloendorff's shattered body or like the living ghouls who are shot on the street for assaulting the rights of the dead. This spatial ecstasy is a deliberate creation, a construction—a product, in Lefebvre's words. Again, it is not that ecstatic space results from natural disaster. It is that the disaster results from the legal and political production of ecstatic space.

Cemeteries

If we turn, for example, to a space that is far more commonly associated with the irrational, the unknowable, and the obscene—a space that is in many ways hyperbolically in ecstasy, if not hidden away, stashed at the margins—we can see these processes playing out much more clearly. The cemetery or graveyard plays a strangely vital role in the shattering of space during moments of crisis. Survivors of disaster, for example, gravitate for no obvious reason to the "safety"[55] of the cemetery—only to be met with the shock and horror of long dead bodies churned up by the convulsed earth. This compulsion to head to the graveyard is, I suggest, one by-product of the link between decomposition and democracy—a result of the political, if not physical, security represented by the mass of dead, democratic subjects. What I argue in this section is that the obscenity of the graveyard, its spatial disintegration, is a particularly political, democratic form of obscenity and disintegration.

I argued earlier that various interpretations or duplications of the decomposing dead body—whether produced by Sophocles, Emerson, or the revolutionary French government—in one way or another positioned this dead body as the bearer of inalienable, transcendental, and incontrovertible rights. These rights in turn placed the decomposing body at the heart of democratic political theory—turning the corpse into a representative of the liberal equality and abstract political identity so fundamental to post-eighteenth-century readings of the democratic state-citizen relationship. I suggest further that the natural space inhabited by the dead body, the graveyard or cemetery, is likewise the natural space of democratic engagement—and that the fascination with the cemetery, with *living* in the cemetery, at moments of crisis is a fascination with this decomposition/democracy relationship. Indeed, the ecstatic space represented by the cemetery—this space beside itself—is space that, like the body beside itself, endows the disaster with meaning.

Lefebvre, in fact, highlights the shattered, unknowable, or disintegrating quality of space in the graveyard or cemetery. When speaking of the cemetery or the tomb as a place in which bodies are buried, for example, he calls it an arena that "give[s] expression to insurmountable separations."[56] When speaking of it as a place of "sanctuary," he calls it "absolute, even in the smallest temple or the most unpretentious village church."[57] The graveyard is thus—perhaps unintentionally in this analysis—both a space that divides, that cuts off, that is rife with walls or barriers, and also, simultaneously, absolute, unqualified and unadulterated, incapable of any division at all. Sanchez-Eppler similarly invokes this multiple nature of the tomb or the graveyard when she talks about "the permeability of the boundary between the living and the dead . . . reiterated within Wordsworth's verse, frequently marking the place where poetry begins."[58] This multiplicity becomes even more explicit when she continues that the tomb or monument "simultaneously aids and hinders access to the dead."[59] Here, in other words, the cemetery is a place deliberately given over to permeable and indefinable boundaries, to spaces and structures that serve opposing ends, to the starting point of "poetry," and to the paradoxically self-conscious endpoint of the rational.

This at once shattered and absolute space inhabited by the dead is, moreover, not just the stuff of poetry but also—and perhaps more so—the stuff of politics and law. I mentioned earlier, for instance, the central role played by the disintegrating aristocratic body in the radically liberal politics of the French Revolution. I argue now that the *space* of the cemetery was similarly key to revolutionary politics.

As Charles A. Tamason has noted in an analysis of one hundred years of funeral riots in the French city of Lille, for example, these were by no means "isolated incident[s]"; during the Revolution, "burial districts by rank were abolished,"[60] and indeed, "revolutionary leaders . . . tried to use funerals to define liberty and equality in terms of the national interest."[61] As Lindsay states in a second article, the destruction of the "tombs and mausoleums" of the aristocracy was an explicit political goal, with "the royal basilica of St. Denis . . . a special target."[62]

The cemetery or graveyard thus became a political place during the crisis that was the French Revolution.[63] The decrees, protests, and riots were by no means issued or staged arbitrarily—they were set deliberately in the spaces of the dead, for deliberate and definite purposes. But two questions nonetheless remain: what could be said in a cemetery that could not be said in a public square or a government building? And why should the indistinct space of the graveyard—the space beside itself, precariously occupied by a tomb—be so fascinating to liberal revolutionaries in a way that other spaces were not?

Again, I think the answers to these questions lie precisely in the ecstatic, inexpressible nature of the funereal space. Like the rights of Polyneices, rights that were made known in or on a tomb were immediately transcendent, aggressively irrational. The democracy they defined was a democracy not subject to argument—a democracy that brooked no rational interference. There were no spaces of discussion and spaces of reflection in this democratic politics—no public and private arenas or areas given over in one case to consent and in the other case coercion. The tomb that simultaneously aided and hindered access to the dead was a tomb that acted quite overtly as a wall without meaning. It was a divide, but the divide merely played up the absence of anything *to* divide, the absoluteness of the space. On one side of the tomb was the scene, on the other side the obscene, but the purpose of the wall was to mark a point of entrance—to make possible the breakdown of any difference between the two. The tomb, in other words, demanded its own desecration—this desecration being the only means of reifying what was already a space beside itself. The French revolutionaries recognized this demand—recognized its incontrovertibly democratic character—and responded to it.

It is true that most governments are not actually in the business—except in crisis situations—of desecrating cemeteries. Ordinarily cemeteries are inviolate space, space that must under any and every circumstance be protected. A great deal of literature has been written over the past thirty years about the dark fear—rather than the patriotic duty—of exposing the dead in their places of rest. In nineteenth-century England especially, "body snatching caught the popular imagination," and

> death practices underwent subtle alterations in response to this perceived threat. An iron coffin was patented which, it was claimed, could not be opened by body-snatchers; others chose thick wood coffins; straw and sticks were added to the soil in order to clog the grave-diggers' space; bodies were buried deep; tombstone and vault design was defensive as well as decorative; grave sites were guarded at night by watchmen.[64]

For those who could pay, "places of burial became like speculative building projects."[65] But even those not rich enough to afford patented coffins or secure burial sites were assured of their "right to be buried in [a] churchyard," given that "a clergyman could not refuse burial because of a failure to pay."[66] There was indeed a movement throughout the nineteenth century toward "burial reform" in England—a reform predicated on two, apparently interrelated, questions. Reformers were concerned first, with "health hazards posed by urban graveyards," and second with "issues of decency."[67] According to reformers, that is, "the promiscuous mingling of the living and the dead invit[ed] moral as well as physical infection," interfering with the graveyard's ideal role as "a place of moral edification."[68]

Here, in other words, there is no desecration of graves, no toppling of tombs, no exposing of decomposing bodies to speak of. There is instead a veritable terror of the possibility of these behaviors and steps taken to prevent them. However, both the fear of body snatchers and the development of patented coffins on the one hand, and the building projects financed and occasionally blocked by burial reformers on the other, point to an attitude toward the space inhabited by the dead not altogether different from the attitude of the more radical French revolutionaries. First of all, it is clear that the cemetery remains a political space—a space ideally that will serve the cause of moral edification, but also a space to be regulated in the name of effective public/private relations. The cemetery is a political space in precisely the same way as the public square—charity can occur there as well as entrepreneurship; the bodies that inhabit it have a right to be free from molestation just as their living counterparts involved in the social contract have.[69]

Again, however, the cemetery is also more exaggeratedly political—or at least democratic—than the public square. The cemetery is, as it was in eighteenth-century France, an arena of meaningless walls and divisions that do nothing more than play up the absoluteness of the space. It is an arena in which space exists beside itself—and in which rights are subject to no argument, no conversation, no self-consciously rational explication. The fear of body snatchers and the iron coffins—the moral threat posed by promiscuous intermingling of living and dead and the guards set up in the cemetery to curb this threat—are as much a result of the multiple nature of the tomb as the revolutionary desecration was. The tomb marks both the division between living and dead and the absence of a division. It marks both a point of access and a point of defense. It marks the possibility of the dead inhabiting the subterranean depths and the possibility of the dead rising up from these depths to inhabit the ground and the air. The fear of the desecration of tombs and the steps taken to prevent it are based, in other words—like the democratic and revolutionary duty to desecrate the tombs—on an acknowledgment of the ecstatic nature of space in the graveyard. Each is an acceptance that space in the graveyard exists beside itself, the scene and the obscene collapsed into one. As a result, here too we have a situation in which the cemetery becomes the space par excellence of democratic rights and duties—a space enclosing the purity of the democratic state-citizen relationship.

I suggest throughout the remainder of this section that the cemetery, like the camp, is an area central to the politics of disaster. The cemetery is a space beside itself, in ecstasy. It is an area in which walls exist only to play up the absoluteness of the space, in which the scene becomes the obscene, and in which death quite literally inhabits all layers of vertical space. Moreover, it is for this reason, I suggest, that the cemetery, like the camp, becomes a place of refuge for disaster victims. There *is* a sort of security in the cemetery—a security, however, far more political than it is physical. It is a security predicated on the idea that space in ecstasy—like the subject in ecstasy—is normative space, that space in ecstasy is a space in which citizens and their rights are incontrovertible. It is a security predicated on the possibility that the live body might be mistaken for the dead and decomposing body—and thus be mistaken for a body inviolate. Finally, it is a security predicated on the idea that recognition of this spatial ecstasy will turn the disaster, and its victims, into something intelligible.

As early as the 1830s and 1840s, for instance, narratives of both the 1755 Lisbon earthquake and various southern Italian disasters made recurrent use of the cemetery trope. As one memoirist wrote about his experiences in Lisbon, he first "ventured down into the city by the safest ways [he] could pick out, to see if there was a possibility of getting anything out of [his] lodgings."[70] Immediately upon entering the city, however, "there came such an intolerable stench from the dead bodies," that "[he] avoided passing near certain places."[71] Nonetheless, "a gentleman told me, that going into town a few days after the earthquake, he saw several bodies lying in the streets, some horribly mangled, as he supposed, by the dogs, others half burnt, some quite roasted; and that in certain places, particularly near the doors of Churches, they lay in vast heaps piled one upon the other."[72] In a description of an earthquake in Calabria published three years earlier, there is a similar reference to "dead bodies imperfectly buried under the ruins that killed them, together with others long since committed to the grave, whose sepulchers the same terrific agent of destruction had torn open, diffused pestiferous exhalations that generated mortal disease."[73]

Neither of these accounts concerns cemeteries—or taking refuge in cemeteries—per se, each nonetheless serves as an effective reference point for discussing the role of actual cemeteries during the Istanbul, San Francisco, and Tokyo earthquakes. In each, for example, the space inhabited by the dead bodies is both political and absolute. In each, there are walls and barriers thrown up, but these walls and barriers do not serve any rational purpose—they in no way divide the scene from the obscene. And in each, the presence of walls and the absence of division serve to play up the overwhelming rights of the decomposing bodies.

In the discussion of the Lisbon earthquake, for instance, the dead bodies have effectively colonized the entire city—the city has become a cemetery, which must be accessed, briefly, by living bodies who "go to town" and then quickly leave. The space is an absolute space of death, but also a space divided by the doors of churches, which simultaneously attract piles of dead bodies but also block their entry. The door of the church serves as a tomb, simultaneously encouraging and denying access to what, under apparently normal circumstances, is the appropriate arena of the dead—simultaneously effecting and breaking down the barriers between the scene and the obscene. Likewise, in the account of the Calabria earthquake, the recently dead and the long dead are thrown together, those who had been buried and those who had yet to be buried occupying the same space and playing the same role. And in the end, again, it is the dead who are the effective inhabitants of the city, the dead who allow the living entry into this absolute space only momentarily, and in forbearance.

Following the 1894 earthquake in Istanbul, the Ottoman government took these narrative tropes of the cemetery as political space, as ecstatic space, and as rightful backdrop for the operation of the normative citizen, as something of a template for its relief of the disaster area. The government's attempts to meet the needs of a population described as "forced to live outside, in open spaces, in gardens and orchards, and even in cemeteries," for example, became a familiar story.[74] In one decree, a question was indeed raised about what to do with the inhabitants of the city, who—seeing most places as dangerous, and terrified of aftershocks—had abandoned their houses and taken refuge in gardens or cemeteries.[75] The partial answer is an interesting one: comparing the spaces inhabited by the living, the wounded, and the dead, the government announced that the dead needed to be buried in "appropriate" areas, but that the wounded could be taken care of by traveling doctors.[76]

In San Francisco, various public squares were described by journalists as "public morgues," where "bodies were laid side by side . . . in the absence of more suitable accommodation. When the flames threatened to reach the square the dead, most of whom were unknown, were removed . . . [and] buried."[77] At the same time, at the morgue itself,

> fifty bodies were lying. The flames rapidly approached this building, and the work of removing the bodies to Jackson Square, opposite, began. While the soldiers and police were carrying the dead to what appeared safe places, a shower of bricks from a building dynamited to check the flames injured many of the workmen and sent soldiers in procession, hurrying to hospitals. The work of removing the bodies stopped and the remainder of the dead were left to possible cremation in the morgue.[78]

Eventually, however, even with these spaces given over to the dead, "the bodies piled up . . . were becoming a menace," and, again, citizens were called upon to dig graves to accommodate them,[79] all the while being horrified at the "scattered" and "putrid corpses" that surrounded them in the "safety" of the cemeteries.[80]

Finally, in Tokyo, the narratives comparing spaces of the dead to spaces of the living—juxtaposing the official morgue or cemetery with impromptu graveyards produced by the crisis situation—were brought to their logical conclusion. On the one hand, for example, the cemeteries themselves were "in a tragic state," with "tombstones flung about and broken and some of the graves yawning where fissures had split the small terraces."[81] "That even the resting place of the dead should be heaved into such disorder," said one commentator, "seemed like pure sadism."[82] On the other hand, there were the *unexpected* graveyards, areas where fires had produced "a solid mass of dead, with twenty thousand still standing on their feet, held up by the other dead around them,"[83] and where, in one "confined space," "thirty two thousand people were roasted to death," their "bodies touching each other as far as the eye could see."[84] Again, the "official" spaces of the dead gradually expanded in these accounts until living wanderers came upon them almost accidentally, shocked into the recognition that the city had in many ways become a cemetery itself.

In each of these disaster narratives, there is thus a constant comparison being made between official or appropriate graveyards and unofficial or impromptu graveyards. The Ottoman government, for example, makes clear that the dead must be moved to appropriate places, shrouded, and then buried. The military government in San Francisco likewise fights a long (if losing) battle to keep the official morgue official. And the memoirists describing their experiences in Tokyo are constantly juxtaposing the disrupted state of the actual graveyards to the ghoulishly ordered state of the burned and standing bodies in public squares. Related to this theme, there is also the deliberateness associated with the spaces occupied by the dead in contrast to the accidental or unexpected quality of the spaces occupied—or passed through—by the living. Again, the Ottoman government produces and regulates "appropriate" areas for the dead, whereas the living chaotically abandon their houses and take refuge without any forethought. In San Francisco, the army repeatedly categorizes certain spaces—the morgue, the public square, the trenches dug by press-ganged citizens—as spaces appropriate for the dead, while the living, again, wander aimlessly. And in Tokyo, the spaces appropriate for the dead are made clear by the emotions they inspired—churned up graveyards are tragic, while charred bodies in open spaces are horrific.

The "tragic" and "sadistic" quality of the convulsed cemetery deserves further attention—especially to the extent that living citizens apparently gravitate toward the tragic cemetery while fleeing the horrific public square. These descriptions of the churned up graveyards suggest certain linkages among the themes I addressed above—the attempt to make the spaces of the dead "appropriate," the deliberate as opposed to aimless quality of these spaces, and the safety represented by the cemetery as opposed to the household.

Both the designation "tragic" and the designation "sadistic" are arguably political as well as aesthetic designations. Both in one way or another get at social or political identities gone awry—at rights, essentially, gone bad. It is true that the first tends to be linked more often to classical political theory,[85] whereas the second tends to be linked to modern liberal political theory.[86] Both, however, describe political life in a way that the "horrific" usually does not. The inevitable destruction of a citizen, for example, is ordinarily a tragic or sadistic thing; the inevitable destruction of a ghoul is, as I noted before, horrific. What this emphasis on the tragic and the sadistic destruction of graveyards in many ways produces, therefore, is, once again, a political statement: the churned up graveyard is a *political* space in agony, and the citizens who take refuge in that graveyard are *political* subjects.

It is for this reason that governments are so careful to maintain a hold over defining the spaces of the dead—are so careful to keep these spaces official, or at least "appropriate." As the dead are moved, transferred, removed, and then buried—as they travel from morgue to square to trench—each of these spaces becomes first and foremost a *political* space. The government's task of defining certain areas as political and certain areas as not-political, that is, overlaps quite comfortably with the designation of new and expanding spaces for the dead.[87] The political acknowledgment—the political *appropriation*—of this spatial disarray is a key element of legal ecstasy and the politics of disaster: churned up bodies on their own cannot be evidence of natural disaster. Churned up bodies that are shifted from the accidental to the political, however—churned up bodies that become a political norm—can and do lend meaning to the crisis.

It is arguably for this reason that the living seek refuge in cemeteries during moments of crisis. Since the desecrated cemetery is both the meaningless by-product of natural violence *and* a political construction, since it marks a transformation from the catastrophic and accidental to the political, it produces both ecstatic, decaying bodies *and* ecstatic, decaying bodies possessed of untrammeled political rights. When the living take refuge in graveyards, therefore, they are quite literally placing themselves into an unquestionably political sphere, surrounding themselves with a space defined by incontrovertible rights rhetoric. The safety represented by the cemetery is above all political safety—it is a safety based on the fact that the bodies found there can *in fact* be tragic, can be the objects of sadistic violence, in a way that the bodies found elsewhere cannot. This is a space that is political in a way that the horrific burned up public square is not. Living citizens seek refuge in cemeteries, that is, in order to conform as much as possible to the (protected) norm represented by the rights-bearing dead body.

When we jump ahead to the end of the twentieth century, we find cemeteries and graveyards playing nearly an identical political role. Although it was less common for victims of the 1999 Istanbul earthquake to seek refuge in cemeteries than it was for their earlier counterparts to do so, the repeated designation and redesignation of certain areas as spaces of the dead—and the ecstatic quality of these spaces—quite definitely remained. The transformation of various collapsed buildings into rhetorical "graveyards," for instance, was arguably much more than simply a poetic way of saying that a number of people had been buried in the rubble. There was also a political statement being made—a political statement that turns disaster areas into ecstatic space, and thus a backdrop for the formulation of ecstatic subjects.

If we start with an article in the Turkish newspaper *Milliyet* titled "Our Pain is Very Great: An Apartment Building in Eskişehir is a Graveyard," for example, we are told precisely how many people were trapped in the wreckage, how many bodies had been removed from it, the names of those who had been identified, and the role of the mayor in identifying the bodies and those who had victimized them.[88] Eight years later, in a retrospective of the earthquake, the newspaper *Zaman* ran an article couched in a (perhaps unexpectedly) similar vocabulary, called "Twenty Thousand People Remain in Tomb-like Houses in Sakarya." In this article, the reporter states:

> in [the working class neighborhood of] Zeytinburnu, Istanbul, one is surrounded with broken and damaged buildings leftover from the Marmara earthquake. Despite the fact that the earthquake happened eight years ago, 376 badly damaged houses in Sakarya are still awaiting demolition. In the same area, 4,362 buildings with core damage need to be reinforced. Scientists say that these houses resemble tombs . . . or "concrete cemeteries." The buildings—which, for legal reasons, have not been repaired—are essentially invitations[89] to death.[90]

Each of these discussions of apartments as graveyards plays up the strangely comforting political character of the shattered spaces of the dead. In the first, the apartment in Eskişehir is turned into a graveyard because dead bodies—and above all identifiable dead bodies—reside beneath it. In the second, perhaps counterintuitively, buildings and houses in Zeytinburnu are concrete cemeteries because the living bodies within them have been summoned or invited to die. What matters in these discussions is not necessarily the actual status—living or dead—of the people inhabiting the spaces, but rather that the spaces in and of themselves are graveyards. The spaces produce the subjects rather than the subjects producing the spaces. In Eskişehir, the bodies are dead, and thus the building is a graveyard. In Zeytinburnu, the bodies are alive, and thus the buildings are graveyards. In each, it is the nature of the space—and not the nature of its inhabitants—that defines its character and potential.

More than this insistence on the preeminent quality of the space as opposed to the status of its inhabitants, however, the political vocabulary used to describe the space identifies it as part of the ecstatic realm of the dead. In the first, for example, it is precisely the fact that identifiable *citizens* are buried under the wreckage—underscored by the turn to the mayor—that reinforces the building's role as a graveyard. In the second, the politicized vocabulary is likely unintentional, but it is worth pointing out that the Turkish word for "cemetery," *tabutluk*, refers both to the courtyard of a mosque where coffins are displayed and, in the vernacular, to a prison or torture chamber in a police station (an area likely familiar to at least some of the working-class population of Zeytinburnu). Likewise, the "invitation," *davetiye*, to death can mean also a summons or subpoena. Interpreted in a different way, that is, the houses in Zeytinburnu resemble prisons or torture chambers, where death presents their inhabitants with a subpoena and summons.

The graveyards described here are thus explicitly political, and likewise explicitly unbounded, unknowable, not subject to meaningful spatial division. The torture chamber is the proverbial ecstatic space—a space where subjects are shattered, moved beyond themselves, a space where death and life, and especially the *desire* for death and the *desire* for life, are intermingled, a space where there is no logic, and a space where it is precisely the subject's *inability* to articulate in a rational manner that makes statements true and believable.[91] That the space inhabited by the working-class residents of Zeytinburnu—and by extension the middle-class residents of Eskişehir—should be both a cemetery *and* a torture chamber plays up its ecstatic character. There is a legal summons, but this is a summons to irrationality. The line between living and dead is erased. And the tomb marks simultaneously the space where the bodies are buried—living or dead—and the inability to reach those bodies—living or dead.

When we turn to preexisting graveyards and cemeteries and their role in the late twentieth-century rhetoric of disaster, we can see further variations on these themes. As an article in *Hürriyet* in the week after the earthquake put it, a place was selected at the side of one municipal cemetery for those who "who shared the same fate on the night of the quake"—a place where nearly 500 people were lined up "side to side," many of them unidentified. Ideally, the article continues, relatives of the unknown victims would be able to identify them based on photographs taken before the bodies were interred.[92]

Move ahead to June 2003, and this narrative is concluded. In a story in the liberal daily *Radikal*, a mother finds her dead son's grave four years after the disaster. The article tells the involved tale of a Ukrainian woman, Natali Obaline (sic), who "finally" found her son Anton, a navy seaman, after years of asking lawyers and politicians for permission to open unidentified graves, going to police stations to look through photographs of unidentified victims, providing documentary evidence that she was a relative of the body she eventually identified, and then finally disinterring the body and taking it home to Ukraine. The article concludes, first, with the words of the mayor of the town in which the body was buried: "she has been reunited (*kavuştu*) with her son. And we did everything in our power to support her." The article then continues, "in the days immediately following the 17 August 1999 earthquake, 69 unidentified people were buried in the Adapazarı Serdivan cemetery. Forty of those people have since been identified by their families, leaving 29 still unknown."[93]

What is this interest, then, first, in photographing the undocumented dead before they are interred, second, in keeping these albums for identification in police stations, and third for telling glowing stories about the success of these policies? Obviously, there is the basic answer that people want closure—want to mourn their relatives—and identifying a body is the surest way to bring this closure about. At the same time, however, this answer does not get at the broader political meaning behind these moves—it does not explain why there should be such an extensive *political* and *legal* framework built up around the process of pre- and postinterment identification. I suggest that these stories also serve to regulate the unregulatable space of the cemetery. The cemetery becomes in these articles once more a hyperbolically political space, a space that remains unbounded and uncertain, and a space that endows the disaster with meaning.

It becomes a space, for example, whose inhabitants have rights—exaggerated rights—as evidenced by the lawyers and politicians with whom "mothers" must speak, and the documentary evidence that these same "mothers" must provide, before the bodies of their sons can be revealed to them. But it is also a space in which the status or state of the dead does not ultimately matter—being living or dead is not all that important. The second passage thus slips easily into a vocabulary of life rather than of death—the mother reunited with her son becomes a picture or image in which the fact of the son's death is less important than the fact that his rights have been respected, and that the security of the cemetery has been maintained.

The dead also become worthy of envy in such stories—as an article published at the anniversary of the disaster, "I'm Jealous of the Dead," makes clear. The point of this article is to play up the pain of those who have been left behind. But there are a number of telling passages in it that, again, suggest there is more going on—suggest that there is more attention being paid to the shattered space of the cemetery than one might initially expect. The article is divided into a number of segments, each anchored by the statements of survivors who lost children or other loved ones in the wreckage. The purpose of these statements is to emphasize the unrelieved bitterness—*and not* the triumph—of remaining alive during and after a disaster. As one grieving mother states, "Should a person be jealous of the dead? I'm jealous . . . [I] ask why I was left behind, I cry every night. I'm jealous of the dead. I wonder, can those who departed actually be the lucky ones?"[94]

The article continues by telling its readers that this mother appealed to the Gölcük Asliye court after the building in which she lived crushed her children. At the court, she received an official statement, signed by an expert, proving that her apartment building had been made of "faulty materials," had been constructed on "soft ground," and had not been in any way up to code. The contractors, however, were not punished.

> Not one of those murderers spent a day in prison and now they're taking jobs repairing the damaged buildings. My mind can't take that sort of thing. They never built a single house—they built graves. And now they are taking contracts for more graves. Is there no one who will punish these killers? Will they punish my husband who spends every evening planning revenge? I don't remotely trust the lawsuit I've started here. So I'm going to take it outside of the country, to the European Court of Human Rights . . . [I]'m not afraid of anything anymore. Because I'm not living. I died on 17 August 1999. I died that day along with my children.[95]

A second grieving parent made a similar comment about the perhaps unexpectedly close relationship between the state and its legal system on the one hand, and the death of her children on the other: "They didn't have a single wound. They died of suffocation. And around that time someone raised a Turkish flag over the wreckage. Is it possible for a person to hate his own country's flag? It is, and at that moment I felt hate and rage in my heart . . . [T]here needs to be an Independence War in this country."[96]

In this article, the elements that produced Natali Obaline's triumphant story of success and closure come together in a different way to produce bitterness and tragedy. The contractors did not build apartment buildings, they built cemeteries—and in these cemeteries rest the children of formerly patriotic citizens. What is it, though, about the nature of these spaces that, in the first case, prompts the grieving mother to seek out the European Court of Human Rights and, in the second, prompts a sudden hatred of a previously honored flag?

The answer to both questions is that arguably these spaces—these cemeteries—are both normative and beyond rational description. It is not just that buildings collapsed and buried helpless citizens. It is more that these buildings effectively became graveyards, remained graveyards, and—more than that—are serving now as models for new graveyards. The only residential space imaginable in either of these stories is the cemetery. Nothing exists in them except cemeteries. Even Natali Obaline, the surviving mother in the first passage, defines herself as dead—as inhabiting a graveyard. The normative quality of the spaces of the dead has reached its logical conclusion in these articles. All space has become the space of the dead. All space has become absolute—space inhabited, or soon to be inhabited, by respectable dead bodies.

Moreover, these spaces are explicitly linked to the state—either via the symbolic act of raising a flag over the wreckage of the collapsed building or via the more legalistic act of granting new building contracts to those responsible for turning them into graveyards in the first place. The politics of disaster in this situation has quite literally revealed the cemetery to be the spatial norm—to be the space protected and defined by the law. For those who refuse to accept the normative nature of this space, therefore, the only move is a move beyond the borders of the nation state and its law—a move toward a sudden hatred of the state's flag, or a move toward the apparent justice represented by the European Court of Human Rights. Unlike Natali Obaline, whose acceptance of the normative function of the graveyard resulted in a cathartic and politically admirable moment of closure, the protagonists in each of these stories refuse to accept the validity of a normative space of the dead. They see it as unjust. And as a result, they remain trapped in a sort of political and legal limbo—denying the centrality of the cemetery even while their envy of the dead plays up its inexorable normativity.

The cemetery, thus, like the camp, gradually becomes a key and necessary political space in the law and politics of disaster. It is indeed as political as it is ecstatic—as much a product of the legal vocabulary of disaster as it is beside itself, indefinable, without any rational divisions or borders. If anything, it is more essential than the camp. Living citizens instinctively gravitate to the cemetery for safety and comfort in a way that they do not gravitate toward the camp—seeking and sensing the same political meaning that the French revolutionaries and British burial reformers did. The cemetery is a space where tragedy can occur. It is a space fraught with meaning and also with indefinable mystery. It is a space where everyone—even and especially the long since dead—possesses incontrovertible political rights. And it is a space that is not graspable through bounded, self-conscious logic—through the political theory that motivated Creon but not Antigone. The tomb represents both access to and a defense of the rights-bearing dead body. The body itself can be either living or dead—its status is less meaningful than the nature of the space. And the nature of this space is simultaneously beside itself and politically central—productive of the ecstatic political subject.

Squares and Monuments

What, then, happens to other political spaces during moments of crisis—what happens to the public squares and monuments, for example, that in liberal theory are responsible for the production of the bounded, self-conscious rational subject?[97] If the camp and the cemetery are the normative spaces of disaster law, do squares or monuments play any role at all? In the final section of this chapter, I argue that, yes, they do—although this role is a complex one. The square and the monument, after all—and in particular the crumbled square or monument—are mentioned repeatedly in the popular, political, and legal texts that surround the crisis or the disaster. The condition of various monuments especially—the question of whether the monument will survive or whether it will require replacement—is a source of anxiety for countless jurists and politicians.

Again, the square or monument plays a less *straightforward* role in the politics of disaster than the camp or the cemetery does. The square in ruins or the monument in pieces represents precisely the threatening sort of space that the camp or the cemetery represents under apparently normal circumstances. Squares and monuments create the wrong *type* of subject—the rational, self-conscious, bounded subject who is in every way marginal to the law and politics of disaster. When disaster writing focuses on squares and monuments, therefore, it ordinarily does so for two reasons: first, it seeks to play up the continuing existence of bounded, rational, and well-defined space even at moments of crisis. And second, it seeks to make this bounded space irrelevant to this crisis.

I note nonetheless that even under apparently ordinary, day-to-day circumstances—even before they have fallen into ruins—squares and monuments are ambivalent spaces. Lefebvre, for instance, spends quite a bit of time describing the contradictions and coercive force possessed by these areas—arguing that "monumentality"

> always embodies and imposes a clearly intelligible message. It says what it wishes to say—yet it hides a good deal more: being political, military, and ultimately fascist[98] in character, monumental buildings mask the will to power, and the arbitrariness of power beneath signs and surfaces which claim to express collective will and collective thought. In the process, such signs and surfaces also manage to conjure away both possibility and time.[99]

He continues by arguing that "monumentality transcends death, and hence also what is sometimes called the 'death instinct,'" its "transcendence" in turn "embeds itself in the monument as its irreducible foundation," and its "atemporality overwhelm[s] anxiety, even—and indeed above all—in funerary monuments."[100] The monument, in other words, represents a "spatial action" that "overcomes conflicts . . . even though it does not resolve them," the monument opens "a way from everyday concerns to collective joy."[101] However, once a monument loses its prestige, "turmoil is inevitable," and this prestige can only be retained "by means of admitted oppression and repression."[102]

If we turn our attention to the monument in ruins—either physically destroyed or deprived of its prestige—we can see one logical conclusion to this narrative of monumental space reached. As Mbembe has argued in his discussion of postcolonial public space and monuments (in crisis), for instance, "bodies can be neutered whenever they are thought to be 'disfiguring' a public place or are considered a threat to public order . . . or whenever the *commandement*, wishing to leave imprinted on the minds of its subjects a mark of its enjoyment, sacrifices them to a firing squad."[103]

In a different context, David Seed has described the physical rather than political crisis of public space in Hiroshima after the detonation of the atomic bomb: "destruction seems freakishly inconsistent; dress patterns are transferred on to the bodies of survivors; the outlines of those near ground zero imprinted on walls, and the sudden growth of plants in the ruins."[104] He continues by arguing that there was created "a lateral panorama of Hiroshima which suggests in still life a complex continuity rather than a total ending."[105]

Both Mbembe and Seed refer implicitly or explicitly to the qualities of monumental space as they were described by Lefebvre—but both also reinterpret these qualities such that the production of political subjects becomes meaningless or dysfunctional. In Lefebvre's analysis, the single defining characteristic of monumental space is that it is knowable and rational. The monument possesses meaning. And this meaning, in its very rationality, "transcends." It in fact transcends both death and time, because its message is a clear, distinct, ordered, and graspable one. It is a message about collective citizenship that denies, through logic, any possibility of irrational conflict. Monumental space is oppressive—"fascist" even—but it is space possessed of a distinct political truth.

When this space is transported to the realm of the postcolony, the war zone, or the disaster area, however, this truth is exploded. In the postcolony, for example, the public nature of the public square itself becomes a threat—and becomes something that cuts into or cuts down, that destroys rather than produces, the citizen. The public itself "disfigures" public space—and so the public must be eliminated. The public square thus loses its political centrality, even while its transcendent ordering potential remains.

In a much more exaggerated way, the atomic bomb similarly transformed public space in Hiroshima. The transcendent atemporality of the square remained—the space continued to suggest "complex continuity rather than a total ending." But the meaning of the space was lost—bodies themselves became graffiti on otherwise purposeless walls. They became space rather than citizens—while the decorative patterns of their clothing became intrinsic parts of the bodies that remained. In each situation, in other words, monumental space remained, its ordering potential survived, but its meaning disintegrated, and the space became marginal—irrelevant to the political violence that created it.

What I suggest in this section is that the rapid restructuring of the public garden, public plaza, public square, or monument in the minutes following a natural disaster is an example of the same sort of process—a likewise abrupt transformation of rational, meaningful, politically central space into rational space at the margins. At the same time, I make clear that, ordinarily, conversation surrounding the use to which public space is put after an earthquake is focused primarily on the breakdown of public/private distinctions,[106] and I discuss what this breakdown means for modern state functioning. My purpose over the following pages, therefore, is not so much to question this focus or to argue that the rhetorical distinction between public and private is an invalid point of departure. Rather, I examine both the collision of the public and private in the disaster area and the *way* in which this collision is articulated. In other words, I situate these narratives within the broader context of spatial ecstasy.

With that in mind, I begin with two anecdotal descriptions of public squares in the days and months following, first, an earthquake that struck Lima in 1746 and, second, an earthquake that struck Naples in 1805. The first of these descriptions is from a scholarly article by Charles F. Walker that focuses on the breakdown and rebuilding of class barriers in the wake of the Lima disaster: "members of Lima's upper core camped in plazas and empty fields," Walker notes, and "the viceroy formed three armed patrols 'to repress the insolence of the people, principally that of blacks and slaves.'"[107] Less than two weeks after the earthquake, he continues, the government began implementing policy to deal with future crisis management, and a committee "recommended widening streets, limiting the height of buildings, prohibiting arched towers, replacing stone structures with wattle and daub, and assuring adequate plazas and public space to serve as refuge in case of disasters."[108]

Sixty years after the Lima disaster, a traveler's account of an earthquake in Naples described the situation as follows:

> when we had got into the street the crowd was immense, and although many voices were heard, some crying 'to the *publick squares*,' and others 'to the *country*' the people seemed confounded, not knowing which way to run. It was with the greatest difficulty we reached the *Lago di Castello*, an open square, and when we had arrived, there was so great a concourse of the inhabitants that there was scarcely room enough for us to stand.[109]

In each of these discussions, the plaza or square plays a key narrative role. In the first, it is precisely the disorder of the plaza that demonstrates the magnitude of the disaster. In the second, it is likewise confusion about whether the public square or the country is the safest option that demonstrates the magnitude of popular panic. These rhetorical moves, however, also emphasize the *marginal* relationship between public space and citizenship formation now that disaster has struck.

In the first article, for example, it is within the open plazas and fields that the supposedly rational class and race categorizations—so fundamental to eighteenth-century political theory—are erased. The police and the government work diligently to redraw and reenforce these categories, but they do so in conflict with the prevailing disorder of the plaza—and not in harmony with it as they would under what were considered normal circumstances. In the second, the square is simply a source of confusion. No one knows whether it is the safest space or the most dangerous—and even upon reaching it, this question remains unanswered. In both passages, that is, the monumental, meaningful, self-conscious aspects of the public square give way to meaningless, confounded, and disordered aspects. The process of citizenship formation continues—the public square is still a space in which political subjects are produced—but this process is more akin to what Mbembe and Seed were describing than to Lefebvre's militaristic, rational transcendence. Public squares in the disaster become marginal space because they perform the same role as, but less effectively than, the cemetery and the camp.

If we turn to the late nineteenth and early twentieth centuries, this reconfiguring of monumental space had become in many ways a formalized aspect of postdisaster record keeping and response. Like the death toll, the list of spaces shattered by the earthquake was organized according to type and political purpose. Following the 1859 Erzurum earthquake, for instance, the official returns (as published by the Royal Geographical Society) made clear that "the Turkish quarters of the town were those which suffered most severely," and that in these neighborhoods, "4500 houses were quite destroyed, or very seriously damaged; 12 mosques suffered more or less; 9 minarets were felled to the ground; 7 Turkish schools were completely destroyed; 5 baths, many of the fountains, and 800 shops, were rendered useless. The khans, in which merchandise is deposited, being almost invariably vaulted, suffered very little."[110]

The fate of shopping areas especially remained a source of concern for Ottoman administrators, and four decades later, after the Istanbul earthquake, the condition of the Covered or Grand Bazaar was the subject of a number of imperial decrees. The monument's multiple—but well established—political roles were explicitly invoked in these documents, its position as a center of trade and commerce, as well as a meeting area, as well as a tourist destination and cultural testimonial, discussed in detail. The decision on the part of the government was eventually to use the disaster as an opportunity, and to repair and redesign the Bazaar such that it was more "regular, uniform, or orderly," and such that it could benefit from "progressive architectural methods," "strong and solid material," and "contemporary building technology." The result would be a shopping area that was simultaneously "more beautiful or graceful," "better ordered," and "safer" than the space that had been destroyed.[111]

The city's open squares and parks were likewise reconfigured or, more deliberately, reimagined in the days following the earthquake—the government's attempts to meet the needs of a population "forced to live outside, in open spaces, in gardens and orchards, and even in cemeteries," once again, a common theme.[112] This theme became more overt a decade later, in San Francisco, where one reporter, Henry Lafler, for instance, described his experiences as follows:

> Portsmouth Square is half a block from my doorway. In its center is a memorial for Robert Louis Stevenson; to the east, facing it, is the hall of justice; to the west was (I use my tenses with care) Chinatown . . . [C]lothed, with the square for a dressing room—in which, by this time, were thousands of persons, mostly mute, gaunt, blankly staring Chinese—a man began to think of his friends and seek them . . . [A]s I write these things, sitting in the opera, in Portsmouth Square, facing gaunt and blackened walls, it seems as though years had passed.[113]

By 1922, the trope of the reconfigured public square had become even more effectively established—the story of the bodies burnt to death in Tokyo's major plazas, for instance, repeatedly invoked, often alongside shattered monuments such as "the granite Memorial Arch to those killed in the Great War," that was thrown over and lying "in a dozen big fragments."[114]

Like the Ottoman and U.S. governments, however, the Japanese government also saw the destruction as an opportunity to reorganize what was now unrecognizable urban public space. In 1930 and 1931, for instance, the Tokyo Municipal Office and various freelance architects were imagining the process of rebuilding as a means "not only to restore the former aspect of the capital, but also to reconstruct an ideal metropolis worthy of the nation's capital."[115] The earthquake, described as "unquestionably a great calamity," was also seen as "a most rare opportunity to undertake the thorough execution of the city plan in a large scene," especially given "the promulgation of the Law of Special City Planning applicable to the Tokyo and Yokohama regions."[116] Focusing particularly on clean, open, public spaces, these documents note, first, that "the evils of modern cities arise principally from congested living conditions," second, that the park, especially, is "an important social institution that seems to remove or at least alleviate these evils," and third, that "parks form the lung of a city."[117]

At the same time, as one contemporary observer noted with respect to these plans, they were to "be regarded as a failure on the part of the Tokyo Municipality" because

> the absolute non-restriction of architectural style has encouraged the combination of style with commercialism . . . [I]t is not impossible in the future to control ugly things such as huge sign boards for a consideration of public morality or by some legal measure, since most of the buildings so far erected in the city are temporary structures. But in the case of permanent buildings, it has become positively impossible to unify them in the future.[118]

In each of these legal and political responses to public squares and monuments shattered by disaster, we can see the same—often simultaneous—process of defining and recognizing what has now become ecstatic space. There is, first of all, a moment of nostalgia for what the space once represented—its day-to-day, normal, historical role in rational, meaningful citizenship formation. Almost immediately, however, there is likewise a recognition of the equally political, but now meaningless, role that the transformed public space is currently playing in the disaster area—a recognition of its subversive potential to disorder and destroy the new political subject. Finally, there is an optimistic turn to the future, in which the meaning of public space will once again be straightforward and transparent—but in which its unquestioned, unmentioned, tacit, and silently accepted character will never again be completely established.

The Ottoman government's focus on shopping areas, for instance, is shot through with a nostalgia for their once meaningful political role. The Grand Bazaar not only served as a commercial center, but as a cultural one. Ottoman citizens as well as tourists visited it, and upon visiting it, they knew objectively and explicitly what it meant to be an Ottoman and also what it meant to be a foreigner. The lines that defined and divided citizens were clear, and the public space that was the Grand Bazaar served as a backdrop against which to draw and redraw them. When this space was destroyed, a significant arena in which political identities could be formed was likewise destroyed. And as a result, there was an enormous anxiety on the part of the government that it be restored—and restored such that it was "better," "more modern," "more organized," and "more graceful" than it had ever been before.

The irony of this growing insistence on a better organized, more effective, and increasingly comprehensible political space, however, is that as it was described and discussed, as it was defined and made knowable, it was likewise made meaningless. As Lefebvre and Mbembe have noted, monumental space is monumental—it serves its political function—precisely because it is *unquestioned*, because its ordering capacity is tacitly and silently accepted. As the Ottoman government sought to produce a modern yet authentic, technologically advanced yet traditionally graceful, replica of the Bazaar, therefore, as it published and discussed these plans, the political capacity of the Bazaar as modern monumental public space was gradually undermined. Unlike the cemeteries and the camps, which were endowed with meaning in the days following the disaster, the Bazaar instead was emptied of meaning. As political subjects beside themselves were formed in the cemeteries, they were made irrelevant to the Bazaar, an area that was in turn irrelevant to the disaster.

This does not mean that public squares or monuments were not sometimes reconfigured as postdisaster political spaces—as areas that could, if perhaps ineffectively, also produce the ecstatic subject. The discussion of Portsmouth Square, the Robert Louis Stevenson monument, and the now nonexistent Chinatown, for instance, is if nothing else a discussion of suddenly marginal space and the extent to which it produces subjects beside themselves. In addition to invoking the usual trope of the collapsed public and private spaces (the square became a "dressing room"), the passage also describes an array of collapsed temporal and physical categories. Chinatown, for example, exists simultaneously in the past, and also to the west, of Portsmouth Square and its monument. Likewise, the "gaunt, blankly staring Chinese" are juxtaposed against the "gaunt and blackened walls" of the opera house—their bodily existence uncertain in precisely the same way that the bodies, transferred as patterns to the ruined walls of Hiroshima, were.

In each case, that is, the purpose and meaning of public spaces are not destroyed, but rather inverted. They still serve as a backdrop for citizenship formation. But there is a shift in this process. Now subject to the law of disaster, these citizens are politically, temporally, and physically beside themselves—citizens in crisis. The inhabitants of Chinatown become quite literally both bodies and backdrop—and the metaphor of the exotic not-quite-citizen as scenery or environment becomes concrete. Likewise, just as the reporter plays up the destructive capacity of the disaster by telling his readers that he shaved and dressed himself in the public/private central square, he also plays up the shattered nature of the square by emphasizing its temporal instability. He is shaving in a space that exists in the present, but alongside it is a space that exists in the past. Whatever political subjects might be formed within this space are thus subjects in flux, uncertain, and above all unrecognizable as rational, bounded, self-conscious beings.

The rhetorical foundations set in 1894, 1906, and 1922 for discussions of disastrous public space remained in place at the end of the twentieth century as the Turkish government responded to the 1999 Marmara earthquake. Just as in 1894, for instance, the fate of various monuments-as-tourist attractions received a great deal of political and public attention—and just as in 1894, the reconfigured political space was a source of anxiety and debate. Four major attractions—the Covered Bazaar, the Hagia Sophia Museum, the Beyazıd Mosque, and the Fatih Mosque—each played different but related roles in the reimagination of public space. The Covered Bazaar, for example, described in one newspaper article as a "historic market," remained "completely sound." Its doors opened almost immediately after the disaster, as soon as it was established that there were no new fissures in the walls—and "visiting foreign tourists" were able to enter it again. The article then concludes that Istanbul's "most important trade centers" had quickly returned to their previous movement and activity in the days after the earthquake.[119]

The Hagia Sophia Museum is likewise described as a building that "will never be destroyed." After first invoking the expertise of Ahmet Çakmak, a building engineer who specializes in earthquake damage, the article moves on to address the destruction caused by the 1894 earthquake, to note that the "fifteen hundred year old structure" has been shaken time and again without suffering damage, and then to praise the wisdom and technical expertise of Byzantine and Ottoman architects such as Anthemius and Sinan. In particular, the article praises the intellectual ability of these architects, and the extent to which they generously shared their knowledge with colleagues while keeping it from those who were untrained—refusing even to reveal their "trade secrets" to the Sultan. After dwelling for some time on these late antique, medieval, and early modern architects and their masterpieces, the article then asks "and what about the new structures?" The answer, according to Çakmak, is that whereas nothing will happen to the newly built skyscrapers, the five- to ten-story apartment buildings constructed throughout the late twentieth century are a different matter—unable to withstand the frequency of seismic waves, constructed of faulty materials, and subject to collapse. Whereas Justinian, Çakmak reminds the reporter, built Hagia Sophia to last forever—indeed until the end of the world—this is not the case with the less monumental buildings, buildings constructed of cement[120] that weakens after less than one hundred years.[121]

The Beyazıd and Fatih Mosques occupied a slightly shifted rhetorical space in these discussions. In an article titled "Beyazıd Mosque Closed to Worship," for instance, we learn that the building did indeed suffer damage—in particular, large fissures in the walls. Whereas it, like Hagia Sofia, is described as "historic," however, it is also held up, along with the Fatih Mosque, as one of four mosques most badly hurt in the earthquake. The local government, the heads of various charitable foundations, and high-ranking müftis were called upon to assess the destruction, which they were "pleased to note" did not include deep structural damage, but did include a great deal of surface cracks and fissures. As the müfti of the Fatih Mosque stated, many of the mosques would be open again for worship once everything had been cleaned up—and in general, the earthquake would not pose any obstacle to prayer.[122]

At the same time, however, an article three days later emphasizes the questionable condition of the most prominent mosques in Istanbul. After noting, for instance, that nearly all of Istanbul's oldest mosques have been destroyed by earthquakes a number of times, it suggests that Fatih Mosque might be the least "lucky" of all of these. Fatih, the article continues, was built on the site of a Byzantine church in the years following Sultan Mehmed II's conquest of Istanbul, and in every earthquake over the past five hundred years, it has suffered extreme damage. The reporter argues that no matter how often Fatih Mosque is repaired in the months and years after a disaster, it always has to be repaired again. As the opening paragraph of the article states, "in the last earthquake Fatih Mosque was damaged [again], and has been closed for worship."

The rest of the article discusses the various moments throughout history that Fatih Mosque has been destroyed and the ways in which Ottoman and Turkish leaders have responded to its destruction. In 1509, for instance, the mosque was badly hurt in an earthquake—its minaret completely broken during what was termed the "little apocalypse." Foreign visitors, the reporter says, commented on the strange existence of a mosque without a minaret for years following the disaster. After the 1766 earthquake, Fatih was once again completely destroyed, and then rebuilt—with much difficulty and bad luck—on the orders of the Sultan. It was reopened for prayer only four years later in 1771. In 1782, it was damaged again during a fire, this time after residents had taken refuge in its courtyard. After commenting once again on the clearly unlucky character of the Mosque, the article concludes by turning more generally to disasters that had hit Byzantine and Ottoman Istanbul, the fear that these disasters had engendered, and those structures (such as the Byzantine walls) that had survived them intact and those structures (like Fatih Mosque) that had not.[123]

In each of these discussions, in other words, a different type of public space is defined, historically contextualized, and described in relation to the disaster. And in each, the disaster is endowed with meaning via reference to a less monumental, less public, less open and rational arena. Indeed, this is the case despite the apparent centrality of the monuments—despite the fact that Hagia Sophia and the Covered Bazaar are praised for their intact "soundness," whereas the two mosques are deprecated as not just subject to damage, but "unluckily" so.[124]

Both Hagia Sophia and the Covered Bazaar, for instance, are defined first and foremost as spaces relevant to tourists. Each is sound and strong, each can be opened immediately following the earthquake, and each can thus continue to serve the foreigners who visit them. This is in direct contradistinction to the two mosques—buildings that despite their historical value are defined by their relevance to Turkish citizens. The mosques, however, relevant to Turkish citizens, are closed—and closed indefinitely. Whereas the monumental spaces that serve to define outsiders are quite accessible during moments of disaster, that is, the monumental spaces that serve to define insiders, Turks, are immediately closed. There is the possibility that these latter structures might be opened again, but—and I emphasize—only when the day-to-day has been reestablished. Monumental space, in other words, has been made explicitly alien in this analysis—national identity formation re-routed to other, less open and public arenas.

Likewise, all four structures lend themselves to minihistory lessons—to discussions not just of contemporary subject formation, but to subject formation in the distant and even antique past. Once again, though, these lessons emphasize simultaneously the historical meaning of various monuments and the historical marginality of public space during times of crisis. Each of these narratives situates the permanence of monumental space within a context of transience and even secrecy. Each in turn plays up the irrelevance of monumental space to the subject of disaster law.

In the case of Hagia Sophia, for instance, it is precisely the privacy and secrecy of early medieval architectural expertise that makes the building sound, capable of withstanding any shock, and beyond the possibility of destruction. This is a building that is sound exactly to the extent that it is the beneficiary of secret, occult knowledge. It is a building whose monumental permanence rests upon an explicitly transient and fleeting knowledge—a building eternal precisely in that no one knew historically, or knows now, how it would, or can, survive so long. To the extent that this is a space in which subjects are formed, therefore, these are subjects in flux. To the extent that they become the focus of disaster law, it is as foreigners, outsiders, or inhabitants of the past.

It is important to emphasize that this status "free from damage," or "always free from damage" is a status that has relevance only during times of crisis. "Free from damage" is a meaningful description only when an earthquake or a disaster is occurring. The very soundness of Hagia Sophia is reliant on the politics of disaster. But it is a soundness likewise irrelevant to the disaster, given that the building has remained intact. Hagia Sophia is free from damage both because of the disaster and in spite of it. It is free from damage because it is simultaneously a public, monumental space and an occult space—the beneficiary of public knowledge and dark, secret, or private knowledge. The political subjects that are formed within the confines of this space are thus simultaneously relevant to the disaster and completely irrelevant to it. As a monumental space, Hagia Sophia can indeed produce subjects of disaster law—but these subjects, again, are ineffective, faulty replicas of the subjects produced in the camp or the cemetery.

When we compare these subjects to those assumed by the discussions of Fatih Mosque, it becomes clear that although the characteristics of monumental space can vary radically, in general all public space produces the same faulty, impermanent replicas of subjects produced in ecstatic space. Fatih, for example, is presented above all as an irrational space—a space that is "unlucky," and beyond notions even of effective or ineffective engineering. Not only is it closed during disasters, but, like Hagia Sophia, even when it is open, it can create nothing but subjects in flux. Far from the straightforward, rational, open space of effective monumentality, it is irrational, unlucky, and confused. It is indeed precisely at moments of crisis that its inability to produce proper public subjects is made manifest.

In each of these discussions, that is, the monument does play a role in the politics of disaster—and is invoked explicitly in narratives of the earthquake. At the same time, however, even in its narrative centrality and importance, the monument is gradually turned marginal, irrelevant, and meaningless to the law of disaster. The public square, museum, or monument can and does produce political subjects. But these subjects are nothing more than ineffective replicas of the ecstatic subjects being produced simultaneously in cemeteries and camps.

In a different kind of flux, these subjects cannot make the disaster intelligible because they are trapped within the irrelevant space of the monument. And the monument thus in turn threatens the disaster in the same way that the cemetery or camp threatens the normal, the ordinary, or the day-to-day.

Conclusion

I end this chapter by returning, first, to one final point Lefebvre makes in his analysis of monumentality, and then to one final anecdote from Wilson's account of the San Francisco earthquake. According to Lefebvre,

> buildings are to monuments as everyday life is to festival, products to works, lived experience to the merely perceived, concrete to stone, and so on . . . [S]uch a space (a monument) is determined by what may take place there, and consequently by what may not take place there (punished/proscribed, scene/obscene). What appears empty may turn out to be full—as is the case with sanctuaries, or with the "ships" or naves of cathedrals. Alternatively, full space may be inverted over an almost heterotopic void at the same location (for instance, vaults, cupolas).[125]

According to Wilson,

> weddings in great number resulted from the disaster. Women, driven out of their homes and left destitute, appealed to the men to whom they were engaged, and immediately marriages were effected. Since the first day of the disaster an increase in the number of marriage licenses issued was noticed by County Clerk Cook. This increase was getting greater. Saturday morning seven licenses were issued in an hour.[126]

We have here two different analyses of the relationship between spaces and festivals. In the first, Lefebvre notes that monuments are in many ways spatial manifestations of festivals—that monuments are spaces defined by events, spectacles, and the codification of prohibited or permitted behavior. In the second, Wilson argues that the destruction of private space (homes) led directly to the celebration of festivals (weddings)—and that essentially all that was left in San Francisco was a spectacular, monumental, public arena, devoid of privacy if not domesticity. In each, public space produced political subjects (the subjects of weddings and festivals), and in each, public space defined these political subjects as rational, self-conscious, individuals (who, for instance, look after their own benefit).

However, these two discussions also hint at a number of alternative manifestations of political space in crisis. When Lefebvre argues that public space is both relentlessly divided or categorized (into the scene/obscene) *and* subject to misinterpretation (as simultaneously empty/full), he is drawing attention to the potential disorder that exists at the heart of even the most well-defined monuments and squares. When Wilson notes that it was precisely that most disquieting of public/private ceremonies, the wedding, [127] that characterized San Francisco's postearthquake squares and plazas, he was similarly suggesting that these public spaces were not as stable as they might initially have appeared to be. As I have argued throughout this chapter, the shift from the rational, well-ordered political space of the day-to-day to the irrational, ecstatic political space of the disaster is a shift that can occur with astonishing rapidity. The camp and the cemetery are certainly not identical to the square and the monument—but neither are they distinctly opposed to one another.

The camp and the cemetery are simply the square and the monument beside themselves. They are public and political spaces given over to the production of ecstatic subjects of disaster law. Like rational public space, they are divided, categorized, and compartmentalized. Walls and borders are thrown up and patrolled. Like rational public space, they produce and assume political subjects—subjects possessed of political rights. The difference between the two is that in the camp or cemetery, the walls serve no purpose *except* to divide—the space on one side of the border identical to the space on the other. The difference between the two is that the rights-bearing subjects of the camp and the cemetery are in ecstasy, beside themselves, dead, or decomposed. The camp and cemetery become spaces of security, in other words, precisely because the not-quite citizen represented by the living body might be mistaken there for the full and hyperbolic citizen represented by the dead one. The camp and the cemetery are democratic spaces in every conceivable way—transcendent and productive of rights that brook no argument, challenge, or debate.

At moments of disaster, the square and the monument thus become rational, public spaces pushed to the margins. Still capable of producing political subjects, they are nonetheless ineffective, in many ways irrelevant, meaningless precisely because they have *not* realized their disordered and disordering potential. Unlike, in this case, the camp or the cemetery, they are producing political subjects, but of the wrong type. As threatening to the politics of disaster as their ecstatic counterparts are to the politics of the day-to-day, these subjects are rational, self-conscious, bounded, and reasonable—or, alternatively, they are simply "foreign." And it is as such that they operate outside the realm of disaster law.

Again, though, even as the fate of the monument suggests a disjuncture between the disaster and the day-to-day, it also suggests a continuity between the two. Just as in the colony, that is, monumental space given over to the grotesque demonstrated the ordinariness of the emergency, so too in the disaster area, the mutability of the monument demonstrates the conflation of the crisis and the everyday. Although I began this chapter by emphasizing the differences (however slight) between spatial manifestations of colonial law and spatial manifestations of disaster law, I conclude by emphasizing their similarities. The simultaneity of the everyday and the crisis, after all, underlies not only the ongoing festival of carnivalesque marriages described by Wilson but also the ongoing security of the permanent emergency. Both marriage and the state of emergency transform a single event, incident, or moment into a permanent situation. Both marriage and the state of emergency claim to protect a prosaic, gendered, domestic space by turning it inside out, exhibiting it, and relentlessly ordering it.

A question to ask is whether this collision of the everyday and the crisis does not—as has been argued by some scholars of colonialism[128]—annihilate the everyday completely. Is it possible for the ordinary, the prosaic, or the commonplace to exist simultaneously with the catastrophe, the crisis, or the festival? Over the course of this chapter, I have suggested that indeed the ordinary and the catastrophe can and do overlap—that the continuity as well as the disjuncture among the monument, camp, and cemetery represents a similar continuity between the everyday and the disaster. This is in part, it is true, because in so many ways the emergency *has* become the norm—especially, but not only, in colonized spaces. More than that, though, it is also because of the variability of ecstatic subjectivity and the vitality of ecstatic space.

Ecstatic subjects and ecstatic spaces operate at the exact point that the everyday gives way to the crisis—they become fixed precisely in the process of their unraveling. And it is for this reason that I have addressed in the concluding sections of each of these chapters both the most apparently ordinary law—torts—and the most apparently extraordinary law—capital punishment and colonial regulation. The catastrophic and the ordinary are not discrete arenas, and once we acknowledge their continuity, we must also acknowledge the impossibility of pinpointing the distinct moment of transition from one to the other.

Judge Andrews, after all, recognized during *Palsgraf* that distinguishing the intelligible from the unintelligible—rational causal relationships from irrational causal relationships—was an arbitrary move. The U.S. Eighth Circuit Court and the European Court of Human Rights likewise recognized that determining a coherent subject of death penalty law required taking death—that most unintelligible of states—as the starting point of law and politics. And finally, colonial administrators have long recognized that coercively enforcing the ordinary or the everyday demands (paradoxically) a permanent state of emergency. In each of these legal frameworks, the intelligible and the unintelligible, the ordinary and the catastrophic, the everyday and the disaster overlap, interact, and seep into one another. And in each, as I have shown, the law assumes subjects and spaces in ecstasy—Schloendorff and Palsgraf, Singleton and Öcalan, the obscene public square and the secure cemetery, alongside the countless (despite the death tolls) inhabitants of disaster areas.

CHAPTER SIX

Conclusion

On September 4, 2007, the *Washington Post* published an article discussing proposed changes to the U.S. government's administration of disaster areas. Titled "ID Would Control Access to Disaster Sites," it states that

> in an effort to provide better control and coordination, the federal government is launching an ambitious ID program for rescue workers to keep unauthorized people from swarming to a disaster scene. A prototype of the new first-responder identification card is already being issued to fire and police personnel in the Washington area. Proponents say the system will get professionals on the scene quicker and keep untrained volunteers from making tough work more difficult.[1]

The article cites the collapse of the World Trade Center buildings on September 11, 2001, as the beginning of a trend away from a more laissez-faire approach to disaster relief,[2] and Hurricane Katrina, in 2005, as the moment when the Federal Emergency Management Agency (FEMA) "came up with the idea . . . [after] countless Americans rushed to help—unasked, undirected, and sometimes unwanted."[3]

This article and the proposal that it addresses raise a number of questions about political control over public space, freedom of information, grassroots activism, and, more basically, whether institutions like FEMA are in fact competent to respond to disasters *without* civilian interference. It is not for this reason that I bring it up here, however. Rather, this new federal initiative is an excellent example of disaster law as I have been discussing it throughout this book. There is, first of all, an insistence underlying the initiative that disaster areas be political spaces, spaces defined and regulated by government agencies, and spaces linked to national identity. This is made clear both in the policy's emphasis on state regulation, and in the rhetorical placement of this policy within the radical state-based nationalism that followed the destruction of the World Trade Center. That FEMA should recommend this new approach to disaster areas only after its incorporation into the Department of Homeland Security, for example, is arguably not a coincidence. The spaces subject to the emergencies and disasters to which FEMA responds are precisely the spaces that demand an articulation of the "homeland"—precarious, vulnerable spaces in need of a stabilizing national narrative.

More than that, though, this redefinition of the disaster area likewise redetermines what type of political subject can legitimately exist within the borders drawn by the crisis. By issuing government ID cards to what are deemed professional rescue workers, the policy makers are creating three distinct categories of citizenship. First there are the civilians outside the disaster area who cannot get in. Second, there are the civilians within the disaster area who cannot get out. And finally, there are the quasi-military professionals, those vetted by the state, who can cross the boundary between the disaster and the not-disaster. What has been created, in other words, is one group of people, visible and clamorous, who are irrelevant to the disaster, a second group of people, invisible and silent, who can define the disaster, and a third group, the professionals, who can speak to the visible on behalf of the invisible. FEMA and Homeland Security, in other words, have managed with this policy to regulate and codify what was previously a threatening and unstable relationship between the subject offstage and the disaster. The invisible, eccentric political subjects who had for three centuries produced the meaning of the crisis can now be effectively represented by professional rescue workers.

By drawing these spatial and political lines, FEMA and Homeland Security have resolved a number of problems that plagued the Ottoman, Japanese, Turkish, and U.S. governments throughout the twentieth century. By regulating the flow of supplies, for instance, the gift of life will now be something easily monitored. There will be no embarrassing incidents of the sort caused by Osman Durmuş. Instead the ecstatic transfer of bodily fluids and body parts will happen in silence—invisible within the walls of the well-patrolled disaster site. Likewise, the death toll will remain official, and only official—there will be no alternative, no private, no unprofessional group challenging the government's ability to compile lists of newly dead citizens. Finally, the throwing up of walls and barriers within the disaster area, the rearticulation of political space, will happen without hindrance, without comment even. Legal ecstasy will now be something, perhaps paradoxically, subject to constant control and regulation.

From this perspective, it makes sense that FEMA officials should introduce their new policy with the counterintuitive comment that their efforts during Hurricane Katrina were "burdened" by civilian interference. It likewise makes sense that these officials should deny civilian claims that the government was unfit to engage in even the most basic disaster relief.[4] If the purpose of disaster response is not, after all, to distribute supplies and to collect information, but rather to distribute supplies and collect information *for a particular political purpose*—a purpose linked to the goals of Homeland Security—then interfering civilians are very much a burden, and the government has been doing an effective job. If the first step in disaster response is to produce an ecstatic, eccentric subject who will bring the political reality of the disaster home, these government agencies have been extraordinarily competent. In the wake of Hurricane Katrina, an entire population of subjects beside themselves, previously offstage or ignored, were suddenly revealed to be living on the roofs of submerged houses or in tents on isolated freeway overpasses—these subjects suddenly became the population at the center of the disaster narrative. And it was FEMA that made this narrative possible.

I emphasize that although this approach to disaster control flies in the face of what, on a gut level, many people understand to be the purpose of effective state engagement, it is not actually far removed from the three-century-long story of crisis and governance that I have been telling in this book. It is also not *only* an example of those who are already marginalized or victimized becoming that much more so when the crisis strikes.[5] Instead, or in addition, the production of the subject in ecstasy—exemplified by FEMA's policies—is a deliberate, meaningful, politically essential process, in no way accidental, and in no way the result of failed legal and political structures. FEMA's unique management of the destruction caused by Hurricane Katrina was not simply a postdisaster exposure of the state violence that under day-to-day circumstances remains for the most part hidden. In addition to that, what the response to Hurricane Katrina and these recent proposals to reimagine and regulate disaster areas hint at is a deliberate form of governance that meets at the intersection of the day-to-day and the crisis.

Although until now I have played up the differences or at least tensions between the politics of the everyday and the politics of disaster, I conclude this book by suggesting that in many ways they are identical—and that the disaster represents a quite normal, or normative, form of democratic engagement. Moreover, as I mentioned briefly in Chapter 1, one lesson to learn from these trends in disaster law is that, rather than aiming at some resolution to crisis or disaster situations, rather than attempting to solve the problem that is the crisis, we might instead try to develop a vocabulary that accepts disaster as the endpoint to law.

What do I mean, though, when I say that the disaster represents a normal or normative form of democratic engagement or that it might be the endpoint to law? In part, I am taking up the point made by Sophocles and embodied by Antigone, Creon, and Polyneices many centuries ago: at the basis of tyranny is confusion or anxiety about the burial of bodies, and at the (implicit) basis of democracy is comfort and reassurance about the burial of bodies. The burial or disinterment of bodies says something very fundamental about the nature of politics—and has, for 2,500 years. In part, however, I also take up the point made in the 2007 *Washington Post* article—a point derived from the linkage between Hurricane Katrina and the destruction of the World Trade Center, between FEMA and Homeland Security, and between, on the one hand, invisible, marginal populations being rescued (or not) from their sinking houses and, on the other, invisible, marginal populations being held in the not quite sovereign space of U.S. camps in Cuba, Afghanistan, Iraq, and elsewhere.

Each of these approaches to democracy—although in many ways quite different—are also in many ways similar. Each takes disintegrating, silent, unbounded subjects as the normative subjects of politics. In the first, the dead body defines democracy; in the second, the invisible occupant of the camp defines democracy. Each likewise takes the crisis as the foundation for everyday politics—each relies on a narrative of disaster (the incest of Oedipus, the tyranny of Creon, the wound to U.S. national pride, the demolition of a historic city) to produce a democracy of the day-to-day. When I say that the disaster represents both a normal and a normative form of democratic engagement, therefore, I mean that quite explicitly: the disaster is normal in that it is part of the everyday. It is normative in that it also *defines* the everyday.

In Chapter One, however, I also talked about the *optimism* embodied by the subject in ecstasy, especially vis-à-vis Agamben's *homo sacer.* It may seem now that this optimism is misplaced—that there can be no optimism in the face of such destruction, there can be no optimism following upon so many stories of subjects ripped apart, buried alive, burned to death, or shot as ghouls and anarchists. I emphasize, however, that the optimism that I associate with the subjects of legal ecstasy is in no way an optimism that sees in the future some end to political violence—be it the political violence of states in crisis or the political violence of so-called healthy states in their day-to-day manifestations.

Rather, the optimism that I associate with subjects in ecstasy is an optimism related to their insistent nature.[6] Not only do subjects in ecstasy have unique access to political truth and reality, but they insist on being heard. Both Mary Schloendorff and the long-dead bodies churned up in shattered cemeteries may have been in a bad physical state—may have lived horrific personal lives—but, politically, they simply could not be ignored. The political life of Mary Schloendorff became the foundation for a century of U.S. legislation on bodily integrity, and the political lives of the dead bodies in the cemetery became the basis of legislation on everything from liberal equality (in France and England) to disease control (in Turkey and the United States). The subject in ecstasy, in other words, represents the possibility at least of enduring and vocal political existence.

Indeed, a second reason to see the ecstatic subject as an optimistic figure is that this subject promises to destabilize the specious rationality that in the past has led so frequently to the demolition or coercive re-creation of political identities. The subject in ecstasy is not a political subject easily turned into an internal refugee. Linked not only to the admission but to the celebration of the relationship between political truth and unbounded irrationality, the subject in ecstasy becomes a figure whose political existence is virtually unassailable.

If we accept legal ecstasy as our starting point, for example, it is difficult to imagine an endpoint at which an individual must maintain *x, y,* or *z* characteristics in order to enjoy full citizenship rights—and in which citizenship rights disappear along with the disappearance of *x, y,* or *z* characteristic. Legal ecstasy involves the blurring of even the most basic distinctions between individual and individual—it demands that *x, y,* and *z* be unknowable, and in constant flux. Again, to make this point concrete, Schloendorff and Polyneices may have been in a bad place, but this was certainly *not* because either had been deprived of a political identity. As subjects in ecstasy, they were indefinable *and therefore* the very basis of politics. If we accept that law ends in disaster—that the subject in ecstasy is the normative subject of politics—we can thus start to think about legal and political structures in a new way. The violence by no means evaporates—but it is resituated, open to alternative analyses.

And it is for this reason that I have both implicitly and explicitly relied on the insights and methodologies provided by feminist theory throughout this book. If there is a field that lends itself to dynamic and multiple analyses of law, subjectivity, and violence, this field is feminist theory. Embedded in each of the stories that I have told—stories of blood transfusion and national identity, of dismemberment as a progressive political act, of disease control used to produce hysterical subjects, of death tolls and disinterment as means of granting rights to corpses, of the living-dead ghouls who assault these rights, and of camps and cemeteries replacing public squares and monuments—is likewise a story of gendered or sexed subjectivity. As Braidotti has argued, it is primarily in the field of feminist theory that the subject in crisis—be it a metaphysical, political, or natural crisis—has been engaged. It is primarily in the field of feminist theory that the relationship between shattered subjects and political or legal structures has been described in detail.

That the rhetoric of feminine hysteria embodied by Mary Schloendorff, for example, should provide the basis for the postdisaster gift of life is something that makes sense only if we recognize the centrality of the gendered or sexed subject. There may or may not be direct mention of women or sexual identity in narratives of this gift—in the narratives of transfusions, transplants, and disease control—but these narratives are nonetheless indebted to three centuries of assumptions about the nature of women's embodied or disembodied sexuality. The connection between Schloendorff's hysteria and dismemberment on the one hand and the gradual elaboration of the democratic subject, possessed of the inviolable right to bodily integrity, on the other, is precisely the sort of connection that feminist theory seeks to analyze. When Henrietta Moore notes, for instance, that from a Lacanian perspective, "the body as it is experienced and perceived by the child is fragmentary, a body-in-bits-and-pieces. Out of this biological chaos of sensation and physiological activity will be constructed a lived anatomy, a psychic map of the body which is given not by biology, but by significations and fantasies (both personal and collective) of the body,"[7] she is commenting on the particularly *political* implications of physical dismemberment and linguistic (or legal) reintegration. When Butler asks three years later, "what does it mean to embrace the very form of power—regulation, prohibition, suppression—that threatens one with dissolution in an effort, precisely to persist in one's own existence,"[8] she is likewise asking a question about the disintegrating subjects of law and politics. Both Moore and Butler are describing a seeming contradiction between the linguistic or legal insistence on coherence that in turn relies on a psychic or even physical incoherence. Each is addressing this contradiction from the perspective of shifting sexed or gendered subjectivity. And each is finding a potential source of optimism in the very confusion that seems to make all activity meaningless.

Although I have written this book primarily as a description of the laws that attempt to bind the ecstatic subject, I have also described the ways in which these laws relate to the subject's potential activity or lack thereof. Butler's question is, again, what does it mean when subjects turn toward the law as the source of both their existence and their disintegration? The question with which I initiated this book was, what does it mean when the law seeks to define a disintegrating or ecstatic subject as the political norm? Although Butler takes the subject as her starting point and I take the law as my starting point, we are nonetheless each drawing on gender studies methodologies as a means of addressing related contradictions in the politics of freedom and security. We are each asking what this particularly gendered form of democracy looks like.

Although the democracy defined by the decomposing, disintegrating corpse from Chapter Four may seem to have little to do with the ways in which women navigate legal and political systems, in fact it is a democracy very much gendered and sexed. If nothing else, Antigone's traditional role as the representative of this *type* of politics—this democracy of dead bodies—suggests a connection between her precarious gendered subjectivity and the likewise precarious subjectivity of her disinterred brother. It is precisely what Nussbaum calls Antigone's "morally superior" desire to be dead and beloved by the dead that leads to the democratic moment at which Antigone (and her brother) become political subjects rather than objects. And it is therefore Antigone's ecstatic, disintegrating, gendered subjectivity that makes her democratic activity possible. As Butler argues, building on her existing work on gender and melancholy,

> melancholia [uncompleted grief] rifts the subject, marking a limit to what it can accommodate. Because the subject does not, cannot, *reflect* on that loss, that loss marks the limit of reflexivity, that which exceeds (and conditions) its circuitry. Understood as foreclosure, that loss inaugurates the subject and threatens it with dissolution.[9]

Democracy defined by the disintegrating, disinterred corpse is thus a melancholic democracy—in which it is precisely the dissolution or shattering of the gendered subject incapable of articulating desire that likewise "inaugurates" this same subject as (I am arguing) a political actor.

In Butler's work, this melancholic, shattered subject is often, although certainly not always, silent—not dissimilar from Agamben's *homo sacer.* As Braidotti has suggested, however, the shattered subject need not necessarily be a quiet one—"non-unitary identity" in her writing is frequently described as a "process of resistance."[10] I must stress, in fact, that although Nussbaum, Butler, and Braidotti are not writers who ordinarily have a great deal in common with one another, they do seem to be moving in similar directions here. Each describes the difficulties or complexities of political engagement, each situates her description within an implicit or explicit story of gendered subjectivity, and each concludes with an implicit or explicit proposal for destabilizing or undermining the narratives that (inappropriately) produce and destroy these subjects. Each has thus appeared throughout this book as I have tried to contextualize the law of disaster—and the democracy that it underlies—within these theories of sexed and gendered subjectivity.

Finally, the camps and cemeteries that serve as ecstatic backdrops to the subjects of disaster law may seem to be spaces defined by a (self-conscious) "masculine" military rule. But they are also spaces in which it is arguably precisely the uncertain, indefinable movements of gendered and sexed actors, actors tied neither to the fantasy of the public nor the fantasy of the private, that are the norm. To the extent, therefore, that there exists a relationship between ecstatic space and the ecstatic subject—a relationship that eventually makes the disaster intelligible—this is a relationship most effectively addressed through the lens of feminist theory. Whether feminist scholars are challenging the notion that representation within knowable space is an act of violence, or whether they are supporting it, they are providing a framework for thinking about the subjects and spaces of disaster law.

In their discussion and critique of Butler's work, for instance, Abigail Bray and Claire Colebrook state that, "by questioning the idea that representation is a 'break' with the fullness of reality, or that the body is, to use Butler's terminology, a 'constitutive outside,' we suggest that feminism rethink its antirepresentationalism. The body is not, we argue, a necessary outside produced by the limiting violence of representation."[11] They continue, "for Butler, discourse cannot include the outside; exteriority may be known or thematized through discourse but is not itself discursive. It is this boundary between signification and the constitutive outside that has produced the feminine *as* a sexed and prerepresentational materiality."[12]

If we understand ecstatic space—like Butler does—as the exterior space that (a) cannot be represented and therefore (b) is a necessary foundation for what must be represented, then its relationship to the law of disaster becomes clear. Ecstatic space in its very inability to be defined, in its very obscenity, makes the disaster politically meaningful. Likewise, if we understand the relationship between—or conflation of—ecstatic space and ecstatic bodies as Butler does, then the paradoxical nature of the subject of disaster law becomes similarly apparent. At the same time, however, if we take Bray's and Colebrook's critique of Butler as a starting point, the relationship among ecstatic spaces, ecstatic bodies, and the subjects of disaster law can likewise be articulated. If representation is not a complete break with reality, if the body as a space can be a site of creative opposition, then legal ecstasy can likewise be a mode of positive activity.

I end, therefore, by revisiting the new policy recommended by FEMA from the perspective of the gendered, sexed, and shattered subject. Again, the notion that disaster areas should be inaccessible to anyone except politically vetted "professionals" raises a number of traditional liberal concerns about freedom of information, freedom of movement, and freedom of speech. If we consider this policy as a prime example of legal ecstasy and the new politics of disaster, however, it can be read less as an assault on liberal freedoms, and more as an assault on the security-based authoritarianism that apparently produced it. FEMA and Homeland Security are now explicitly recognizing the subject in ecstasy as the normative subject of disaster law and the law of the day-to-day. More than that, they are attempting both to regulate and codify—to define and to bind—this subject. By definition indefinable and unbounded, however, the ecstatic subject necessarily eludes this process—and thereby highlights the fractures in FEMA's policy. Just as the gendered subject of liberal politics gradually came to personify the crisis of liberalism, in other words, the ecstatic subject of the politics of security arguably personifies the disintegration of any effective authoritarianism. Again, the violence does not disappear. But a new vocabulary for addressing it does become possible. As Butler has suggested, "perhaps only by risking the *incoherence* of identity is connection possible . . . [perhaps] only the decentered subject is available to desire."[13]

Reference Matter

Notes

Chapter One

1. Unless otherwise noted, all translations are my own.

2. See, for instance, the extensive analysis of ecstasy in Judith Butler, *Undoing Gender.* New York and London: Routledge, 2004. pp. 19–21, 32–33, 148–151.

3. See, among others, Andrew M. Greeley, *Ecstasy: A Way of Knowing.* Englewood Cliffs, N.J.: Prentice-Hall, 1974; Carl W. Ernst, *Words of Ecstasy in Sufism.* Albany: State University of New York Press, 1985; James Rolleston, *Narratives of Ecstasy: Romantic Temporality in Modern German Poetry.* Detroit: Wayne State University Press, 1987; Felicitas D. Goodman, *Ecstasy, Ritual, and Alternate Reality: Religion in a Pluralistic World.* Bloomington: Indiana University Press, 1988; John J. Collins and Michael Fishbane, eds., *Death, Ecstasy, and Other Worldly Journeys.* Albany: State University of New York Press, 1995; Jill Marsden, *After Nietzsche: Notes Towards a Philosophy of Ecstasy.* New York: Palgrave, 2002.

4. Although this idea was a common theme among classical Greek, Roman, and medieval thinkers. See "Ecstasy and Subjectivity" in this chapter..

5. As in Daniel A. Farber and Jim Chen, *Disasters and the Law: Katrina and Beyond.* New York: Aspen Publishers, 2006.

6. As Nikolas Rose, Pat O'Malley, and Mariana Valverde argue in their discussion of Foucault's theories of governmentality, "the intrinsic relationship between government and ethics linked Foucault's arguments into the lively debates at that time [the early 1980s] concerning the question of the subject. During the 1970s, many had argued that the constitution of subjectivity was a key political issue; that capitalism required the production of subjects who imagined themselves to be autonomous, self-possessed, bounded, agentive individuals; and that radical thought needed to question this imaginary relation through semiotics or through a certain version of (French) psychoanalysis."

Nikolas Rose, Pat O'Malley, and Mariana Valverde, "Governmentality," *Annual Review of Law and Social Science* 2 (2006): 83–104. p. 90.

7. Antony Anghie, "Finding the Peripheries: Sovereignty and Colonialism in Nineteenth Century International Law," *Harvard International Law Journal* 40 (1999): 1–80. p. 27.

8. Hannah Arendt, *The Origins of Totalitarianism*. New York: Harcourt, 1976. p. 300.

9. For instance, Butler, *Undoing*, pp. 31–34.

10. See the discussion of bodily integrity and national boundaries in Luise White, "The Traffic in Heads: Bodies, Borders, and the Articulation of Regional Histories," *Journal of South African Studies* 23 (3) (1997): 325–338. pp. 326, 332.

11. Although a number of scholars writing from a psychoanalytical framework have noted the paradoxical nature of subjectivity in legal thought. David Caudill, for example, has made the convincing case that Lacanian analysis might be an effective way to address the complexity of the legal subject. (David Caudill, *Lacan and the Subject of Law: Toward a Psychoanalytical Critical Legal Theory*. Atlantic Highlands, N.J.: Humanities Press, 1997.) It is worth pointing out, however, that Caudill likewise recognizes the relative paucity of sustained work on shattered, multiple, or shifting subjects of law. In his discussion of Pierre Schlag, for instance—a scholar who has addressed the problematic nature of legal subjectivity in some detail—Caudill notes that "there is some ambiguity in Schlag's use of the term 'self.' The rational, autonomous 'self' is a rhetorical fiction in the form of American legal thought . . . [I]n Schlag's treatment of these paradoxes, he is more philosophical than he is psychological, more oriented to text as psyche than to psyche as text, and more attuned to social than psychoanalytical theory." Caudill, p. 72. Schlag does nonetheless provide an excellent foundation for many of the ideas that I explore in my own (also more philosophical than psychoanalytical) approach to legal subjectivity. See Pierre Schlag, "The Problem of the Subject," *Texas Law Review* 69 (1991): 1627–1743.

12. As it is defined in Carl Schmitt, *Political Theology: Four Chapters on the Concept of Sovereignty*. Trans. George Schwab. Chicago: University of Chicago Press, 2005. p. 12.

13. See Giorgio Agamben, *State of Exception*. Trans. Kevin Attell. Chicago: University of Chicago Press, 2005. "In this way, the impossible task of welding norm and reality together, and thereby constituting the normal sphere, is carried out in the form of the exception, that is to say, by presupposing their nexus. This means that in order to apply a norm it is ultimately necessary to suspend its application, to produce an exception." p. 40.

14. My hope is that this introductory summary of the state of ecstasy will serve as a foundation for the more detailed analysis of the ecstatic subject that comes next. Moreover, to the extent that this book describes the ways in which legal ecstasy defines ecstatic subjects—rather than the ways in which subjects in ecstasy define ecstatic law—I think it is useful to attempt to theorize, at least, a state of ecstasy that exists prior to subjectivity.

15. See, for example, Judith Butler's analysis of ecstasy in the work of Hegel and Benjamin: "In my view, Hegel has given us an ek-static notion of the self, one which is, of necessity, outside itself, not self-identical, differentiated from the start . . . [T]o be a self is, on these terms, to be at a distance from who one is, not to enjoy the prerogative of self-identity (what Hegel calls self-certainty), but to be cast, always, outside oneself, Other to oneself." Butler, *Undoing*, p. 148.

16. I should emphasize that Butler is at pains to differentiate between the self and the subject in these passages: "the 'self' here is not the same as the subject, which is a conceit of autonomous self-determination. The self in Hegel is marked by a primary enthrallment with the Other, one in which that self is put at risk." Butler, *Undoing*, p. 149. This differentiation is key to my argument as well, and I address it in more detail in the section that follows. For more on the difference between the subject and the self in psychoanalytical theory, see Henrietta Moore, "'Divided We Stand': Sex, Gender, and Sexual Difference," *Feminist Review* 47 (Summer, 1994): 78–95, where Moore notes that "the Lacanian subject should not be confused either with the person or the self." p. 92.

17. As, for example, Pheng Cheah describes each in the work of Kant and Hegel. Pheng Cheah, *Spectral Nationality: Passages of Freedom from Kant to Postcolonial Literatures of Liberation*. New York: Columbia University Press, 2003. pp. 151–152.

18. See, for example, Rosi Braidotti, *Patterns of Dissonance: A Study of Women in Contemporary Philosophy*. Trans. Elizabeth Guild. New York: Routledge, 1991. p. 52. For a defense or reimagining of the Cartesian subject, see Slavoj Zizek, *The Ticklish Subject: The Absent Centre of Political Ontology*. London: Verso, 1999.

19. And in which "the universality of the knowing thing and the processes of knowing" rendered "this Cartesian subject a transcendental one." Matthew L. Jones, "Descartes' Geometry as Spiritual Exercise," *Critical Inquiry* 28 (1) (Autumn, 2001): 40–71. pp. 40–41.

20. For example, "[Descartes] continually asserted that mathematics is an exercise, perhaps the best that we have. In taking this claim seriously, we can clarify Descartes' geometry. Simultaneously we will escape the long tradition of equating the subject Descartes aimed to create through his exercise with the so-called Cartesian and modern subjects." Jones, p. 46.

21. Ibid, p. 42.

22. Ibid, p. 53. Italics in original.

23. Longinus, *On the Sublime*. Trans. James A. Arieti and John M. Grossett. New York: Edwin Mellen Press, 1985. p. 6 [1.2].

24. Ibid, p. 9 [1.3].

25. Ibid, p. 87 [15.1].

26. Longinus, Arieti and Grossett, note p. 10.

27. Ibid, note p. 87

28. For a variation on this interpretation of the sublime in Longinus, see Wai Chee Dimock:

"this temporal disagreement between reader and author is noted by Longinus, perhaps the first critic to link resonance to an interactive process that, in its exuberance, can give rise to a democratic contest between the recipient and the originator. Celebrating the sublimity of literature, Longinus praises its aural longevity, understood as the persistence of sound not originating in texts but vibrating in response to them . . . [T]his enduring resonance is a function of the listening ear, which, moved by the sublime text, is moved to take 'a proud flight and is filled with joy and vaunting, as though it had itself produced what it has heard' . . . [I]n foregrounding the agency of hearing and predicating it on the potential disagreement between author and reader, the Longinian theory of the sublime seems to honor literature less for its originary act than for subsequent acts of inflection, inversion, dissension . . . [L]onginus seems to make listening and not listening strangely cognate, indeed conflatable. The ear is not a passive receptacle; it is a force that remakes what it hears. The aesthetics associated with Longinus, Frances Ferguson notes, 'culminates in a dissolution of the subject in the person of the author and in a reinscription of the subject in the person of the reader.'" Wai Chee Dimock, "A Theory of Resonance," *PMLA* 112 (5) (Oct. 1997): 1060–1071. p. 1067.

29. In invoking these lectures, I am not insisting on a direct link between ecstatic subjects in the fifth century BCE and ecstatic subjects today—or, for that matter, arguing that Foucault's analysis of classical law and politics is accurate. Rather, I am trying to highlight some running themes that appear in discussions of ecstasy and subjectivity—and, eventually, truth—in more general terms.

30. He brings up alchemy as an example of science operating within the realm of spirituality—but distinct from theology: "that alchemy, for example, and a whole stratum of knowledge, was at this time thought to be obtainable only at a cost of a modification in the subject being clearly proves that there was no constitutive or structural opposition between science and spirituality. The opposition was between theological thought and the requirement of spirituality. Thus the disengagement did not take place abruptly with the appearance of modern science." Michel Foucault, *The Hermeneutics of the Subject: Lectures at the Collège de France, 1981–1982*. Trans. Graham Burchell. New York: Picador, 2001. p. 27.

31. Ibid, p. 15.

32. Ibid, p. 17. See also, p. 178: "during the Hellenistic and Roman period there is the increasingly marked absorption of philosophy (as thought concerning truth) into spirituality (as the subject's own transformation of his bode of being). With this there is, of course, an expansion of the cathartic theme . . . [H]ow must I transform my own self so as to be able to have access to the truth?" This is also, according to Jones, the starting point of much of Descartes' work: "Descartes' geometry was such a spiritual exercise [*askesis*], meant to counter instability, to produce and secure oneself despite outside confusion

through the production of real mathematics. Descartes' famous quest to find a superior philosophy took place within this therapeutic model." Jones, p. 44. The difference is that whereas *askesis* in the work of Descartes leads to a "securing" of the self, in the work of the classical philosophers, as interpreted by Foucault, it leads to a losing of the self.

33. Ibid, p. 17.

34. "You *metanoei* (you change opinion) when you have been persuaded by someone. You also find the notion of *metanoia*, the idea of a *metanoein* with the meaning of regret and the experience of remorse. In this usage it always has a negative connotation, a negative value. *Metanoia* always has a negative rather than a positive meaning in the Greek literature of that period. Thus, in Epictetus you find the idea that we must get rid of the erroneous judgments we may have in our heads. Why must we get rid of these judgments? Because otherwise we will be forced to reproach ourselves, to struggle against ourselves, and to repent on account of and as a consequence of these judgments. We will be forced to repent: *metanoein*." Ibid, pp. 214–215.

35. Ibid, p. 14.

36. Ibid, p. 17.

37. Michel Foucault, *Fearless Speech*. Ed. Joseph Pearson. Los Angeles: Semiotext(e), 2001. p. 15. Italics in original.

38. Foucault, *Hermeneutics*, p. 317.

39. Ibid, p. 318.

40. Ibid, p. 447.

41. Butler, *Undoing*, p. 19. Italics in original.

42. Ibid, p. 20.

43. Ibid, pp. 32–33. Italics in original.

44. Ibid, pp. 26–27.

45. Butler develops and complicates this notion in her analysis of language and subjectivity in *The Psychic Life of Power*. She argues, for instance, that "the genealogy of the subject as a critical category . . . suggests that the subject, rather than being identified strictly with the individual, ought to be designated as a linguistic category, a place holder, a structure in formation. Individuals come to occupy the site of the subject (the subject simultaneously emerges as a 'site'), and they enjoy intelligibility only to the extent that they are, as it were, established in language." Judith Butler, *The Psychic Life of Power: Theories in Subjection*. Stanford: Stanford University Press, 1997. p. 10.

46. Rosi Braidotti, *Nomadic Subjects: Embodiment and Sexual Difference in Contemporary Feminist Theory*. New York: Columbia University Press, 1994. p. 77. Italics in original.

47. Ibid, p. 166.

48. Ibid, p. 130.

49. Ibid, p. 196.

50. Ibid, p. 52.

51. Giorgio Agamben, *Homo Sacer: Sovereign Power and Bare Life*. Trans. Daniel Heller-Roazen. Stanford: Stanford University Press, 1998. (Original publication Giulio Einaudi, 1995.)

52. Foucault, *Hermeneutics*, p. 178.

53. Jones, p. 44.

54. For an elaboration of this point, see the section, "Natural Disasters and Metaphysical Disasters" in this chapter.

55. Schmitt, *Political Theology*, p. 5.

56. Ibid, p. 36.

57. Agamben, *State of Exception*, p. 35.

58. Ibid, p. 40.

59. Ibid, p. 71.

60. Ibid, p. 73.

61. Ellen Kennedy, "Hostis not Inimicus: Toward a Theory of the Public in the Work of Carl Schmitt," *The Canadian Journal of Law & Jurisprudence* 10 (January 1997): 35–48. p. 40.

62. "The Insurrection Act of 1807," 10 U.S.C. § 333(a)(1)(A).

63. See "Historical Disaster Writing" in the next chapter: *The American Red Cross Annual Report for the Year Ended June 30, 1918*. Washington, D.C.: The Arbor Press, 1918. p. 86.

64. Kennedy, p. 40.

65. The sacred man who occupies the space of indistinction produced by Agamben's state of exception.

66. As Agamben argues, "together with the process by which the exception everywhere becomes the rule, the realm of bare life . . . gradually begins to coincide with the political realm." Agamben, *Homo Sacer*, p. 9.

67. In the sense elaborated by Foucault above.

68. "Bare life" in Agamben's work.

69. Rosi Braidotti, *Transpositions: On Nomadic Ethics*. Cambridge: Polity Press, 2006. p. 265. Braidotti also states, "my affinity for *zoe* as generative pre-human vitality, against the negative rendition made of it by Agamben and others who are influenced by Heidegger, rests on the fact that *zoe* has historically been feminized. Women were classified alongside natives, animals, and others as referents of a generative force that was reduced to a mere biological function and deprived of political and ethical relevance." p. 270.

70. Unlike Braidotti, who makes a convincing case for decentering Thanatos, I focus in some detail on death as an aspect of legal ecstasy. At the same time, however, I also suggest that death need not be understood as necessarily negative in this context.

71. See, for example, Veena Das, Arthur Kleinman, Mamphela Ramphele, and Pamela Reynolds, *Violence and Subjectivity*. Berkeley: University of California Press, 2000. "Because most of the essays [in this collection] are located in spaces in which ongoing

violence has blurred boundaries between violence, conflict, and peaceful resolution, they look at these issues from an off-the-center position in two senses. First, they ask how people engage in the tasks of daily living, rehabiting the world in the full recognition that perpetrators, victims, and witnesses come from the same social space. Second, they seek to analyze not only the explicit acts of bodily harm that occur in violent conflict but also the more subtle forms of violence perpetrated by institutions of science and the state . . . [T]hese ethnographies reveal that larger social actors . . . are all implicated in the actualization of the violence that transforms the everyday life of local communities." p. 2.

72. W. H. Hobbs, "The Messina Earthquake," *Bulletin of the American Geographical Society* 41 (7) (1909): 409–422. p. 409.

73. *The American Red Cross Annual Report for the Year Ended June 30, 1918*, p. 86.

74. This is perhaps a deliberate echo of Rousseau's response to Voltaire's horror at the 1755 Lisbon earthquake, in which he argued that "earthquakes did happen in deserts, but they caused no comparable damage because the local 'savages' were scattered across the land and therefore endangered by neither 'the fall of housetops, nor the conflagration of houses.' The problem, in other words, was not earthquakes, but reckless urbanization . . . [C]ivilization, in short, was less a cure for disasters than a cause." As paraphrased and analyzed in Kevin Rozario, *The Culture of Calamity: Disaster and the Making of Modern America*. Chicago: University of Chicago Press, 2007. p. 19.

75. For a careful, well researched example of this genre, see Dayna Bowen Matthew, "Disastrous Disasters: Restoring Civil Rights Protections for Victims of the State in Natural Disasters," *Journal of Health and Biomedical Law* 2 (2006): 213–248.

76. Again, my goal here is by no means to deny the unquestionably racist or imperial nature of much modern disaster response.

77. See, for instance, George A. Finch, "Piracy in the Mediterranean," *American Journal of International Law* 31 (4) (Oct. 1937): 659–665, and Raoul Genet, "The Charge of Piracy in the Spanish Civil War," *American Journal of International Law* 32 (2) (April 1938): 255–256.

78. Braidotti, *Patterns of Dissonance*, p. 52.

79. Ibid, p. 52.

80. Ibid, p. 52.

81. Ibid, p. 38.

82. Ibid, p. 74.

83. I should emphasize that although I rely on the work of scholars in each camp, I am very much aware that there is (or was) a divide between gender theorists and sexual difference theorists, especially in the early 1990s. I am also very much aware that Braidotti represents for the most part sexual difference theory, rather than gender studies. I nonetheless refer to "gender studies" in a broad way in this book as a field that also includes those sexual difference theorists who critique gender as an effective analytical category. For more on this conversation, see Johanna Foster, "An Invitation to Dialogue: Clarifying

the Position of Feminist Gender Theory in Relation to Sexual Difference Theory," *Gender and Society* 13 (4) (August 1999): 431–456. See also, "reacting even more passionately against the supposed idealism or 'mentalism' of gender as a cultural norm, there have been arguments that sexual difference is ontological and constitutive of the subject (Braidotti 1989, 102), and that the body should be thought in its sexual specificity (Grosz 1994, 19) . . . [S]exuality would not be one issue among others, precisely because sexual difference is fundamental to the production of subjectivity in general." Abigail Bray and Claire Colebrook, "The Haunted Flesh: Corporeal Feminism and the Politics of (Dis)Embodiment," *Signs* 24 (1) (Autumn, 1998): 35–67. p. 41. For Braidotti's own succinct analysis of sexual difference theory, see Rosi Braidotti, *Metamorphoses: Toward a Materialist Theory of Becoming.* Cambridge: Polity Press, 2002. pp. 28–34.

84. For example, "while we are bound to recognize, following Nietzsche, that at times of crisis every culture tends to turn to its 'others,' to become feminized, in the sense of having to face its limitations, gaps, and deficiencies, on the other hand it should also be said that the thought, speech, and actual agency of these same 'others,' namely feminist theory and practice, do play an important function in bringing about this 'crisis.'" Braidotti, *Patterns of Dissonance*, p. 11.

85. Braidotti, *Patterns of Dissonance* p. 218.

86. As Mary Hawkesworth has argued with regard to Butler's theories of gender and desire, "Butler denounces the modes of power that produce homosexuality as necessary, yet prohibited; within culture, yet marginalized." Mary Hawkesworth, "Confounding Gender," *Signs* 22 (3) (Spring, 1997): 649–685. p. 666.

87. I should emphasize that when I talk about the ecstatic subject, I am not talking about the "condition of dispossession of the bodily self, a structurally splintered position which is historically associated with femininity as a symbolic mark of absence and with women as its empirical referent." Braidotti, *Metamorphoses*, p. 76. As will become clear over the following chapters, my understanding of ecstatic subjectivity is more complex—and more active—than this traditional notion of splintered feminine dispossession.

88. For more on this function of law in critical theory, see the previous section on legal ecstasy. For more on this function of law in liberal theory, see, for instance, the work of Jean-Jacques Rousseau: "as to the associates, they collectively take the name *people*; individually they are called *citizens*, insofar as participants in the sovereign authority, and *subjects*, insofar as they are subjected to the laws of the state. But these terms are often confused and mistaken for one another." Jean-Jacques Rousseau, *On the Social Contract.* Trans. Donald A. Cress. Indianapolis: Hackett Publishing Co., 1987. p. 25. Italics in original.

89. As Lawrence Rosen puts it: "law is so inextricably entwined in culture that, for all its specialized capabilities, it may, indeed, best be seen not simply as a mechanism for attending to disputes or enforcing decisions, not solely as articulated rules or as evidence of differential power, and not even as the reification of personal values or superordinate be-

liefs, but as a framework for ordered relationships, an orderliness that is itself dependent on its attachment to all the other realms of its adherents' lives." Lawrence Rosen, *Law as Culture: An Invitation*. Princeton: Princeton University Press, 2006. p. 7.

90. Rousseau's theory of participatory democracy, for instance, "rests on his ideas of consent and membership: on his conception of consent as being constantly re-affirmed through the continuous participation of the members, and not that of any body of officials or representatives, that consent gives rise to." E. D. Watt, "Rousseau Réchaufée—Being Obliged, Consenting, Participating, and Obeying only Oneself," *Journal of Politics* 43 (4) (August 1981): 707–719. p. 707.

91. "The subject always faces the risk of slipping away from the symbolic into the Real. A final merger with the Real is 'ceasing-to-be'—negative becoming, or psychosis. The subject resists this descent into darkness by striving to recognize itself symbolically . . . [L]anguage and law provide a refuge against psychosis. Yet the materials found there are never adequate to the subject. If I am purely symbolic, I have no identity whatsoever. Rather, I reduce myself to the point where I am just an object to others. Too much objectification is a bad thing—the indicium of hysteria. It is pornography as such." David Gray Carlson, "The Traumatic Dimension in Law," *Cardozo Law Review* 24 (August 2003): 2287–2329. pp. 2292–2293.

92. Interpellation as it was initially theorized by Louis Althusser: "this account appears to imply that social existence, existence as a subject, can be purchased only through a guilty embrace of the law, where guilt guarantees the intervention of the law and, hence, the continuation of the subject's existence. If the subject can only assure his/her existence in terms of the law, and the law requires subjection for subjectivation, then, perversely, one may (always already) yield to the law in order to continue to assure one's own existence. The yielding to the law might then be read as the compelled consequence of a narcissistic attachment to one's continuing existence." Butler, *Psychic Life of Power*, pp. 112–113.

93. It is true, as I have noted, that the line between disaster law and everyday law is not as distinct as it might appear to be—and that I blur that line further in the chapters that follow.

94. See the section "Natural Disasters and Metaphysical Disasters" in this chapter.

95. "Women, it is held, are a source of disorder because their being, or their nature, is such that it necessarily leads them to exert a disruptive influence in social and political life. Women have a disorder at their very centres—in their morality—which can bring about the destruction of the state." Carole Pateman, *The Disorder of Women: Democracy Feminism, and Political Theory*. Stanford: Stanford University Press, 1989. p. 18

96. We can see this especially in the elaboration of international human rights law. Ruth A. Miller, *The Limits of Bodily Integrity: Abortion, Adultery, and Rape Legislation in Comparative Perspective*. Aldershot: Ashgate Press, 2007. pp. 172–173.

97. As Butler argues in a more Lacanian vein, "what constitutes the limit of the thinkable, the narratable, the intelligible? What constitutes *the limit of what can be thought as true*? These are, I believe, questions that psychoanalysis has always interrogated precisely because it relies on a form of analytic listening and a form or 'reading' which takes for granted that what is constituted as the thinkable realm is predicated on the exclusion (repression or foreclosure) of what remains difficult or impossible to think. This is, of course, not to say that nothing is thought, that no story is told, and no representation made, but only to say that whatever story and representation emerge to account for this event, which is no event, will be subject to this same catachresis that I perform when I speak about it improperly as an event; it will be one that must be read for what it indicates, but cannot say, or for the unsayable in what is said. What remains crucial is a form of reading that does not try to find the truth of what happened, but, rather, asks, what has this non-happening done to the question of truth? For part of the effect of that violation, when it is one, is precisely to make the knowing of truth into an infinitely remote prospect; this is its epistemic violence. To insist, then, on verifying the truth is precisely to miss the effect of the violation in question, which is to put the knowability of truth into enduring crisis." Butler, *Undoing*, pp. 156–157.

98. Pheng Cheah, *Inhuman Conditions: On Cosmopolitanism and Human Rights*. Cambridge: Harvard University Press, 2006. p. 13.

99. Fatma Ürekli, *İstanbul'da 1894 Depremi*. Istanbul: İle̦sitim Yayınları, 1995. p. 15.

Chapter Two

1. Rozario, p. 13.

2. Again, "there was no constitutive or structural opposition between science and spirituality. The opposition was between theological thought and the requirement of spirituality. Thus the disengagement did not take place abruptly with the appearance of modern science." Foucault, *Hermeneutics*, p. 27.

3. Leopold Wettersteint de Hodenstein, "A Full Account of the Great and Terrible Earthquake in Germany, Hungary and Turkey." Trans. Rich Alcock. London: R. C., 1673. p. 8. Italics in original.

4. "The Light in Which We Are Taught by the World of God to Consider Earthquakes," *Gentleman's Magazine* 20 (April 1750): 169.

5. Maxine Van de Wetering, "Moralizing in Puritan Natural Science: Mysteriousness in Earthquake Sermons," *Journal of the History of Ideas* 43 (3) (July–Sept. 1982): 417–438. pp. 423–424.

6. Ibid, pp. 423–424.

7. Ibid, p. 429.

8. Ibid, p. 436.

9. For a further variation on the supernatural characteristics of the sovereign (in the Ottoman context), his role in law making, and how this relates to moments of disaster, see: "In his memoirs, Lutfi Simavi, a high palace functionary, mentions the common belief that raging fires in the city would at once be extinguished as soon as the Sultan personally arrived on the scene. The documentary record suggests the Sultans in fact routinely sped to sites of fires, even at night. Sultan Selim III, for example, immediately boarded his imperial boat on seeing smoke rising from the Asian side of Istanbul on July 9, 1791. He reached the place and stayed there until the fire was extinguished. On his way back to the palace he spotted another fire and raced to that location as well." Hakan Karateke, "Opium for the Subjects? Religiosity as a Legitimizing Factor for the Ottoman Sultan." Eds. Hakan Karateke and Maurus Reinkowski. *Legitimizing the Order: The Ottoman Rhetoric of State Power.* Leiden: Brill, 2005. pp. 114–115.

10. Rita Goldberg, "Voltaire, Rousseau, and the Lisbon Earthquake," *Eighteenth Century Life* 13 (2) (1989): 1–20, p. 1.

11. Ibid, pp. 1–2.

12. Ibid, p. 1.

13. For more on the particularly chaotic nature of Lisbon, "It is scarcely hyperbolic to say, that the very fabric of nature seems ready to be resolved into its primary elements, and the reign of chaos threatens to return . . . [A] new quay, covered with a vast concourse of people, sunk in an instant, to an unfathomable depth. It is remarkable, that not a single corpse out of the whole number ever rose to the surface." "Observations on Earthquakes," *The Port-Folio,* 7 (5) (May 1812): 421–436, pp. 422–423, 427.

14. David Hume, "An Essay on Civil Liberty," *The Columbia Magazine* (January 1788): 9–14. p. 11. Emphasis in original.

15. See, for instance, "Ancient and Modern Eloquence," *Blackwood's Edinburgh Magazine* 68 (422) (Dec. 1850): 655.

16. "Free Trade at its Zenith," *Blackwood's Edinburgh Magazine* 66 (410) (Dec. 1849): 776.

17. "Sir Robert Peel," *Blackwood's Edinburgh Magazine* 68 (419) (Sept. 1850): 358.

18. "Results of Revolution in Europe" *Blackwood's Edinburgh Magazine* 7 (436) (Feb. 1852): 242–257, p. 249. See also, pp. 244–245.

19. "The European Crisis," *Saturday Evening Post* (Sept. 26, 1857): 2.

20. "Wars Between France and England," *The Friend of Peace* 4 (1815): 34–5. p. 35.

21. Ibid, p. 35. Italics in original.

22. Sheila Hones, "Natural and Unnatural Wars." Eds. James D. Proctor and David M. Smith. *Geography and Ethics: Journeys in a Moral Terrain.* London and New York: Routledge, 1999, pp. 163–175. pp. 167, 172–173.

23. Ibid, pp. 167, 172–173.

24. Thus producing a link to Burke's well-traveled "moral earthquake."

25. C. H. D. "The Moral Effects of Earthquakes," *New Peterson Magazine* (3) (March, 1894): 293–294. p. 294.

26. For a contemporary variation on this argument, see Jared Diamond, *Guns, Germs and Steel: The Fates of Human Societies*. New York: W. W. Norton, 2005.

27. "Germany in Earthquake," *Current Opinion* 6 (Dec 1. 1923): 654–657. p. 654.

28. I emphasize that these are two different texts, separated by a number of years. My point here is more a point about the broader discourse in which these two articles are engaging.

29. Stephen Bonsal, "The Philippines—After an Earthquake," *The North American Review* 174 (March, 1902): 409–421. p. 410.

30. Bediüzzaman Said Nursi, "Deprem ve Hikmetleri," *Risale-i Nur Külliyatında*. Istanbul: Bayrak Mat., 1999. p. 7. For more on Said Nursi and his work, see Şerif Mardin, *Religion and Social Change in Modern Turkey: The Case of Bediuzzaman Said Nursi*. Albany: State University of New York Press, 1990, and Ibrahim M. Abu-Rabi, ed. *Islam at the Crossroads: On the Life and Thought of Bediuzzaman Said Nursi*. Albany: State University of New York Press, 2003.

31. Said Nursi, pp. 2–3.

32. Ibid, p. 11.

33. Susan J. Napier, "Panic Sites: The Japanese Imagination of Disaster from Godzilla to Akira," *Journal of Japanese Studies* 19(2) (Summer 1993): 327–351. p. 331.

34. Daniel A. Farber and Jim Chen, *Disasters and the Law: Katrina and Beyond*. New York: Aspen Publishers, 2006. pp. 2–3. See also, "Weber's body of work seems relevant to sociological studies of disaster. His conceptualization of ideal types provides a way to explain why the term 'disaster,' culturally identified with multiple simultaneous deaths (or the threat thereof) perceived to be the result of natural forces, is so resistant to redefinition (such as to encompass the crimes of a serial killer or the crash of a stock market) . . . [D]isasters are invaluable opportunities to study sense-making mechanisms, at both collective and individual levels, in their most visible forms." Robert A. Stallings, "Weberian Political Sociology and Sociological Disaster Studies," *Sociological Forum* 17 (2) (June 2002): 281–305. pp. 283, 300.

35. J. Michael Allen, "The Price of Identity: The 1923 Kantō Earthquake and Its Aftermath," *Korean Studies* 20 (1996): 64–93. pp. 64–65.

36. Ibid, pp. 64–65.

37. Anthony Oliver-Smith, "Peru's Five-Hundred year Earthquake: Vulnerability in Historical Context." Eds. Anthony Oliver-Smith and Susanna M. Hoffman. *The Angry Earth: Disaster in Anthropological Perspective*. London: Routledge, 1999, pp. 74–89. p. 84.

38. Ibid, p. 84.

39. A related theme that appears in the field of catastrophe studies is that disasters occur around vulnerable populations or, more explicitly, at centers of vulnerability. A disaster is endowed with meaning in these analyses upon the invocation of vulnerable

spaces or vulnerable bodies, and thus it is not cultural centrality that makes the disaster intelligible, but rather exposure to violence. Greg Bankoff, for instance, has critiqued geographies that seek to define "defenseless spaces" and "spaces of vulnerability"—"regions . . . where a population's vulnerability is enhanced by the operation of despotic or illegitimate governments," and where populations are "at risk, not simply because they are exposed to hazard, but as a result of a marginality that makes their life a 'permanent emergency.'" Greg Bankoff, *Cultures of Disaster: Society and Natural Hazard in the Philippines*. London: Routledge Curzon, 2003. pp. 12–13. As Robert Bolin and Lois Stanford have argued in a less critical vein, "while physical exposure to risk is a necessary element in vulnerability, it is people's lack of capacities that transform environmental hazard into a disaster." Robert Bolin and Lois Stanford, "Constructing Vulnerability in the First World: The Northridge Earthquake in Southern California, 1994," in Oliver-Smith and Hoffman, pp. 89–113. p. 90.

40. Gregory V. Button, "The Negotiation of Disaster: The Media Response to Oil Spills in Great Britain," in Oliver-Smith and Hoffman, pp. 113–133. p. 129–130.

41. John Taylor, *Body Horror: Photojournalism, Catastrophe, and War*. New York: New York University Press, 1998. p. 87.

42. Elana Gomel, "The Plague of Utopias: Pestilence and the Apocalyptic Body," *Twentieth Century Literature* 46 (4) (Winter, 2000): 405–433. pp. 405.

43. Ibid, pp. 405–406.

44. Stallings, pp. 283, 300.

45. Veena Das, "The Act of Witnessing: Violence, Poisonous Knowledge, and Subjectivity." Eds. Veena Das, Arthur Kleinman, Mamphela Ramphele, and Pamela Reynolds. *Violence and Subjectivity*. Berkeley: University of California Press, 2000. pp. 203–225. p. 208.

46. Maureen Fordham and Anne-Michele Ketteridge, "'Men Must Work and Women Must Weep': Examining Gender Stereotypes in Disasters." Eds. Elaine Enarson and Betty Hearn Morrow. *The Gendered Terrain of Disaster: Through Women's Eyes*. Westport, C.T.: Praeger, 1998, pp. 81–95. pp. 83, 89.

47. Another work that at least implicitly seeks the truth of the disaster in the realm of the everyday is Kevin Rozario's *The Culture of Calamity: Disaster and the Making of Modern America*. Taking as a starting point the idea that there is "an intimate connection between calamity and modern American economic, political, and cultural developments" (p. 24), Rozario situates various U.S. progress narratives within a history of successive disaster—pointing out, for example, that many early twentieth-century industrialists viewed the San Francisco earthquake as an "opportunity" for progress and expansion (pp. 75–76), and that disaster narratives were often viewed as a means of rescuing Americans from an "inauthentic" daily life. Rozario, pp. 114, 166–167.

48. Mike Davis, *Dead Cities*. New York: The New Press, 2002. p. 402.

Chapter Three

1. “Mary E. Schloendorff v. The Society of the New York Hospital,” Court of Appeals of New York, 211 N.Y. 125; 105 N.E. 92 (1914). One of the most well-known passages from this case is the following: “In the case at hand, the wrong complained of is not merely negligence. It is trespass. Every human being of adult years and sound mind has a right to determine what shall be done with his own body; and a surgeon who performs an operation without his patient’s consent, commits an assault, for which he is liable in damages. (*Pratt v. Davis, 224 Ill. 300*; *Mohr v. Williams, 95 Minn. 261.*) This is true except in cases of emergency where the patient is unconscious and where it is necessary to operate before consent can be obtained. The fact that the wrong complained of here is trespass rather than negligence, distinguishes this case from most of the cases that have preceded it. In such circumstances the hospital’s exemption from liability can hardly rest upon implied waiver. Relatively to this transaction, the plaintiff was a stranger. She had never consented to become a patient for any purpose other than an examination under ether. She had never waived the right to recover damages for any wrong resulting from this operation, for she had forbidden the operation. In this situation, the true ground for the defendant’s exemption from liability is that the relation between a hospital and its physicians is not that of master and servant. The hospital does not undertake to act through them, but merely to procure them to act upon their own responsibility.” pp. 93–94.

2. See, for instance, Elaine Scarry, “Consent and the Body: Injury, Departure, and Desire,” *New Literary History* 21 (Autumn, 1990): 867–896. p. 868.

3. Paul A. Lombardo, “Phantom Tumors and Hysterical Women: Revising our View of the Schloendorff Case,” *Journal of Law, Medicine & Ethics,* Winter 33 (2005): 791–800. p. 795.

4. Ibid, p. 795.

5. Ibid, p. 795.

6. Ibid, p. 795.

7. For an interesting theoretical take on dismemberment as a mode of subjectivity, see Braidotti’s point that Deleuze redefines “the interface between intentionality and desire at a historical time when the subject is dismembered and re-located along multiple axes.” Braidotti, *Metamorphoses*, p. 101.

8. See, for instance, Schloendorff’s further testimony: “Upon making his rounds Dr. Stimson (the surgeon) ‘playfully punched me with his fist in the abdomen; in a playful way he said, How are you, how do you feel old girl? I screamed in agony at the pain he gave me.’ The same explanations for her ‘imagined’ pain were given to her son Evan Gamble. ‘She was suffering no pain’ the doctor said, ‘she only imagined it.’” Lombardo, pp. 796–797.

9. This process is arguably one logical conclusion to the processes discussed by Edward H. Levi and Cardozo himself when they address the construction of “legal con-

cepts": "It may be that this analysis of legal reasoning places too much emphasis on the comparison of cases and too little on the legal concepts which are created. It is true that similarity is seen in terms if a word, and inability to find a ready word to express similarity or difference may prevent change in the law. The words which have been found in the past are much spoke of, have acquired a dignity of their own, and to a considerable measure control results. As Judge Cardozo suggested in speaking of metaphors, the word starts out to free thought and ends by enslaving it. [fn. 10: Berkey v. Third Ave. Ry. Co., 244 N.Y. 84, 94, 155 N.E. 58, 61 (1926).] . . . [B]ut it is not simply deductive. In the long run a circular motion can be seen. The first stage is the creation of the legal concept which is built up as cases are compared . . . [T]he second stage is the period when the concept is more or less fixed, although reasoning by example continues to classify items inside and out of the concept. The third stage is the breakdown of the concept, as reasoning by example has moved so far ahead as to make it clear that the suggestive influence of the word is no longer desired." Edward H. Levi, *An Introduction to Legal Reasoning*. Chicago: University of Chicago Press, 1949. pp. 8–9.

10. Frederick H. Dewey, "How an Earthquake Looks and Feels," *Lippincott's Monthly Magazine* (April 1899): 527–531. p. 531.

11. F. Peyre Porcher, "Influence of the Charleston Earthquakes on Health," *Medical News* 50 (5) (Jan. 29, 1887): 138. p. 138. Italics in original.

12. "Effects of Earthquake on the Emotions," *Current Literature* (49) (4) (1910): 6–7. p. 6.

13. I am not arguing that liberal rights-rhetoric is a particularly effective vocabulary for articulating women's political identity. In the context of this piece, however, political identity is couched in liberal language, and I am trying to engage with the text on its own terms.

14. For a more detailed analysis of the relationship between the shattered subject and the shattered or dismembered body (and the erotic potential of this relationship) see the work of George Bataille. In his *Tears of Eros*, especially, there is a three-page spread of photographs from April 1905 detailing the "Chinese torture" of the "*Hundred Pieces*," in which a body is slowly dismembered, and in which, Bataille argues, the subject exhibits unquestionable moments of "ecstasy." Georges Bataille, *Tears of Eros*. Trans. Peter Conner. San Francisco: City Light Books, 1989. pp. 204–206.

15. Emiko Ohnuki-Tierney, "Brain Death and Organ Transplant: Cultural Bases of Medical Technology," *Current Anthropology* 35 (3) (June 1994): 233–254, p. 233.

16. Ibid, p. 234.

17. Ibid, p. 237. Italics in original.

18. Ibid, p. 234. Italics in original.

19. Ibid, p. 233.

20. Margaret Locke, "Deadly Disputes: Hybrid Selves and the Calculation of Death in Japan and North America," *Osiris* 13 (1998): 410–429. pp. 412–13.

21. This point is something of a play on Braidotti's argument that, "for Deleuze the body is a surface where forces play. They are not the expression of in-depth interiority or the enactment of transcendental models; there is nothing essentialist or primordial about Deleuzian bodies. They are the play of different forces, and as such they are pure simulacra. The bodily surface is to be thought as repetition or the external return of these forces, without, however, a model or a single pattern that gets repeated; it is an intensive discontinuity in which the subject disintegrates. This definition of multiplicity on the dispersion of the subject opens up the question of the void. Given that, in the tradition of Western metaphysics, thinking always means thinking about something, how are we to understand the new intransitive status reached by contemporary theories of subjectivity such as Deleuze's?" Braidotti, *Patterns of Dissonance*, p. 74.

22. Braidotti, *Nomadic Subjects*, pp. 52–53. Braidotti is using a Deleuzian framework here to make what I think is a more Foucauldian point about bodies, populations, and biopower.

23. Pheng Cheah, *Spectral Nationality*, p. 153.

24. Ibid, p. 352.

25. Butler, *Undoing*, p. 66.

26. Ibid, p. 66.

27. Ibid, p. 66.

28. See the analyses of Achille Mbembe and Antony Anghie in "Ecstatic Space," Chapter Five.

29. Claude Bernard, *Les Proprièt̀ès Physiologiques et Les Altérations Pathologiques des Liquides de L'organisme*, vol. 1. Paris: J. B. Baillière et Fils, 1859. p. 45.

30. Ibid, p. 469.

31. Ibid, p. 44.

32. Ibid, p. 470.

33. Esin Kâhya, *Ondokuzunca Yüzyılda Osmanlı İmparatorluğu'na Tip Eğitimi ve Türk Hekimleri*. Ankara: Atatürk Kültür Merkezi Başkanlığı, 1997. p. 17.

34. From Şanizade Mehmet Ataullah, Hamse-i Şanizade, vol. 2, in Kâhya, p. 26.

35. Kâhya, p. 50.

36. According to Mehmet Şakir in Kâhya, pp. 50–51.

37. "Blood," *Blackwood's Edinburgh Magazine* 83 (512) (June 1858): 687–696. p. 692.

38. Ibid, p. 692. Italics in original.

39. For more on political subjectivity and pregnancy, see Miller, *The Limits of Bodily Integrity*.

40. "The first transfusion center was created in a Parisian hospital in 1923. At the time, transfusions were carried out from 'arm to arm.' Those who provided blood were paid for their 'donations.' Private doctors as well as public hospitals developed networks of professional donors who would provide blood on demand." Eric A. Feldman, "HIV and Blood in Japan: Transforming Private Conflict into Public Scandal." Eds. Eric A.

Feldman and Ronald Bayer. *Blood Feuds: AIDS, Blood, and the Politics of Medical Disaster.* New York: Oxford University Press, 1999, pp. 59–95. p. 68.

41. Nermin Aygen, *Türklerin Kan Grupları ve Kan Gruplarının Antropolojik Karakterlerle İlgisi Üzerine bir Araştırman.* Ankara: İdeal Basımevi, 1946. pp. 2–3.

42. Ibid, p. 12.

43. Luise White, "Cars Out of Place: Vampires, Technology, and Labor in East and Central Africa," *Representations* 43 (Summer 1993): 27–50. pp. 30–31.

44. For more on the literary relationship between blood and fears of (reverse) colonialism, see Stephen Arata, "The Occidental Tourist: Dracula and the Anxiety of Reverse Colonization," *Victorian Studies* 33 (1990): 621–645.

45. Amy Lyford, "The Aesthetics of Dismemberment: Surrealism and the Musée de Val-de-Grace in 1917," *Cultural Critique* 46 (Autumn 2000): 45–79. p. 52. Italics in original.

46. Ibid, p. 52.

47. Ibid, p. 67.

48. We can see a related (if less critical) reinterpretation of the dismembered body—and its artistic potential—in the following passage from the 1918 report of the American Red Cross: "The booklets on reconstructing the wounded soldier and rehabilitating the war cripple were widely distributed and the staff of the Institute delivered many lectures and provided many pictures, lantern slides, etc. for civic bodies interested in the work . . . [A]t the Institute in New York various departments for training cripples have been inaugurated, such as artificial limb making, drafting, oxy-acetylene welding, printing, etc. and civilian cripples have been and are now being trained." *American Red Cross Annual Report*, pp. 74–75.

49. James Russell Wilson, *San Francisco's Horror of Earthquake and Fire.* New York: G. W. Bertron, 1906. pp. 36–37.

50. As Butler paraphrasing (and critiquing) Althusser puts it, "in the infamous example that Althusser offers, a policeman hails a passerby on the street, and the passerby turns and recognizes himself as the one who is hailed. In the exchange by which recognition is proffered and accepted, interpellation—the discursive production of the social subject—takes place." Judith Butler, *The Psychic Life of Power*, p. 5.

51. Otis Manchester Poole, *The Death of Old Yokohama in the Great Japanese Earthquake of Sept. 1, 1923.* London: George Allen and Unwin, Ltd. 1968. p. 120.

52. R. O. Matheson, "Through the Inferno of the Japanese Earthquake," *McClure's Magazine* 56 (1) (Jan. 1924): 8–21. p. 17.

53. See "Cemeteries" in Chapter Five, especially, for more on the complexity of the monument as something that demonstrates the reality of the disaster.

54. "Cahil olabılırım," *Hürriyet* (August 24, 1999): http://arama.hurriyet.com.tr/arsivnews.aspx?id=-97804.

55. Ibid.

56. Ibid.

57. "Basını, Yunanlılara şikayet etti," *Hürriyet* (September 20, 1999): http://arama.hurriyet.com.tr/arsivnews.aspx?id=-102913.

58. Ibid.

59. "Yunan Sağlık Bakanı: 'Biz Türk kanı alırız,'" *Milliyet* (Eylül 11, 1999): http://www.milliyet.com.tr/1999/09/11/index.html.

60. "Organ mafyası kimsesiz çocuk peşinde, uyarısı," *Hürriyet* (August 27, 1999): http://arama.hurriyet.com.tr/arsivnews.aspx?id=-98545.

61. Ahmet Şik, "'Öleni kıskanıyorum,'" *Radikal* (August 17, 2000): http://www.belgenet.com/deprem/170800_r17.html.

62. See below for more on looters and "ghouls."

63. Noah Webster, "A Brief History of Epidemic and Pestilential Diseases," *The Medical Repository of Original Essays and Intelligence* 3 (3) (1800): 278–288. pp. 278–279.

64. Ibid, p. 283.

65. Noah Webster, "On the Connection of Earthquakes and Epidemic Diseases," *The Medical Repository of Original Essays and Intelligence* 4 (1801): 350–345. p. 342.

66. "Earthquake at Lisbon," *The American Magazine of Useful and Entertaining Knowledge* 3 (12) (Sept. 1, 1837): 452–455. p. 455.

67. Ürekli, p. 27.

68. BOA İrade Hus. 180/18 M 1312, as reproduced in Mehmet Genç and Mehmet Mazak, eds. *İstanbul Depremleri: Fotoğraf ve Belgelerde 1894 Depremi*. İstanbul: İğdaş Kültürel Yayınları, 2000. pp. 208–209. A note is needed here to explain the nature of Genç and Mazak's work. On facing pages are reproduced photographs of documents from the 1894 earthquake kept in a special file in the Başbakanlık Archive and the editors' modern Turkish translations/transliterations of these documents. Throughout this book, I rely equally on both the modern Turkish translations and my own reading of the documents shown in the photographs.

69. Maj. Gen. Adolphus W. Greely, *Earthquake in California—April 18, 1906—Special Report*. Washington, D.C.: Government Printing Office, 1906. p. 34.

70. Ibid, p. 33.

71. Ibid, p. 34.

72. S. P. Jocelyn, General Orders, Provost General, April 22, 1906 in Greely, p. 57.

73. Wilson, *San Francisco's Horror*, pp. 236–237. Here, in other words, the fear or possibility of infectious disease gave way to the reality of mental disease—and the thing that was particularly horrific was that, with the sane but potentially infected people occupying the camps, there was no place to put the demented.

74. Bureau of Social Affairs, *The Great Earthquake of 1923 in Japan*. Japan: The Home Office, 1926. p. 75.

75. Ibid, p. 96.

76. I am by no means arguing that various disease control measures do not prevent the spread of disease. Nor am I arguing that the medical and legal institutions that respond to disasters do not seek the health and prosperity of the populations they serve. Rather, I am suggesting that an equally important aspect of medico-legal disease control is the designation—or even creation—of ecstatic, eccentric subjects of law. I am arguing that even as medical institutions define the marginal as the most vulnerable to disease, as these institutions develop methods of protecting marginal groups, they are also producing or creating both marginality and vulnerability—and thus the reality of the disaster.

77. "Salgın hastalık tehlikesi," *Hürriyet* (August 22, 1999): http://arama.hurriyet.com.tr/arsivnews.aspx?id=-97540.

78. "Bobrek tehlikesi," *Hürriyet* (August 31, 1999): http://arama.hurriyet.com.tr/arsivnews.aspx?id=-99338.

79. "Depremzedede uyuz ve fare korkusu," *Hürriyet* (August 31, 1999): http://arama.hurriyet.com.tr/arsivnews.aspx?id=-99307.

80. "Deprem, çocuklarda psiko travma nedeni," *Hürriyet* (August 31, 1999): http://arama.hurriyet.com.tr/arsivnews.aspx?id=-99267.

81. "Deprem, erkek doğumlarını azaltır," *Hürriyet* (August 28, 1999): http://arama.hurriyet.com.tr/arsivnews.aspx?id=-98749.

82. For more on women citizens and the right to bodily integrity, see Miller, *The Limits of Bodily Integrity.*

83. "A man carrying a package jumped aboard a car of a moving train and, seeming unsteady as if about to fall, a guard on the car reached forward to help him in and another guard on the platform pushed him from behind, during which the package was dislodged and falling upon the rails exploded, causing injuries to plaintiff, an intending passenger, who stood on the platform many feet away. There was nothing in the appearance of the package to give notice that it contained explosives. In an action by the intending passenger against the railroad company to recover for such injuries, the complaint should be dismissed. Negligence is not actionable unless it involves the invasion of a legally protected interest, the violation of a right, and the conduct of the defendant's guards, if a wrong in relation to the holder of the package, was not a wrong in its relation to the plaintiff standing many feet away." "Palsgraf v. Long Island Railroad," Court of Appeals of New York 248 N.Y. 339 (1928). p. 339.

84. What particular rights these are I will discuss in a moment.

85. "Palsgraf" (dissent), p. 349.

86. "Palsgraf," p. 341.

87. "Palsgraf" (dissent), p. 352.

88. "The man [who started the chain of events—not Palsgraf herself] was not injured in his person nor even put in danger. The purpose of the act, as well as its effect, was to make his person safe. If there was a wrong to him at all, which may very well be doubted,

it was a wrong to a property interest only, the safety of his package. Out of this wrong to property, which threatened injury to nothing else, there has passed, we are told, to the plaintiff by derivation or succession a right of action for the invasion of an interest of another order, the right to bodily security. The diversity of interests emphasizes the futility of the effort to build the plaintiff's right upon the basis of a wrong to some one else." "Palsgraf," p. 343.

89. "Palsgraf" (dissent), p. 355.

90. The passage continues, "One who seeks redress at law does not make out a cause of action by showing without more that there has been damage to his person. If the harm was not willful, he must show that the act as to him had possibilities of danger so many and apparent as to entitle him to be protected against the doing of it though the harm was unintended. Affront to personality is still the keynote of the wrong." "Palsgraf," p. 345.

91. It is worth pointing out that one of the principal symptoms Palsgraf suffered after the injury was a "stuttering condition induced by the accident." Andrew L. Kaufman, *Cardozo*. Cambridge: Harvard University Press, 1998. pp. 286–287.

Chapter Four

1. Edouard Conte and Cornelia Essner, *La Quête de la Race: Une Anthropologie du Nazisme*. Paris: Hachette, 1995. p. 151.

2. Ibid, p. 173.

3. Art. 410. "If the guilty person disfigures or mutilates the corpse, or in any manner commits upon it acts of brutality or obscenity he shall be punished with penal servitude from 3 to 6 years." Italy, *Penal Code of the Kingdom of Italy*. London: His Majesty's Stationery Office, 1931. pp. 113–114. (art. 408–413)

4. Literally, a ghoul is a demon or monster who inhabits graveyards and eats the dead.

5. "What does having the right of life and death actually mean? In one sense, to say that the sovereign has a right of life and death means that he can, basically, either have people put to death or let them live, or in any case that life and death are not natural or immediate phenomena which are primal or radical, and which fall outside the field of power. If we take the argument a little further, or to the point when it becomes paradoxical, it means that in terms of his relationship with the sovereign, the subject is, by rights, neither dead nor alive. From the point of view of life and death, the subject is neutral, and it is thanks to the sovereign that the subject has the right to be alive or, possible, the right to be dead." Michel Foucault, *"Society Must Be Defended": Lectures at the Collège de France, 1975–1976*. Trans. David Macey. New York: Picador, 2003. p. 240.

6. Ibid, p. 241.

7. Ibid, p. 245.

8. "Death is outside the power relationship. Death is beyond the reach of power, and power has a grip on it only in general, overall, or statistical terms . . . [P]ower no longer recognizes death. Power literally ignores death." Ibid, p. 248.

9. *American Red Cross Annual Report for the Year Ending June 30, 1920*. p. 16.

10. *American Red Cross Annual Report for the Year Ending June 30, 1919*. p. 60.

11. For an excellent analysis of this process, see Robert E. Goodin, Carole Pateman, and Roy Pateman, "Simian Sovereignty," *Political Theory* 25 (6) (Dec. 1997): 821–849.

12. Slavoj Zizek, "Melancholy and the Act," *Critical Inquiry* 26 (4) (Summer 2000): 657–681. p. 661.

13. "Then did the little maid reply / 'Seven boys and girls are we / Two of us in the church-yard lie / Beneath the church-yard tree' / 'You run about, my little maid / Your limbs they are alive / If two are in the church-yard laid / then ye are only five.'" Karen Sanchez-Eppler, "Decomposing: Wordsworth's Poetry of Epitaph and English Burial Reform," *Nineteenth Century Literature* 42 (4) (March 1988): 415–431. p. 415.

14. Ibid, p. 421.

15. Ibid, p. 420.

16. I go into more detail about the relationship between decomposition and democracy in the section "Decomposition, Disinterment, and Democracy" in this chapter. For now, I note that I am defining "democracy" broadly, as a system in which, as Agamben argues, "man as a living being presents himself no longer as an *object* but as the *subject* of political power." Agamben continues, "if anything characterizes modern democracy as opposed to classical democracy, then, it is that modern democracy presents itself from the beginning as a vindication and liberation of *zoē* [bare life], and that it is constantly trying to transform its own bare life into a way of life and to find, so to speak, the *bios* [political life] of *zoē*." Agamben, *Homo Sacer*, p. 9.

17. Christine Quigley, *The Corpse: A History*. North Carolina: McFarland and Co., 1996. p. 2.

18. Zizek makes a related point when he argues that "the ultimate Sadeian image of an 'undead' victim of torture who can bear endless pain without having escape into death at his or her disposal is also waiting to become reality." Slavoj Zizek, *Welcome to the Desert of the Real: Five Essays on September 11th and Related Dates*. New York: Verso, 2002. p. 12.

19. Dr. Krugelstein, "Presumption of Survivorship," *The Western Journal of Medicine and Surgery* 7 (5) (May 1843): 352–356. p. 352.

20. Ibid, p. 353–354.

21. For example, "Not so with mothers who perished with their offspring; these all appeared to have been careless as to themselves, devoting all their thoughts to the preservation of the infant." In "The Effects of an Earthquake in Calabria: Burying," *Journal of Belles Lettres* (Sept. 11, 1838): 2–3, p. 2. "A wretched mother at Plistena was in a room with

her two children . . . [T]he situation in which the three bodies were found is a plain demonstration that the mother had abandoned herself to destruction in striving to protect her children . . . and in this attitude she was found under the rubbish." "Some account of the Earthquake in Calabria, in the year 1783, in a letter from a gentleman on his travels through Calabria in 1786," *The Philadelphia Magazine and Review* (Jan. 1799): 11–13. p. 13. "The mothers made vaulted roofs of their own bodies, to protect their offspring from the falling masses." In "The Calabria Earthquake," *Monthly Magazine of Belles-Lettres and the Arts.* (March 1834): 153–156. p. 154. "Un bébé après avouisé journé plusiers heures en contact avec sa mere écrasée a été trouvé vivant auprès sa." BOA, Y. E. E. 11/24/15 Ağostos 1894, [report by Enginitis in French], in Genç and Mazak, pp. 106–109, p. 107. And, a variation, "[my wife] clasped her arms over my head to shield me from the danger of falling masonry, to which she herself thus remained exposed . . . [H]ad my wife hastened to the door on feeling the shock, she would probably have been struck down at the moment of emergence, as happened in so many other cases that day." Vaughan Cornish, "The Jamaica Earthquake," *The Geographical Journal* 31 (3) (March 1908): 245–271. p. 246.

22. "Portugal," *Blackwood's Edinburgh Magazine* 56 (345) (Oct. 1844): 100–105. p. 103.

23. P. Martin Duncan, "Earthquakes," *Frank Leslie's Popular Monthly* 11 (4) (April 1881): 503–510. p. 507.

24. Charles Davison, *A Study of Recent Earthquakes.* London: The Walter Scott Publishing Co., 1905. pp. 24–25.

25. R. D. Oldham, "The Italian Earthquake of December 28, 1909," *The Geographical Journal* 33 (2) (Feb. 1909): 185–188. p. 185.

26. Giorgio Martara, "The Economic Revival of Messina," *The Economic Journal* 23 (91) (Sept. 1913): 438–442. p. 438.

27. Robert A. O. Dalyell, "Memorandum. Earthquake of Erzurum, June, 1859," *Journal of the Royal Geographical Society of London* 33 (1863): 234–237. p. 235.

28. Genç and Mazak, p. 41.

29. BOA İrade Hus. 18/19 M 1312 in Genç and Mazak, pp. 178–179.

30. Ibid.

31. BOA, İrade Hus. 54/13 M 1312 in Genç and Mazak, pp. 180–181.

32. BOA, Hus. 170/6 M 1312 in Genç and Mazak, ed. pp. 128–129.

33. BOA, Y. A. Hus. 302/53/7 M 1312 in Genç and Mazak, pp. 158–159.

34. Wilson, p. 126.

35. Ibid, p. 62.

36. Ibid, p. 192.

37. Ibid, p. 60.

38. Ibid, p. 175.

39. Ibid, p. 175.

40. Bureau of Social Affairs, Home Office Japan, 1926, p. 17.

41. J. C. Balet, "Lettres Du Japon," *L'Illustration* (January 5, 1924): 6.

42. Poole, p. 38.

43. Ibid, p. 39.

44. Ibid, p. 83.

45. Ibid, p. 98.

46. "An Eye Witness Describes the Japanese Catastrophe," *Current Opinion* (November 1, 1923): 590. p. 590. Seven years later, the mayor of Tokyo concluded the narrative by taking a page from the story of Messina—situating the "marvelous prosperity Tokyo has witnessed in the last 50 years" and "the outstanding growth of [its] population," within the destruction of the disaster and the work of reconstruction. For instance: "To realize the marvelous prosperity Tokyo has witnessed in the last 50 years, one has only to consult the population growth for that period. The following figures indicate the outstanding growth of the population in Tokyo." Tokyo Municipal Office, *Tokyo: Capital of Japan—Reconstruction Work*. Tokyo: Toppan Printing Co, 1930. p. 12.

47. For more on discrimination against the Chinese, especially in U.S. immigration policy, see Lucy E. Salyer, *Laws Harsh as Tigers: Chinese Immigrants and the Shaping of Modern Immigration Law*. Chapel Hill: University of North Carolina Press, 1995, and Erika Lee, *At America's Gates: Chinese Immigration During the Exclusion Era, 1882–1943*. Chapel Hill: University of North Carolina Press, 2003.

48. Although he is notably undisturbed by live *Chinese* bodies beneath the wreckage.

49. In this case the living/dead body buried under the rubble is not dissimilar from *homo sacer* as he is manifested in the "Muselmann" of the Nazi death camp. Agamben continues by arguing that in the case of the Muselmann in the camp, "a law that seeks to transform itself entirely into life finds itself confronted with a life that is absolutely indistinguishable from law, and it is precisely this indiscernibility that threatens the *lex anima* of the camp." Agamben, *Homo Sacer*, p. 185.

50. "Dakikada bir mezar," *Hürriyet* (August 20, 1999): http://arama.hurriyet.com.tr/arsivnews.aspx?id=-97318.

51. Ibid.

52. Ibid.

53. "182 asker enkaz altında," *Hürriyet* (August 18, 1999): http://arama.hurriyet.com.tr/arsivnews.aspx?id=-96786.

54. Ibid.

55. "Adalar bo¸saldı," *Hürriyet* (August 30, 1999): http://arama.hurriyet.com.tr/arsivnews.aspx?id=-99036.

56. Ibid.

57. Ibid.

58. I should be clear: my point here is not that the Ottoman or Turkish governments neglected the Islands in 1894 or in 1999—in many ways they were the subject of

particularly intense scrutiny and concern. (See, for example, BOA İrade Şehremaneti 6/4 Ş 1312, Genç and Mazak, pp. 136–137 and BOA Y. A. Hus. 302/53/7 M 1312, Genç and Mazak, pp. 158–159. See also BOA İrade Hus. 18/3 S 1312, on "appointing Ohannes Efendi from the Armenian Community to the Aid Commission," in Genç and Mazak, pp. 168–169.) Instead, I emphasize the rhetorical force of the death toll in discussions of disasters separated by over a century.

59. What *is* known is that a huge number of people are taking on this new status every day, that someone must keep track of them, and that this status is of the utmost interest to the government and its bureaucrats.

60. It was, for instance, "a theme established in the English-speaking academy by Sir Richard Jeb's introduction to his 1888 redaction of the Greek text . . . [M]oreover this interpretation of Sophokles's tragedy acquired profound influence among philosophers of nineteenth-century Europe, evidenced especially in the writings of Hegel, Holderlin, Schelling, and Kierkegaard." James Comas, "War and the Anima of Criticism," *Rhetoric Review* 16 (2) (Spring, 1998): 188–225.

61. Zizek, "Melancholy," p. 667.

62. "We have, then, two narrowly limited practical worlds, two strategies of avoidance and simplification. In one, a single human value has become *the* final end; in the other, a single set of duties has eclipsed all others. But we can acknowledge that we admire Antigone, nonetheless, in a way that we do not admire Creon . . . [T]he dishonour to civic values involved in giving pious burial to an enemy's corpse is far less radical than the violation of religion involved in Creon's act. Antigone shows a deeper understanding of the community and its values than Creon does when she argues that the obligation to bury the dead is an unwritten law, which cannot be set aside by the decrees of a particular ruler." Martha Nussbaum, *The Fragility of Goodness: Luck and Ethics in Greek Tragedy and Philosophy*. Cambridge: Cambridge University Press, 1986, 2001. p. 66.

63. Ibid, p. 63.

64. Ibid, p. 63.

65. Ibid, p. 65.

66. Sophocles, *Antigone*. Trans. Theodore H. Banks. New York: Oxford University Press, 1956. lines 370–375. p. 13.

67. Suzanne Glover Lindsay, "Mummies and Tombs: Turenne, Napoleon, and Death Ritual," *The Art Bulletin* 82 (3) (Sept. 2000): 476–502. p. 476.

68. Ibid, p. 476.

69. Lindsay analyzes this statement as follows: "treated literally, such an account dismissed these elite dead as evidence of an acknowledged urban problem. Spurred by scientific arguments about the threat of Paris' overcrowded tombs to public health, proven by the toxic effect on many who approached them, the city administrators began moving remains to remote underground sites in the 1760s to protect residents from the miasma of incomplete decomposition. Considered symbolically, this chronicle of the corpse's state

when exhumed was morally judgmental. The putrid embalmed royals were palpable witnesses to the mortality of the monarchy and to their moral threat." Ibid, p. 478.

70. John T. Matteson, "Grave Discussions: The Image of the Sepulcher in Webster, Emerson, and Melville," *New England Quarterly* 74 (3) (Sept. 2001): 419–446. p. 434.

71. Ibid, p. 434.

72. See Chapter Three for example, where Mary Schloendorff's right to bodily integrity meant precisely that her bodily borders should be trespassed.

73. Elizabeth Hallam, Jenny Hockey, and Glennys Howarth, *Death and Social Identity.* London and New York: Routledge, 1999. p. 138.

74. *ARC Annual Report for the Year Ending June 30, 1920.* p. 97.

75. *ARC Annual Report for the Year Ending June 30, 1918.* p. 42.

76. Carol Acton, "Bodies Do Count." Eds. Peter Gray and Kendrick Oliver. *The Memory of Catastrophe* Manchester: Manchester University Press, 2004. p. 161.

77. As opposed to sisters revealing the bodies of their brothers, as in Antigone.

78. A variation, in other words, on Lyford's analysis of the subversive role of post–World War I surrealism: "just as the body could be manipulated for the purposes of instilling order and unity, so it could be torn apart in order to underscore the violence being done to individuals in the name of social stability." Lyford, pp. 52–53.

79. BOA İrade Şehremaneti 6/4 Ş 1312 and BOA İrade Şehremaneti 6/4 Ş 1312 in Genç and Mazak, pp. 136–137 and 138–139.

80. Quigley, p. 162. For a variation on this theme, see: "the springs of wells were corrupted or lost. And the dead bodies imperfectly buried under the ruins that killed them, together with others long since committed to the grave, whose sepulchers the same terrific agent of destruction had torn open, diffused pestiferous exhalations that generated mortal disease." "The Calabria Earthquake," p. 153.

81. Wilson, p. 121–122.

82. "New Means of Perpetuating Memorials: Scientific Methods Ensuring Continuance for 10,000 Years," *The Illuminated London News* Sept. 5, 1931. p. 30.

83. For an inverted variation on this notion, in which (a) the decomposition of the dead body is a means of supplanting one political ideology for another, and (b) the *absence* of a death toll is associated with the political illegitimacy of fascist—as opposed to liberal democratic—governance, see: "Perón's superiors saw the earthquake as a means for denouncing and uprooting liberalism once and for all . . .. [W]ithin a day of the tragedy, the military authorities decided to quickly cremate the bodies of all the dead, apparently because they feared infection. On the edge of the vast common grave—or sometimes just on street corners—soldiers and volunteers doused piles of bodies with kerosene and set them aflame. In the rush, few provisions were made for identifying or keeping track of the dead: nothing resembling a list of victims would ever be compiled. Such actions of profound symbolic violence only compounded the horror and powerlessness of the aftermath of mass death." Mark Alan Healey, "The Fragility of the Moment: Politics and Class

in the Aftermath of the 1914 Argentine Earthquake," *International Labor and Working Class History* 62 (2002): 50–59. pp. 52–53.

84. Agamben, *Homo Sacer*, p. 9. Italics in original.

85. Ibid, p. 9.

86. "Salgın hastalık tehlikesi."

87. I understand "the people" in a broadly political way—inclusive of all subject/citizens, living or dead.

88. "Portugal," p. 103.

89. As it is described, for example, by Arendt, p. 286.

90. Wilson, p. 61.

91. Ibid, p. 126.

92. Matheson, pp. 20–21.

93. For a variation on this "madness" theme in San Francisco, see "the Chinese came out of their underground burrows like rats and tumbled into the square, beating such gongs and playing such noisy instruments as they had snatched up. They were met on the other side by the refugees of the Italian quarter. The panic became madness. At least two Chinamen were taken to the morgue dead of knife wounds, given for no other reason, it seems, than the madness of panic." Wilson, p. 48.

94. "Yıkılan binanın müteahhiti Evren'in evini de yapmış," *Hürriyet* (August 18, 1999): http://arama.hurriyet.com.tr/arsivnews.aspx?id=-96920.

95. Although this refers specifically to those who opened the grave of the famous entrepreneur, Vehbi Koç. "Çetelere teşvik müteahhide af," *Hürriyet* (August 29, 1999): http://arama.hurriyet.com.tr/arsivnews.aspx?id=-98777.

96. Ibid.

97. For a more nuanced discussion of this issue, see Austin Sarat, *Mercy on Trial: What it Means to Stop an Execution*. Princeton: Princeton University Press, 2005.

98. Mirja Trilsch and Alexandra Rüth, "Öcalan v Turkey. App. No. 46221/99," *The American Journal of International Law* 100 (1) (Jan. 2006): 180–186. p. 180.

99. And, more specifically, activities aimed at bringing about the secession of a part of Turkish national territory.

100. Singleton v. Norris, 319 F.3d 1018 (8th Cir. 2003).

101. Ibid, p. 1031.

102. Ibid, p. 1032.

103. See, for example, John Parry's discussion of the Kantian proposition that citizens claim punishment as an equal moral right in John T. Parry, "Finding a Right to be Tortured," *Law and Literature* 19 (2) (2007): 207–228. pp. 219, 221.

104. And, given the de facto end to capital punishment in Turkey as of 1984, the difference between the two was indeed not insignificant. Nonetheless, Turkish jurists and politicians were forced between 1999 and 2002 to vacillate between assuring the public

that this time around the sentence would in fact lead to execution and assuring the European Union that, in Turkey, sentencing prisoners to death was by no means identical to executing them. For more on this conversation, see: "Oy birliğiyle idam," *Hürriyet* (Nov. 26, 1999): http://arama.hurriyet.com.tr/arsivnews.aspx?id=-115548, "Batı basını: İdamda, Türk politikacılar zorlanacak," *Hürriyet* (Nov. 27, 1999): http://arama.hurriyet.com.tr/arsivnews.aspx?id=-115883, "Avrupa: AB'yi düşünün," *Hürriyet* (Nov. 26, 1999): http://arama.hurriyet.com.tr/arsivnews.aspx?id=-115550.

105. Trilsch and Rüth, pp. 183–184.

Chapter Five

1. C. H. D., p. 294.

2. Bankoff, pp. 12–13.

3. Consider, for example, the seventy-year long "temporary emergency" that served as a foundation for British colonial policy in Egypt.

4. My discussion of Lefebvre may seem problematic in that I address a number of his arguments outside of the context of the Marxist theory that is so central to his work. I believe, however, that many of the points he makes lend themselves likewise to a variation on postcolonial analysis.

5. Anghie, p. 27.

6. Henri Lefebvre, *The Production of Space*. Trans. Donald Nicholson-Smith. Oxford: Blackwell, 1991. p. 36. Italics in original.

7. Achille Mbembe, *On the Postcolony*. Berkeley: University of California Press, 2001. p. 103.

8. Achille Mbembe, "Necropolitics." Trans. Libby Meintjes. *Public Culture* 15 (1) (2003): 11–40. p. 25.

9. Lefebvre, p. 396.

10. Ibid, p. 236.

11. Ibid, p. 35.

12. Ibid, p. 375.

13. Mbembe, "Necropolitics," p. 29.

14. Mbembe, *Postcolony*, 104.

15. Mbembe, "Necropolitics," p. 23.

16. Ibid, p. 25.

17. Ibid, p. 25.

18. Anghie, p. 21.

19. Ibid, p. 22.

20. Ibid, p. 24.

21. Mbembe, *Postcolony*, p. 102.

22. Ibid, p. 118.

23. Mbembe likewise argues, for instance, that "in a postcolony of this kind, then, I am concerned with the ways state power (1) *creates*, through administrative and bureaucratic practices, its own world of meanings—a master code that, while becoming the society's primary central code, ends by governing, perhaps paradoxically, the logics that underlie all other meanings within that society; (2) attempts to institutionalize this world of meanings as a 'socio-historical world,' and to make that world real, turning it into a part of people's 'common sense,' not only by instilling it into the minds of the *cibles*, or 'target population,' but also by integrating it into the period's consciousness." Mbembe, *Postcolony*, p. 103.

24. Ibid, p. 124.

25. Ibid, p. 109.

26. Recall the Red Cross reports and their ambivalent relationship with "nature."

27. Lefebvre, p. 110.

28. Ibid, p. 402–403.

29. Ibid, pp. 70–71.

30. Ibid, p. 83. Italics in original.

31. Ibid, p. 101.

32. Ibid, pp. 83–84.

33. Mbembe, "Necropolitics," p. 24.

34. See again, "[Warfare] is not subject to any rule in the colonies. In the colonies, the sovereign might kill at any time, or in any manner. Colonial warfare is not subject to legal and institutional rules. It is not a legally codified activity. Instead, colonial terror constantly intertwines with colonially generated fantasies of wilderness and death and fictions that create the effect of the real." Mbembe, "Necropolitics," p. 25.

35. Agamben, *Homo Sacer*, pp. 108–109, 120–121.

36. For example, Mbembe, "Necropolitics," passim.

37. Greely, p. 35.

38. General Orders #29, S. P. Jocelyn, May 13, 1906 in Greely, p. 73.

39. For more on the importance of "attractiveness," see "the conditions under which lived many, outside of the army camps, were often insanitary (sic), and it was speedily evident that concentration into large camps under military supervision would best insure the public health. Although recommending this scheme to the Major, it was with the distinct announcement that the army would use neither moral stress nor physical force, relying upon the attractiveness of properly constructed, well-policed, and orderly camps against the others of heterogeneous character." Greely, p. 34. (Note the relationship between "unattractive" and "heterogeneous" spaces.)

40. And thus, one could argue, it defines the space outside as ecstatic.

41. Greely, p. 46.

42. Ibid, p. 52.

43. For more on the late nineteenth- and early twentieth-century U.S. doctrine of "separate but equal" as "equal protection," see Plessy v. Ferguson, 163 U.S. 537 (1896).

44. Wilson, p. 48. See also, "Chinatown had debauched into these streets; coolies in blue blouses lay beside the huge wicker baskets packed with their effects, or went swiftly along at a curious trot." Henry Anderson Lafler, "My Sixty Sleepless Hours: A Story of the San Francisco Earthquake," *McClure's Magazine* vol. 27 (3) (July 1906): 275–282. p. 278, and many others.

45. "Erdek Açılıyor," *Hürriyet* (August 22, 1999): http://arsiv.hurriyetim.com.tr/hur/turk/99/08/22/gundem/15gun.html.

46. "Çadır aynı çadır," *Hürriyet* (August 27, 1999): http://arama.hurriyet.com.tr/arsivnews.aspx?id=-98527.

47. For example, "what is spatial practice under neocapitalism? It embodies a close association, within perceived space, between daily reality (daily routine) and urban reality (the routes and networks which link up the places set aside for work, 'private' life and leisure). This association is a paradoxical one, because it includes the most extreme separation between the places it links together . . . [I]n order to dominate space, technology introduces a new form into a pre-existing space—generally a rectilinear or rectangular form such as a meshwork or chequerwork. A motorway brutalizes the countryside and the land, slicing through space like a great knife. Dominated space is usually closed, sterilized, emptied out." Lefebvre, pp. 38, 165.

48. Ibid, pp. 38, 165.

49. For an earlier narrative of the road as a barrier, see "the reply of a grizzled fire engineer, standing at the corner of O'Farrell Street and Van Ness Avenue, beside a blackened engine, may not have been as tense as Hugo's guard at Waterloo, but the pathos of it could have been no greater. In answer to the question of what he proposed to do, he said: 'we are waiting for it [the fire] to come. When it gets here we will make one more stand. If it crosses Van Ness Avenue, the city is gone.'" Wilson, p. 101.

50. "Otoyollar ücretsizdi," *Hürriyet* (August 18, 1999): http://arama.hurriyet.com.tr/arsivnews.aspx?id=-96910.

51. "Karayolu kılavuzu," *Hürriyet* (August 19, 1990): http://arama.hurriyet.com.tr/arsivnews.aspx?id=-97109.

52. "Avcılar'da trafik felç," *Hürriyet* (August 20, 1999): http://arama.hurriyet.com.tr/arsivnews.aspx?id=-97307.

53. "Gölcük'te karantina," *Hürriyet* (August 22, 1999): http://arama.hurriyet.com.tr/arsivnews.aspx?id=-97480.

54. Even the virtual manifestations of these roads—the networks rather than the routes—underwent a spatial transformation. Following the 1894 earthquake, the Ottoman Telegraph and Post Ministry building was destroyed, and immediately afterward, the undamaged machines were moved into gardens so that the lines still intact could continue their operation. A little over a century later, Turkish cell phone companies were

similarly concerned with maintaining their networks, and with maintaining them in spatially unexpected and confusing contexts. The Turkcell company, for example, issued a statement to the mass media a week after the earthquake, in which it explained why its cell phones were inoperative in the disaster areas—blaming a lack of electricity to its primary stations and the nature of the GSM network. Rather than displacing the grids and networks onto space devoted to agriculture or pleasure like the nineteenth-century Telegraph Ministry had, in other words, the Turkcell company produced an implicit analogy between its virtual grid and the highway grid. Like the highways, the purpose of the cell phone network was to dominate space and to forge connections between the rhetorical center and the rhetorical periphery. Also like the highways, however, the network could paradoxically and simultaneously sever these connections. The mass of the population in Istanbul and İzmit owned and carried a cell phone—in this way they were intimately connected with one another, any distance between them eliminated. At the same time however, actual communication was impossible—a spatial network existed in the ownership of the phones, but it simultaneously alienated phone owners in the absence of communication. Like the roads, therefore, the cell phone network also turned in upon itself and served to destabilize, in this case, the virtual manifestation of space. There was occasional talk of cell phone calls being placed from under the rubble, but these narratives, far from playing up the effectiveness of virtual space, instead highlighted its meaningless, alienating character. Ürekli, p. 16, and "Turkcell'den deprem savunması," *Hürriyet* (August 30, 1999): http://arama.hurriyet.com.tr/arsivnews.aspx?id=-98966.

55. Quigley, p. 162.

56. Lefebvre, p. 137.

57. Ibid, p. 236.

58. Sanchez-Eppler, p. 420.

59. Ibid, p. 422.

60. Charles A. Tamason, "From Mortuary to Cemetery: Funeral Riots and Funeral Demonstrations in Lille, 1779–1870," *Social Science History* 4 (1) (Winter 1980): 18–31. pp. 16.

61. Ibid, p. 23.

62. Lindsay, p. 476.

63. Although the public and political nature of cemeteries was something common to a number of culture contexts. In the early modern Ottoman Empire, for example, first, "the principle of the sacredness and inviolability of the grave was applied with such severity as to render impossible the use of common graves or the reuse of individual sepulchral space," second "Ottoman authorities had systematically promoted the development of *extra muros* or suburban burial grounds, much in the style of western cemeteries of the late eighteenth and nineteenth centuries," and third, as a gradual result, Ottomans "transform[ed] an individual and religious marker into a social one, and . . . turn[ed] their epitaphs into extensions of the public image of the deceased and of their entourage,"

viewing "the cemetery as an extension of public space." Edhem Eldem, "Urban voices from beyond: identity, status and social strategies in Ottoman Muslim funerary epitaphs of Istanbul (1700–1850)." Eds. Virginia H. Aksan and Daniel Goffman. *The Early Modern Ottomans: Remapping the Empire.* Cambridge: Cambridge University Press, 2007, pp. 233–255. pp. 234, 254–255.

64. Mary Bradbury, *Representation of Death: A Social Psychological Perspective.* London and New York: Routledge, 1999. p. 11.

65. Thomas Laqueur, "Bodies, Death, and Pauper Funerals," *Representations* 1 (Feb. 1983): 109–131. pp. 115–116.

66. Ibid, p. 115.

67. Sanchez-Eppler, p. 416.

68. Ibid, p. 416.

69. For an Ottoman variation on these processes, "Ottoman cemeteries [in the early modern period] were an extension of the urban public space, linking the dead to the living through a social discourse of status, genealogy, and biography." Eldem, p. 240.

70. "Earthquake at Lisbon," p. 455.

71. Ibid, p. 455.

72. Ibid, p. 455.

73. "The Calabria Earthquake," p. 153.

74. Ürekli, pp. 99–100.

75. BOA, Y.A. 302/53/7 M 1312 in Genç and Mazak, pp. 158–159.

76. Ibid.

77. Wilson, p. 121.

78. Ibid, p. 54.

79. Ibid, pp. 121–122.

80. Quigley, p. 162. For a variation on this theme, see above, "The Calabria Earthquake," p. 153.

81. Poole, p. 48.

82. Ibid, p. 48.

83. Matheson, p. 17.

84. Poole, p. 120.

85. See, for instance, my discussion of Antigone in Chapter Four. .

86. For example, "Sade's modernity does not consist in his having foreseen the unpolitical primacy of sexuality in our unpolitical age. On the contrary, Sade is as contemporary as he is because of his incomparable presentation of the absolutely political (that is, 'biopolitical') meaning of sexuality and physiological life itself. Like the concentration camps of our century, the totalitarian character of the organization of life in Silling's castle—with its meticulous regulations that do not spare any aspect of physiological life (not even the digestive function, which is obsessively codified and publicized)—has its root in the fact that what is proposed here for the first time is a normal and collective (and

hence political) organization of human life founded solely on bare life." Agamben, *Homo Sacer*, p. 135.

87. At the same time, it is worth pointing out that all three governments gradually lost control over this process of designation. Indeed, the spaces of the dead quickly ran beyond their boundaries and colonized other spaces, previously occupied by the living. As the living entered the cemeteries and set up housekeeping there, in other words—and as the dead populated public square after public square—the government's neat lines and divisions remained, but remained without purpose. There was no longer any actual distinction between the political space of the cemetery and the apparently apolitical space of the household. The scene and the obscene, again, became one—the divisions between the two serving merely to emphasize this absoluteness.

88. The mayor then continues with an exegesis of the situation, especially given the faulty building techniques. "Acımız çok büyük" *Milliyet* (August 18, 1999): http://www.milliyet.com.tr/1999/08/18/haber/haboo.html.

89. A "davetiye" can be a summons or subpoena as well as written invitation.

90. "Sakarya'da 20 bin kişi mezar evlerde kalıyor" *Zaman* (February 23, 2007): http://www.zaman.com.tr/webapp-tr/haber.do?haberno=504358.

91. As Foucault argues in *Discipline and Punish*, "If torture was so strongly embedded in legal practice, it was because it revealed truth and showed the operation of power. It assured the articulation of the written on the oral, the secret on the public, the procedure of investigation on the operation of the confession; it made it possible to reproduce the crime on the visible body of the criminal; in the same horror, the crime had to be manifested and annulled. It also made the body of the condemned man the place where the vengeance of the sovereign was applied, the anchoring point for a manifestation of power, an opportunity of affirming the dissymmetry of forces. We shall see later that the truth-power relation remains at the heart of all mechanisms of punishment and that it is still to be found in contemporary penal practice—but in a quite different form and with very different effects." Michel Foucault, *Discipline and Punish*. Trans. Alan Sheridan. New York: Vintage, 1995. p. 55.

92. "Mezar dili," *Hürriyet* (August 25, 1999): http://webarsiv.hurriyet.com.tr/1999/08/25/138858.asp.

93. Zafer Tokuş, "Nihayet oğlunu buldu: Ukraynalı anne Obaline, Marmara depreminde ölen oğlunun mezarını 4 yıl sonra buldu. Obaline'nin oğlu, kimsesizlerin gömüldüğü bir başkasına ait mezarda çıktı," *Radikal* (June 26, 2003): http://www.radikal.com.tr/haber.php?haberno=79473.

94. Şik, "'Öleni kıskanıyorum.'"

95. Ibid.

96. Ibid.

97. See, for example, Jürgen Habermas, *The Structural Transformation of the Public Sphere: An Inquiry into a Category of Bourgeois Society.* Trans. Thomas Burger. Cambridge: MIT Press, 1989.

98. See also Lefebvre's point that plazas and public squares are deliberately blank such that they mirror military parade grounds. Lefebvre, p. 50.

99. Ibid, p. 143.

100. Ibid, p. 221.

101. Ibid, p. 222.

102. Ibid, p. 222.

103. Mbembe, *Postcolony*, 114.

104. David Seed, "The Dawn of the Atomic Age." Ed. David Seed. *Imagining Apocalypse: Studies in Cultural Crisis.* London: Macmillan, 2000, pp. 88–103, p. 100.

105. Ibid, p. 100.

106. But interestingly not scene/obscene distinctions. Depending on the politics of the narrative, this public/private breakdown is described either as an excellent example of the discipline of the subject, or as a "sacrifice" on the part of the free citizen. See, for example, the following after the 1906 San Francisco earthquake: "with few exceptions those who had homes responded readily to the new call made upon them, and when they did not the butt ends of rifles quickly forced a way through inhospitable doors." Wilson, p. 208.

107. Charles F. Walker, "The Upper Classes and their Upper Stories: Architecture and the Aftermath of the Lima Earthquake of 1746," *Hispanic American Historical Review* 83 (1) (February 2003): 53–82. p. 64.

108. Ibid, p. 68.

109. "Extract of a Letter Giving an Account of the Earthquake, Which Took Place at Naples, July 25th 1805," *The Monthly Anthology* 2 (12) (Dec. 1805): 628–630, p. 629. Italics in original.

110. Dalyell, p. 235.

111. BOA İrade Hus. 198/14 M 1312 in Genç and Mazak, pp. 204–207.

112. Ürekli, pp. 99–100.

113. Lafler, pp. 275–276. For a variation on the narrative of apparent spatial dislocation in San Francisco, see "At the time of the earthquake and fire in San Francisco the soldiers rescued from the slave pens in Chinatown about three hundred Japanese girls, many of them mere children. The soldiers said these girls did not know in what part of the world they were living!" Elinor H. Stoy, "Chinatown and the Curse that Makes it a Plague Spot in the Nation," *The Arena* 38 (215) (Oct. 1907): 360–365. p. 363.

114. Poole, p. 48.

115. Tokyo Municipal Office, p. 42.

116. Ibid, p. 53.

117. Ibid, p. 63.

118. Ino Dan, "The Reconstruction of Tokyo and Aesthetic Problems of Architecture," *Tokyo: Japan Council of the Institute of Pacific Relations*, 1931. p. 3.

119. "Kapalıçarşı sağlam çıktı," *Hürriyet* (August 20, 1999): http://arama.hurriyet.com.tr/arsivnews.aspx?id=-97214.

120. It is worthwhile to compare this late twentieth-century commentary on the ephemeral nature of cement to the lauding of cement as a building material that would designate Turkey as modern, strong, and civilized in the early twentieth century: "The 'arrival' of the New Architecture (*Yeni Mimari*, as the Modern Movement came to be called in Turkey) was celebrated with a double-page feature article in the official republican daily *Hakimiyet-i Milliye* (National Sovereignty) in 1930. The article hailed recent construction in Ankara as 'the new architecture of this century,' an expression of 'the new truth' that was spreading through all parts of the world . . . [T]he crucial role of *simenarme* (literally, 'reinforced cement,' a word later replaced by *betonarme*, or 'reinforced concrete,' still in use in modern Turkish) was highlighted as a major factor informing the principles and aesthetic of the New Architecture." Sibel Bozdoğan, *Modernism and Nation Building: Turkish Architectural Culture in the Early Republic*. Seattle and London: University of Washington Press, 2001. pp. 153–154.

121. "Ayasofya asla yıkılmaz," *Hürriyet* (August 19, 1999): http://arama.hurriyet.com.tr/arsivnews.aspx?id=-96991.

122. "Beyazıd Camii ibadete kapandı," *Hürriyet* (August 19, 1999): http://arama.hurriyet.com.tr/arsivnews.aspx?id=-97043.

123. "Fatih Camii depreme şerbetli," *Hürriyet* (August 22, 1999): http://arama.hurriyet.com.tr/arsivnews.aspx?id=-97537.

124. An editorial convention indicative at the very least of the newspaper *Hürriyet's* basis in Turkish Republican secularism and nationalism.

125. Lefebvre, p. 223–224.

126. Wilson, p. 194.

127. Bataille, for example, argues that transgression "persists at the very basis of marriage," that the marriage ceremony is in fact no different from the blood sacrifice: "laws that allow an infringement and consider it legal are paradoxical. Hence, just as killing is simultaneously forbidden and performed in sacrificial ritual, so the initial sexual act constituting marriage is a permitted violation." Bataille, pp. 109–110.

128. See "Ecstatic Space" in this chapter for more on the colony as a lawless space, subject to a constant state of emergency.

Chapter Six

1. Devlin Barrett, "ID Would Control Access to Disaster Sites," *Washington Post* (Tuesday, September 4, 2007): A06.

2. Where, for example, one retired soldier accessed the wreckage simply by showing his U.S. Marines tattoo and passing into the area. Ibid. The article continues, "Dickinson said the government is not trying to discourage volunteers, but he thinks there should come a time, within a few days of a disaster, when civilians step back and let the professionals take control. Supporters say the ID cards could be checked at a disaster area with a card-reader device and used to verify a person's unique skills. For example, if police officers have been trained to handle hazardous materials, officials at the scene could deploy the officers to an area where their skills would be best put to use."

3. Ibid. The article continues, "many of those volunteers angrily dispute the notion they were a burden. They insist that in many instances they were able to deliver respirators, hard hats and protective boots to workers when no one else seemed able."

4. "Similar frustrations arose after Katrina, when people were shocked that the government struggled to take basic supplies such as water to the worst areas." Ibid.

5. Although it is clearly *in part* a result of this prior marginalization.

6. For an alternative but related reading of the relationship between (political) existence and insistence, consider Zizek's point that "the opposite of *existence* is not nonexistence, but *insistence*: that which does not exist, continues to *insist*, striving toward existence. Zizek, *Welcome*, p. 22.

7. Henrietta Moore, "'Divided We Stand': Sex, Gender, and Sexual Difference," *Feminist Review* 47 (Summer, 1994): 78–95. p. 89. In this passage, Moore is relying heavily on the work of Elizabeth Grosz. Moore then continues, "there are some resonances here with Braidotti's 'feminine corpor(e)ality,' although in order to provide a workable theory of embodied subjectivity we would need to combine Braidotti's emphasis on materiality with Lacan's insistence on the symbolic. This might prove extremely difficult, not to say risky, since there is nothing that links Braidotti's female body to Lacan's feminine except some residual and unresolved problem about anatomy." Moore, pp. 89–90.

8. Butler, *Psychic Life of Power*, p. 9.

9. Ibid, p. 23. She continues, a few pages later, "as a stopgap against a sadistic destruction, guilt signals less the psychic presence of an originally social and external norm than a countervailing desire to continue the object one wishes dead. It is in this sense that guilt emerges in the course of melancholia not only, as the Freudian view would have it, to keep the dead object alive, but to keep the living object from 'death,' where death means the death of love, including occasions of separation and loss." Ibid, p. 25. Italics in original.

10. Braidotti, *Metamorphoses*, pp. 40–41.

11. Abigail Bray and Claire Colebrook, "The Haunted Flesh: Corporeal Feminism and the Politics of (Dis)Embodiment," *Signs* 24 (1) (Autumn, 1998): 35–67. p. 38.

12. They conclude by citing Butler: "'the feminine exceeds its figuration . . . [and] this unthematizeability constitutes the feminine as the impossible yet necessary foundation of what can be thematized and figured.' This opposition between representation and exteriority is enabled by seeing discourse as language and signification (as representation) that always refers to some nondiscursive exterior." Bray and Colebrook, p. 43. Italics in original.

13. Butler, *Psychic Life of Power*, p. 149. Italics in original.

Bibliography

Abu-Rabi, Ibrahim M., ed. *Islam at the Crossroads: On the Life and Thought of Bediuzzaman Said Nursi*. Albany: State University of New York Press, 2003.

Acton, Carol. "Bodies do Count." Eds. Peter Gray and Kendrick Oliver. *The Memory of Catastrophe*. Manchester: Manchester University Press, 2004.

Agamben, Giorgio. *Homo Sacer: Sovereign Power and Bare Life*. Trans. Daniel Heller-Roazen. Stanford: Stanford University Press, 1998.

Agamben, Giorgio. *State of Exception*. Trans. Kevin Attell. Chicago: University of Chicago Press, 2005.

Allen, J. Michael. "The Price of Identity: The 1923 Kantō Earthquake and Its Aftermath," *Korean Studies* 20 (1996): 64–93.

Anghie, Antony. "Finding the Peripheries: Sovereignty and Colonialism in Nineteenth Century International Law," *Harvard International Law Journal* 40 (1999): 1–80.

American Red Cross. *American Red Cross Annual Report for the Year Ended June 30, 1918*. Washington, DC: The Arbor Press, 1918.

American Red Cross. *American Red Cross Annual Report for the Year Ended June 30, 1919*. Washington, DC: The Arbor Press, 1919.

American Red Cross. *American Red Cross Annual Report for the Year Ended June 30, 1920*. Washington, DC: The Arbor Press, 1920.

Arata, Stephen. "The Occidental Tourist: Dracula and the Anxiety of Reverse Colonization," *Victorian Studies* 33 (1990): 621–645.

Arendt, Hannah. *The Origins of Totalitarianism*. New York: Harcourt, 1968, 1976.

Aygen, Nermin. *Türklerin Kan Grupları ve Kan Gruplarının Antropolojik Karakterlerle İlgisi Üzerine bir Araştırman*. Ankara: İdeal Basımevi, 1946.

Balet, J. C. "Lettres Du Japon," *L'Illustration* (January 5, 1924): 6.

Bankoff, Greg. *Cultures of Disaster: Society and Natural Hazard in the Philippines*. London: Routledge Curzon, 2003.

Barrett, Devlin. "ID Would Control Access to Disaster Sites," *Washington Post* (September 4, 2007): A06.

Bataille, Georges. *Tears of Eros*. Trans. Peter Conner. San Francisco: City Light Books, 1989.

Bernard, Claude. *Les Propriètès Physiologiques et Les Altérations Pathologiques des Liquides de L'organisme*, vol. 1. Paris: J. B. Baillière et Fils, 1859.

Bolin, Robert, and Stanford, Lois. "Constructing Vulnerability in the First World: The Northridge Earthquake in Southern California, 1994." Eds. Anthony Oliver-Smith and Susanna M. Hoffman. *The Angry Earth: Disaster in Anthropological Perspective*. London: Routledge, 1999. pp. 89–113.

Bonsal, Stephen. "The Philippines—After an Earthquake," *The North American Review* 174 (March, 1902): 409–421.

Bozdoğan, Sibel. *Modernism and Nation Building: Turkish Architectural Culture in the Early Republic*. Seattle and London: University of Washington Press, 2001.

Bradbury, Mary. *Representation of Death: A Social Psychological Perspective*. London and New York: Routledge, 1999.

Braidotti, Rosi. *Metamorphoses: Toward a Materialist Theory of Becoming*. Cambridge: Polity Press, 2002.

Braidotti, Rosi. *Nomadic Subjects: Embodiment and Sexual Difference in Contemporary Feminist Theory*. New York: Columbia University Press, 1994.

Braidotti, Rosi. *Patterns of Dissonance: A Study of Women in Contemporary Philosophy*. Trans. Elizabeth Guild. New York: Routledge, 1991.

Braidotti, Rosi. *Transpositions: On Nomadic Ethics*. Cambridge: Polity Press, 2006.

Bray, Abigail, and Colebrook, Claire. "The Haunted Flesh: Corporeal Feminism and the Politics of (Dis)Embodiment," *Signs* 24 (1) (Autumn, 1998): 35–67.

Bureau of Social Affairs. *The Great Earthquake of 1923 in Japan*. Japan: Home Office, 1926.

Butler, Judith. *The Psychic Life of Power: Theories in Subjection*. Stanford: Stanford University Press, 1997.

Butler, Judith. *Undoing Gender*. New York and London: Routledge, 2004.

Button, Gregory V. "The Negotiation of Disaster: The Media Response to Oil Spills in Great Britain." Eds. Anthony Oliver-Smith and Susanna M. Hoffman. *The Angry Earth: Disaster in Anthropological Perspective*. London: Routledge, 1999. pp. 113–133.

Carlson, David Gray. "The Traumatic Dimension in Law," *Cardozo Law Review* 24 (August 2003): 2287–2329.

Caudill, David S. *Lacan and the Subject of Law: Toward a Psychoanalytical Critical Legal Theory*. Atlantic Highlands, N.J.: Humanities Press, 1997.

C. H. D. "The Moral Effects of Earthquakes," *New Peterson Magazine* (3) (March, 1894): 293–294.

Cheah, Pheng. *Inhuman Conditions: On Cosmopolitanism and Human Rights.* Cambridge: Harvard University Press, 2006.

Cheah, Pheng. *Spectral Nationality: Passages of Freedom from Kant to Postcolonial Literatures of Liberation.* New York: Columbia University Press, 2003.

Collins, John J., and Fishbane, Michael, eds., *Death, Ecstasy, and Other Worldly Journeys.* Albany: State University of New York Press, 1995.

Comas, James. "War and the Anima of Criticism," *Rhetoric Review* 16 (2) (Spring, 1998): 188–225.

Conte, Edouard, and Essner, Cornelia. *La Quête de la Race: Une Anthropologie du Nazisme.* Paris: Hachette, 1995.

Cornish, Vaughan. "The Jamaica Earthquake," *The Geographical Journal* 31 (3) (March 1908): 245–271.

Dalyell, Robert A. O. "Memorandum. Earthquake of Erzurum, June, 1859," *Journal of the Royal Geographical Society of London* 33 (1863): 234–237.

Dan, Ino. "The Reconstruction of Tokyo and Aesthetic Problems of Architecture," *Tokyo: Japan Council of the Institute of Pacific Relations,* 1931.

Das, Veena. "The Act of Witnessing: Violence, Poisonous Knowledge, and Subjectivity." Eds. Veena Das, Arthur Kleinman, Mamphela Ramphele, and Pamela Reynolds. *Violence and Subjectivity.* Berkeley: University of California Press, 2000. pp. 203–225.

Davis, Mike. *Dead Cities.* New York: The New Press, 2002.

Davison, Charles. *A Study of Recent Earthquakes.* London: The Walter Scott Publishing Co., 1905.

Dewey, Frederick H. "How an Earthquake Looks and Feels," *Lippincott's Monthly Magazine* (April 1899): 527–531.

Diamond, Jared. *Guns, Germs and Steel: The Fates of Human Societies.* New York: W. W. Norton, 2005.

Dimock, Wai Chee. "A Theory of Resonance," *PMLA* 112 (5) (October 1997): 1060–1071.

Duncan, P. Martin. "Earthquakes," *Frank Leslie's Popular Monthly* 11 (4) (April 1881): 503–510.

Eldem, Edhem. "Urban voices from beyond: identity, status and social strategies in Ottoman Muslim funerary epitaphs of Istanbul (1700–1850)." Eds. Virginia H. Aksan and Daniel Goffman. *The Early Modern Ottomans: Remapping the Empire.* Cambridge: Cambridge University Press, 2007. pp. 233–255.

Ernst, Carl W. *Words of Ecstasy in Sufism.* Albany: State University of New York Press, 1985.

Farber, Daniel A. and Chen, Jim. *Disasters and the Law: Katrina and Beyond.* New York: Aspen Publishers, 2006.

Feldman, Eric A. "HIV and Blood in Japan: Transforming Private Conflict into Public Scandal." Eds. Eric A. Feldman and Ronald Bayer. *Blood Feuds: AIDS, Blood, and the Politics of Medical Disaster.* New York: Oxford University Press, 1999. pp. 59–95.

Finch, George A. "Piracy in the Mediterranean," *American Journal of International Law* 31 (4) (October 1937): 659–665.

Fordham, Maureen and Ketteridge, Anne-Michele. "'Men Must Work and Women Must Weep': Examining Gender Stereotypes in Disasters." Eds. Elaine Enarson and Betty Hearn Morrow. *The Gendered Terrain of Disaster: Through Women's Eyes*. Westport, Ct: Praeger, 1998. pp. 81–95.

Foster, Johanna. "An Invitation to Dialogue: Clarifying the Position of Feminist Gender Theory in Relation to Sexual Difference Theory," *Gender and Society* 13 (4) (August 1999): 431–456.

Foucault, Michel. *Discipline and Punish*. Trans. Alan Sheridan. New York: Vintage, 1995.

Foucault, Michel. *Fearless Speech*. Ed. Joseph Pearson. Los Angeles: Semiotext(e), 2001.

Foucault, Michel. *History of Sexuality: The Care of the Self*. Trans. Robert Hurley. New York: Vintage, 1988.

Foucault, Michel. *"Society Must Be Defended": Lectures at the Collège de France, 1975–1976*. Trans. David Macey. New York: Picador, 2003.

Genç, Mehmet and Mazak, Mehmet, eds. *İstanbul Depremleri: Fotoğraf ve Belgelerde 1894 Depremi*. İstanbul: İğdaş Kültürel Yayınları, 2000.

Genet, Raoul. "The Charge of Piracy in the Spanish Civil War," *American Journal of International Law* 32 (2) (April 1938): 255–256.

Goldberg, Rita. "Voltaire, Rousseau, and the Lisbon Earthquake," *Eighteenth Century Life* 13 (2) (1989): 1–20.

Gomel, Elana. "The Plague of Utopias: Pestilence and the Apocalyptic Body," *Twentieth Century Literature* 46 (4) (Winter, 2000): 405–433.

Goodin, Robert E., Pateman, Carole, and Pateman, Roy. "Simian Sovereignty," *Political Theory* 25 (6) (December 1997): 821–849.

Goodman, Felicitas D. *Ecstasy, Ritual, and Alternate Reality: Religion in a Pluralistic World*. Bloomington: Indiana University Press, 1988.

Greeley, Andrew M. *Ecstasy: A Way of Knowing*. Englewood Cliffs, N.J.: Prentice-Hall, 1974.

Greely, Maj. Gen. Adolphus W. *Earthquake in California—April 18, 1906—Special Report*. Washington, D.C.: Government Printing Office, 1906.

Habermas, Jürgen. *The Structural Transformation of the Public Sphere: An Inquiry into a Category of Bourgeois Society*. Trans. Thomas Burger. Cambridge: MIT Press, 1989.

Hallam, Elizabeth, Hockey, Jenny, and Howarth, Glennys. *Death and Social Identity*. London and New York: Routledge, 1999.

Hawkesworth, Mary. "Confounding Gender," *Signs* 22 (3) (Spring, 1997): 649–685.

Healey, Mark Alan. "The Fragility of the Moment: Politics and Class in the Aftermath of the 1914 Argentine Earthquake," *International Labor and Working Class History* 62 (2002): 50–59.

Hobbs, W. H. "The Messina Earthquake," *Bulletin of the American Geographical Society* 41 (7) (1909): 409–422.

Hones, Sheila. "Natural and Unnatural Wars." Eds. James D. Proctor and David M. Smith. *Geography and Ethics: Journeys in a Moral Terrain*. London and New York: Routledge, 1999.

Hume, David. "An Essay on Civil Liberty," *The Columbia Magazine* (January 1788): 9–14.

Italy. *Penal Code of the Kingdom of Italy*. London: His Majesty's Stationery Office, 1931.

Jones, Matthew L. "Descartes' Geometry as Spiritual Exercise," *Critical Inquiry* 28 (1) (Autumn, 2001): 40–71.

Kâhya, Esin. *Ondokuzunca Yüzyılda Osmanlı İmparatorluğu'na Tip Eğitimi ve Türk Hekimleri*. Ankara: Atatürk Kültür Merkezi Başkanlığı, 1997.

Karateke, Hakan. "Opium for the Subjects? Religiosity as a Legitimizing Factor for the Ottoman Sultan." Eds. Hakan Karateke and Maurus Reinkowski. *Legitimizing the Order: The Ottoman Rhetoric of State Power*. Leiden: Brill, 2005. pp. 111–130.

Kaufman, Andrew L. *Cardozo*. Cambridge: Harvard University Press, 1998.

Kennedy, Ellen. "Hostis not Inimicus: Toward a Theory of the Public in the Work of Carl Schmitt," *The Canadian Journal of Law & Jurisprudence* 10 (January 1997): 35–48.

Krugelstein, Dr. "Presumption of Survivorship," *The Western Journal of Medicine and Surgery* 7 (5) (May 1843): 352–356.

Lafler, Henry Anderson. "My Sixty Sleepless Hours: A Story of the San Francisco Earthquake," *McClure's Magazine* vol. 27 (3) (July 1906): 275–282.

Laqueur, Thomas. "Bodies, Death, and Pauper Funerals," *Representations* 1 (February 1983): 109–131.

Lee, Erika. *At America's Gates: Chinese Immigration During the Exclusion Era, 1882–1943*. Chapel Hill: University of North Carolina Press, 2003.

Lefebvre, Henri. *The Production of Space*. Trans. Donald Nicholson-Smith. Oxford: Blackwell, 1991.

Levi, Edward H. *An Introduction to Legal Reasoning*. Chicago: University of Chicago Press, 1949.

Lindsay, Suzanne Glover. "Mummies and Tombs: Turenne, Napoleon, and Death Ritual," *The Art Bulletin* 82 (3) (September 2000): 476–502.

Locke, Margaret. "Deadly Disputes: Hybrid Selves and the Calculation of Death in Japan and North America," *Osiris* 13 (1998): 410–429.

Lombardo, Paul A. "Phantom Tumors and Hysterical Women: Revising our View of the Schloendorff Case," *Journal of Law, Medicine & Ethics* 33 (2005): 791–800.

Longinus. *On the Sublime*. Trans. James A. Arieti and John M. Grossett. New York: Edwin Mellen Press, 1985.

Lyford, Amy. "The Aesthetics of Dismemberment: Surrealism and the Musée de Val-de-Grace in 1917," *Cultural Critique* 46 (Autumn 2000): 45–79.

Mardin, Şerif. *Religion and Social Change in Modern Turkey: The Case of Bediuzzaman Said Nursi*. Albany: State University of New York Press, 1990.

Marsden, Jill. *After Nietzsche: Notes Towards a Philosophy of Ecstasy*. New York: Palgrave, 2002.

Martara, Giorgio. "The Economic Revival of Messina," *The Economic Journal* 23 (91) (September 1913): 438–442.

Matheson, R. O. "Through the Inferno of the Japanese Earthquake," *McClure's Magazine* 56 (1) (January 1924): 8–21.

Matteson, John T. "Grave Discussions: The Image of the Sepulcher in Webster, Emerson, and Melville," *New England Quarterly* 74 (3) (September 2001): 419–446.

Matthew, Dayna Bowen. "Disasterous Disasters: Restoring Civil Rights Protections for Victims of the State in Natural Disasters," *Journal of Health and Biomedical Law* 2 (2006): 213–248.

Mbembe, Achille. "Necropolitics." Trans. Libby Meintjes. *Public Culture* 15 (1) (2003): 11–40.

Mbembe, Achille. *On the Postcolony*. Berkeley: University of California Press, 2001.

Miller, Ruth A. *The Limits of Bodily Integrity: Abortion, Adultery, and Rape Legislation in Comparative Perspective*. Aldershot: Ashgate Press, 2007.

Moore, Henrietta. "'Divided We Stand': Sex, Gender, and Sexual Difference," *Feminist Review* 47 (Summer 1994): 78–95.

Napier, Susan J. "Panic Sites: The Japanese Imagination of Disaster from Godzilla to Akira," *Journal of Japanese Studies* 19 (2) (Summer 1993): 327–351.

Nussbaum, Martha. *The Fragility of Goodness: Luck and Ethics in Greek Tragedy and Philosophy*. Cambridge: Cambridge University Press, 1986, 2001.

Ohnuki-Tierney, Emiko. "Brain Death and Organ Transplant: Cultural Bases of Medical Technology," *Current Anthropology* 35 (3) (June 1994): 233–254.

Oldham, R. D. "The Italian Earthquake of December 28, 1909," *The Geographical Journal* 33 (2) (February 1909): 185–188.

Oliver-Smith, Anthony. "Peru's Five-Hundred Year Earthquake: Vulnerability in Historical Context." Eds. Anthony Oliver-Smith and Susanna M. Hoffman. *The Angry Earth: Disaster in Anthropological Perspective*. London: Routledge, 1999.

Parry, John T. "Finding a Right to be Tortured," *Law and Literature* 19 (2) (2007): 207–228.

Pateman, Carole. *The Disorder of Women: Democracy Feminism, and Political Theory*. Stanford: Stanford University Press, 1989

Poole, Otis Manchester. *The Death of Old Yokohama in the Great Japanese Earthquake of Sept. 1, 1923* London: George Allen and Unwin, Ltd., 1968.

Porcher, F. Peyre. "Influence of the Charleston Earthquakes on Health," *Medical News* 50 (5) (January 29, 1887): 138.

Quigley, Christine. *The Corpse: A History*. Jefferson, N.C.: McFarland and Co., 1996.

Rolleston, James. *Narratives of Ecstasy: Romantic Temporality in Modern German Poetry*. Detroit: Wayne State University Press, 1987.

Rose, Nikolas, O'Malley, Pat, and Valverde, Mariana. "Governmentality." *Annual Review of Law and Social Science* 2 (2006): 83–104.

Rosen, Lawrence. *Law as Culture: An Invitation*. Princeton: Princeton University Press, 2006.

Rousseau, Jean-Jacques. *On the Social Contract*. Trans. Donald A. Cress. Indianapolis: Hackett Publishing Co., 1987.

Rozario, Kevin. *The Culture of Calamity: Disaster and the Making of Modern America*. Chicago: University of Chicago Press, 2007.

Said Nursi (Bediüzzaman). "Deprem ve Hikmetleri," *Risale-i Nur Külliyatında*. Istanbul: Bayrak Mat., 1999.

Salyer, Lucy E. *Laws Harsh as Tigers: Chinese Immigrants and the Shaping of Modern Immigration Law*. Chapel Hill: University of North Carolina Press, 1995.

Sanchez-Eppler, Karen. "Decomposing: Wordsworth's Poetry of Epitaph and English Burial Reform," *Nineteenth Century Literature* 42 (4) (March 1988): 415–431.

Sarat, Austin. *Mercy on Trial: What it Means to Stop an Execution*. Princeton: Princeton University Press, 2005.

Scarry, Elaine. "Consent and the Body: Injury, Departure, and Desire," *New Literary History* 21 (Autumn, 1990): 867–896.

Schlag, Pierre. "The Problem of the Subject," *Texas Law Review* 69 (1991): 1627–1743.

Schmitt, Carl. *Political Theology: Four Chapters on the Concept of Sovereignty*. Trans. George Schwab. Chicago: University of Chicago Press, 2005.

Seed, David. "The Dawn of the Atomic Age." Ed. David Seed. *Imagining Apocalypse: Studies in Cultural Crisis*. London: Macmillan, 2000, pp. 88–103.

Şik, Ahmet. "'Öleni kıskanıyorum,'" *Radikal* (August 17, 2000): http://www.belgenet.com/deprem/170800_r17.html.

Sophocles. *Antigone*. Trans. Theodore H. Banks. New York: Oxford University Press, 1956.

Stallings, Robert A. "Weberian Political Sociology and Sociological Disaster Studies," *Sociological Forum* 17 (2) (June 2002): 281–305.

Stoy, Elinor H. "Chinatown and the Curse that Makes it a Plague Spot in the Nation," *The Arena* 38 (215) (October 1907): 360–365.

Tamason, Charles A. "From Mortuary to Cemetery: Funeral Riots and Funeral Demonstrations in Lille, 1779–1870," *Social Science History* 4 (1) (Winter 1980): 18–31.

Taylor, John. *Body Horror: Photojournalism, Catastrophe, and War*. New York: New York University Press, 1998.

Tokuş, Zafer. "Nihayet oğlunu buldu: Ukraynalı anne Obaline, Marmara depreminde ölen oğlunun mezarını 4 yıl sonra buldu. Obaline'nin oğlu, kimsesizlerin gömüldüğü bir başkasına ait mezarda çıktı," *Radikal* (June 26, 2003): http://www.radikal.com.tr/haber.php?haberno=79473.

Tokyo Municipal Office. *Tokyo: Capital of Japan—Reconstruction Work.* Tokyo: Toppon Printing Co., 1930.

Trilsch, Mirja, and Rüth, Alexandra. "Öcalan v Turkey. App. No. 46221/99," *The American Journal of International Law* 100 (1) (January 2006): 180–186.

Ürekli, Fatma. *İstanbul'da 1894 Depremi.* Istanbul: İleşitim Yayınları, 1995.

Van de Wetering, Maxine. "Moralizing in Puritan Natural Science: Mysteriousness in Earthquake Sermons," *Journal of the History of Ideas* 43 (3) (July–September 1982): 417–438.

Walker, Charles F. "The Upper Classes and their Upper Stories: Architecture and the Aftermath of the Lima Earthquake of 1746," *Hispanic American Historical Review* 83 (1) (February 2003): 53–82.

Watt, E. D. "Rousseau Réchaufée—Being Obliged, Consenting, Participating, and Obeying only Oneself," *Journal of Politics* 43 (4) (August 1981): 707–719.

Webster, Noah. "A Brief History of Epidemic and Pestilential Diseases," *The Medical Repository of Original Essays and Intelligence* 3 (3) (1800): 278–288.

Webster, Noah. "On the Connection of Earthquakes and Epidemic Diseases," *The Medical Repository of Original Essays and Intelligence* 4 (1801): 350–345.

Wettersteint de Hodenstein, Leopold. "A Full Account of the Great and Terrible Earthquake in Germany, Hungary and Turkey." Trans. Rich Alcock. London: R. C., 1673.

White, Luise. "Cars Out of Place: Vampires, Technology, and Labor in East and Central Africa," *Representations* 43 (Summer 1993): 27–50.

White, Luise. "The Traffic in Heads: Bodies, Borders, and the Articulation of Regional Histories," *Journal of South African Studies* 23 (3) (1997): 325–338.

Wilson, James Russell. *San Francisco's Horror of Earthquake and Fire.* New York: G. W. Bertron, 1906.

Zizek, Slavoj. "Melancholy and the Act," *Critical Inquiry* 26 (4) (Summer 2000): 657–681.

Zizek, Slavoj. *The Ticklish Subject: The Absent Centre of Political Ontology.* London: Verso, 1999.

Zizek, Slavoj. *Welcome to the Desert of the Real: Five Essays on September 11th and Related Dates.* New York: Verso, 2002.

Anonymous Essays, Articles, and Cases

"182 asker enkaz altında," *Hürriyet* (August 18, 1999): http://arama.hurriyet.com.tr/arsivnews.aspx?id=-96786.

"Acımız çok büyük" *Milliyet* (August 18, 1999): http://www.milliyet.com.tr/1999/08/18/haber/haboo.html.

"Adalar boşaldı," *Hürriyet* (August 30, 1999): http://arama.hurriyet.com.tr/arsivnews.aspx?id=-99036.

"An Eye Witness Describes the Japanese Catastrophe," *Current Opinion* (November 1, 1923): 590.

"Ancient and Modern Eloquence," *Blackwood's Edinburgh Magazine* 68 (422) (December 1850): 655.

"Avcılar'da trafik felç," *Hürriyet* (August 20, 1999): http://arama.hurriyet.com.tr/arsivnews.aspx?id=-97307.

"Avrupa: AB'yi düşünün," *Hürriyet* (November 26, 1999): http://arama.hurriyet.com.tr/arsivnews.aspx?id=-115550.

"Ayasofya asla yıkılmaz," *Hürriyet* (August 19, 1999): http://arama.hurriyet.com.tr/arsivnews.aspx?id=-96991.

"Basını, Yunanlılara şikayet etti," *Hürriyet* (September 20, 1999): http://arama.hurriyet.com.tr/arsivnews.aspx?id=-102913.

"Batı basını: İdamda, Türk politikacılar zorlanacak," *Hürriyet* (November 27, 1999): http://arama.hurriyet.com.tr/arsivnews.aspx?id=-115883.

"Beyazıd Camii ibadete kapandı," *Hürriyet* (August 19, 1999): http://arama.hurriyet.com.tr/arsivnews.aspx?id=-97043

"Blood," *Blackwood's Edinburgh Magazine* 83 (512) (June 1858): 687–696.

"Bobrek tehlikesi," *Hürriyet* (August 31, 1999): http://arama.hurriyet.com.tr/arsivnews.aspx?id=-99338.

"Çadır aynı çadır," *Hürriyet* (August 27, 1999): http://arama.hurriyet.com.tr/arsivnews.aspx?id=-98527.

"Cahil olabılırım," *Hürriyet* (August 24, 1999): http://arama.hurriyet.com.tr/arsivnews.aspx?id=-97804.

"Çetelere teşvik müteahhide af," *Hürriyet* (August 29, 1999): http://arama.hurriyet.com.tr/arsivnews.aspx?id=-98777.

"Dakikada bir mezar," *Hürriyet* (August 20, 1999): http://arama.hurriyet.com.tr/arsivnews.aspx?id=-97318.

"Deprem, çocuklarda psiko travma nedeni," *Hürriyet* (August 31, 1999): http://arama.hurriyet.com.tr/arsivnews.aspx?id=-99267.

"Deprem, erkek doğumlarını azaltır," *Hürriyet* (August 28, 1999): http://arama.hurriyet.com.tr/arsivnews.aspx?id=-98749.

"Depremzedede uyuz ve fare korkusu," *Hürriyet* (August 31, 1999): http://arama.hurriyet.com.tr/arsivnews.aspx?id=-99307.

"Earthquake at Lisbon," *The American Magazine of Useful and Entertaining Knowledge* 3 (12) (September 1, 1837): 452–455.

"Effects of Earthquake on the Emotions," *Current Literature* (49) (4) (1910): 6–7.

"Erdek Açılıyor," *Hürriyet* (August 22, 1999): http://arsiv.hurriyetim.com.tr/hur/turk/99/08/22/gundem/15gun.html.

"Extract of a Letter Giving an Account of the Earthquake, Which Took Place at Naples, July 25th 1805," *The Monthly Anthology* 2 (12) (December 1805): 628–630.

"Fatih Camii depreme şerbetli," *Hürriyet* (August 22, 1999): http://arama.hurriyet.com.tr/arsivnews.aspx?id=-97537.

"Free Trade at its Zenith," *Blackwood's Edinburgh Magazine* 66 (410) (December 1849): 776.

"Germany in Earthquake," *Current Opinion* 6 (December 1, 1923): 654–657.

"Gölcük'te karantina," *Hürriyet* (August 22, 1999): http://arama.hurriyet.com.tr/arsivnews.aspx?id=-97480.

"Kapalıçarşı sağlam çıktı," *Hürriyet* (August 20, 1999): http://arama.hurriyet.com.tr/arsivnews.aspx?id=-97214.

"Karayolu kılavuzu," *Hürriyet* (August 19, 1990): http://arama.hurriyet.com.tr/arsivnews.aspx?id=-97109.

"Mary E. Schloendorff v. The Society of the New York Hospital," Court of Appeals of New York, 211 N.Y. 125; 105 N.E. 92 (1914).

"Mezar dili," *Hürriyet* (August 25, 1999): http://webarsiv.hurriyet.com.tr/1999/08/25/138858.asp.

"New Means of Perpetuating Memorials: Scientific Methods Ensuring Continuance for 10,000 Years," *The Illuminated London News* (September 5, 1931): 30.

"Observations on Earthquakes," *The Port-Folio*, 7 (5) (May 1812): 421–436.

"Organ mafyası kimsesiz çocuk peşinde, uyarısı," *Hürriyet* (August 27, 1999): http://arama.hurriyet.com.tr/arsivnews.aspx?id=-98545.

"Otoyollar ücretsizdi," *Hürriyet* (August 18, 1999): http://arama.hurriyet.com.tr/arsivnews.aspx?id=-96910.

"Oy birliğiyle idam," *Hürriyet* (November 26, 1999): http://arama.hurriyet.com.tr/arsivnews.aspx?id=-115548.

"Palsgraf v. Long Island Railroad," Court of Appeals of New York 248 N.Y. 339 (1928).

"Plessy v. Ferguson," 163 U.S. 537 (1896).

"Portugal," *Blackwood's Edinburgh Magazine* 56 (345) (October 1844): 100–105.

"Results of Revolution in Europe" *Blackwood's Edinburgh Magazine* 7 (436) (February 1852): 242–257.

"Sakarya'da 20 bin kişi mezar evlerde kalıyor," *Zaman* (February 23, 2007): http://www.zaman.com.tr/webapp–tr/haber.do?haberno=504358.

"Salgın hastalık tehlikesi" *Hürriyet* (August 22, 1999): http://arama.hurriyet.com.tr/arsivnews.aspx?id=-97540.

"Singleton v. Norris," 319 F.3d 1018 (8th Cir. 2003).

"Sir Robert Peel," *Blackwood's Edinburgh Magazine* 68 (419) (September 1850): 358.

"Some account of the Earthquake in Calabria, in the year 1783, in a letter from a gentleman on his travels through Calabria in 1786," *The Philadelphia Magazine and Review* (January 1799): 11–13.

"The Calabria Earthquake," *Monthly Magazine of Belles-Lettres and the Arts.* (March 1834): 153–156.

"The Effects of an Earthquake in Calabria: Burying," *Journal of Belles Lettres* (September 11, 1838): 2–3.

"The European Crisis," *Saturday Evening Post* (September 26, 1857): 2.

"The Insurrection Act of 1807," 10 U.S.C. § 333(a)(1)(A).

"The Light in Which we are Taught by the World of God to Consider Earthquakes," *Gentleman's Magazine* 20 (April 1750): 169.

"Turkcell'den deprem savunması," *Hürriyet* (August 30, 1999): http://arama.hurriyet.com.tr/arsivnews.aspx?id=-98966.

"Wars Between France and England," *The Friend of Peace* 4 (1815): 34–35.

"Yıkılan binanın müteahhiti Evren'in evini de yapmış," *Hürriyet* (August 18, 1999): http://arama.hurriyet.com.tr/arsivnews.aspx?id=-96920.

"Yunan Sağlık Bakanı: 'Biz Türk kanı alırız,'" *Milliyet* (Eylül 11, 1999): http://www.milliyet.com.tr/1999/09/11/index.html.

Index

THE CULTURAL LIVES OF LAW

Austin Sarat, Editor

The Cultural Lives of Law series brings insights and approaches from cultural studies to law and tries to secure for law a place in cultural analysis. Books in the series focus on the production, interpretation, consumption, and circulation of legal meanings. They take up the challenges posed as boundaries collapse between as well as within cultures, and as the circulation of legal meanings becomes more fluid. They also attend to the ways law's power in cultural production is renewed and resisted.

The Affective Life of Law: Legal Modernism and the Literary Imagination
Ravit Reichman
2009

Fault Lines: Tort Law as Cultural Practice
Edited by David M. Engel and Michael McCann
2008

Lex Populi: The Jurisprudence of Popular Culture
William P. MacNeil
2007

The Cultural Lives of Capital Punishment: Comparative Perspectives
Edited by Austin Sarat and Christian Boulanger
2005